MARANGA MAI!

MARANGA MAI!
TE REO AND MARAE IN CRISIS?

**EDITED BY
MERATA KAWHARU**

AUCKLAND
UNIVERSITY
PRESS

First published 2014

Auckland University Press
University of Auckland
Private Bag 92019
Auckland 1142
New Zealand
www.press.auckland.ac.nz

Text © The contributors
Photographs © Krzysztof Pfeiffer

ISBN 978 1 86940 805 3

National Library of New Zealand Cataloguing-in-Publication Data
Maranga mai! : te reo and marae in crisis? / edited by Merata Kawharu.
Includes index
ISBN 978-1-86940-805-3
1. Maori language—Revival. 2. Maori language—Social aspects—New Zealand—Northland—Case studies. 3. Maori language—Social aspects. 4. Maori (New Zealand people)—Social life and customs—21st century. 5. Language maintenance—New Zealand. [1. Reo Māori. reo 2. Mātauranga. reo 3. Marae. reo 4. Kōhanga. reo 5. Matareo. reo 6. Māoritanga. reo]
I. Kawharu, Merata.
306.4408999442—dc 23

Publication is assisted by the Marsden Fund Council from government funding, administered by the Royal Society of New Zealand.

This book is copyright. Apart from fair dealing for the purpose of private study, research, criticism or review, as permitted under the Copyright Act, no part may be reproduced by any process without prior permission of the publisher.

Internal design: Katrina Duncan
Cover design: Spencer Levine
Photographs: Krzysztof Pfeiffer; many courtesy of Māori Maps / Te Potiki National Trust Limited

Printed by 1010 Printing International Ltd

CONTENTS

Wāhinga Kōrero *Erima Henare*		vi
Introduction *Merata Kawharu*		1
1	Ko te Rere o te Reo / The Decline of the Language *Merimeri Penfold*	11
2	Tribal Marae: Crisis? What Crisis? *Paul Tapsell*	35
3	Te Memeha Haere o ngā Kaikōrero Tohunga ki Runga i ngā Marae / The Dearth of Competent Speakers on the Marae *Hōne Sadler*	65
4	Te Reo Māori and Māori Identity: What's in a Maunga? *Arapera Ngaha*	71
5	Motutī Road: At the End of the Road, or Just the Beginning? *Kevin Robinson*	97
6	Te Reo Māori and Schooling *Margie Hōhepa*	103
7	Auē, Taukiri ē: The Changing Face of Marae *Fraser Toi*	129
8	Te Reo Māori and the Tamariki of Te Tai Tokerau: A Twenty-first-century Demography *Stephen McTaggart*	139
9	Renaissance and Re-Engagement: A Rangatahi Perspective *Kiri Toki*	175
10	Casting a New Net: Connecting Marae and te Reo in the Information Age *Merata Kawharu, with Paratene Tane*	181
11	Made of Many Threads: Identity as a Vibrant Tapestry *Pounamu Jade Aikman-Dodd*	211
12	Ngā Taonga Kōrero and the Modern World *Michael Hennessy*	219
Acknowledgements		246
Index		248

WĀHINGA KŌRERO

Ruia, ruia, tahia, tahia,
Kia hemo ake te kākoakoa,
Kia herea mai i te kawau korokī,
Kia tātaki mai i roto i te pūkorokoro whaikoro.
Te kūaka he kūaka mārangaranga,
Kotahi te manu i tau ki te tāhuna, tau atu, tau atu, tau atu!

Me mihi rā ki te hunga nā rātou nei i whāriki ēnei tuhinga hei whakaoho ake i te wairua, i te manawa o Te Tai Tokerau ki tōna reo e ngaro haere nei i te tirohanga kanohi.

Mai i tōku ao, i kite au i te wā e maru ana ngā marae o Te Tai Tokerau i ngā kaikōrero ka taea te tū ki ngā marae maha o te motu. Ko Tūrei Heke o Te Rāwhiti e mau taiaha ana, e oma ana me te whakatakoto i ana kōrero ātaahua, ko Hone Heke Rankin arero koi, ko Anaru Ngāwaka kaumātua mōhio ki te Kawenata Tawhito, ko Te Riri Maihi Kawiti te mana o te kupu. Whai muri mai i a rātou ko Raniera Te Korohū Whiu, Himi Hēnare, Piri Irāia, Manga Tau, Haimona Snowden, Nicky Conrad ngā kaiwhakakapi whārua mahue mai i te ao tawhito. Uiui kau, rapurapu kau, kei hea rā rātou e ngaro nei? 'E hinga ana he tētē kura, e ara mai ana he tētē kura.' Ko rātou ēnā!

Ka āta tirohia e ahau ngā marae o Te Tai Tokerau i tēnei wā, ka toko ake te whakaaro ki roto i a au, kei te tika ngā kōrero o te hunga nei mō te hemo haere o te reo ki roto i a tātou? Kua eke te wā kia pēnei ai taua whakataukī rā, 'E hinga ana he tētē kura, e ara mai ana he tētē noa iho?'

E tamara mā, kāti te manawa kiore, kua tae kē mai te wā kia manawa kūaka tātou. Mārangaranga mai! Ko te hauora o te reo, kaua ko te haumate o te reo, kei roto i te hiakai o tēnā, o tēnā!

Nāku iti nei
Erima Henare

INTRODUCTION

'Maranga mai,' exclaimed Tai Tokerau kuia Merimeri Penfold. 'Wake up!'

The 94-year-old was at her home in the Far North on the phone to me in Dunedin. 'Sometimes I just do not understand,' she lamented. 'Our people. We have become complacent. Our language and our marae are struggling. Yet we are asleep. We need to wake up!'

These sentiments more or less capture the tenor of this collection of essays. As the title of the book suggests, we present a challenge. Or *re*-present a challenge: kaumātua and other Māori leaders laid it down well before words were formed on these pages. Simply, the challenge is how to come to terms with deepening crises within Māori communities: the crisis of the Māori language and the crisis of our most central institution of identity, the tribal marae. An overarching question needs to be asked first: how real are the problems so claimed? Then there are critical questions of detail. If these crises are observable by and within Māori communities, where do the responsibilities lie in responding to them? Is it with marae communities, whānau, schools, Māori organisations and/ or government? Who shoulders what obligations? Our book responds to these challenges and begins to address the issues directly. We do this by looking at what the concerns are, and how and why they have developed.

We also consider novel ways of addressing them: the development of web-based educational resources, Maorimaps.com and Tewehinui.com.

We are not suggesting that marae and te reo are consigned to a fatal decline. That would be simply wrong. But Māori kin-group communities, and New Zealand as a whole, are at a new cultural crossroads. We need to better understand what that is if we are to respond properly to the challenges of maintaining and enhancing our indigenous identity; an identity that marks New Zealand out from the rest of the world. At a more personal level, too, we are asking, what kind of future do we want for our tamariki, our children? They are descendants of a cultural heritage where marae and te reo have previously been cornerstones but which may no longer be so crucial in their day-to-day lives.

Over the past 30 years or so, many Māori-language initiatives have been implemented which have worked to combat language poverty in communities. One of the major causes of the language decline, especially since the 1930s, was its silencing in the education system. Of the widely reported ban in schools from that time, the noted Māori leader and te reo promoter Sir James Henare succinctly said: 'The facts are incontrovertible. If there was no such policy there was an extremely effective gentlemen's agreement!' (Waitangi Tribunal, 1986, p. 16). Sir James and many others recognised that concerted responses were needed to address the language crisis.[*] And so in the early 1980s, Māori-medium schooling was established. The sense of alarm also saw, in 1986, the Waitangi Tribunal reporting on the major Treaty of Waitangi claim regarding te reo. Following the tribunal's recommendations, just one year later, in 1987, te reo Māori became an official language of New Zealand and the Māori Language Commission was established. Māori media such as Māori radio stations and Māori Television have expanded the range of forums where te reo is heard and promoted. And since the early 1990s, wānanga or Māori tertiary institutions have emerged. These are major achievements. But, 30 years

---

[*] Richard Benton, a pioneer of Māori-language research, particularly in the 1970s and 1980s, had long highlighted the difficulties facing the Māori language. His work of the 1970s, published in 1991, set a crucial evidential base confirming the perilous state of the language. See Benton, 1991.

since the first initiatives, a complacency about the language has also crept into communities. How is this possible? Perhaps because people feel the language is being taken care of by 'the experts' – the teachers, the lecturers, the kaumātua and other fluent speakers of te reo? Revitalisation is in good hands, people think, so there is no need for major concern or alarm. But with complacency have come closures of Māori-language programmes and schools, and fewer Māori children now learn their language.

The facts speak for themselves. In October 2012, the Waitangi Tribunal concluded that the case of the kōhanga reo (preschool Māori-language learning nests) claimant was well founded. It said that the Crown had not fulfilled its duties as a Treaty partner. The Ministry of Education had assimiliated the kōhanga reo movement, stifling its progress and, critically, resulting in a long decline in its number of participants. The tribunal found that the funding regime, quality measures and other policies had effectively failed kōhanga reo. Another tribunal report records page after page of language decline problems, with claimants from Ngāti Porou, Ngāti Kahungunu, Te Tai Tokerau and Ngāti Koata describing the difficulties facing their people. These include the aging demographic of native speakers; difficulties in learning regional forms of te reo, especially for those who live outside the tribal district; and a very limited number of trained teachers, particularly those trained in region-specific language, or 'te mita' (Waitangi Tribunal, 2010, pp. 389–391). Although the increased availability of language courses over recent years has undoubtedly contributed towards language revitalisation, the courses by themselves are inadequate to equip students to converse proficiently (Waitangi Tribunal, 2010, p. 436).

The tribunal described a grim trend, over recent years, in Māori-language learning. The initial gains made by kōhanga reo and kura kaupapa (total immersion Māori schools) have simply not been capitalised upon. The numbers of Māori children learning te reo in Māori-medium education are now declining. From the peak of 14,514 tamariki at 809 kōhanga reo throughout the country in 1993, a dramatic drop occurred so that by 2009 only 9288 children were attending kōhanga. Many kōhanga had closed by then, too: only 464 were officially open (and 27 puna reo; another Māori-language-learning preschool).

From six kura in 1990, there were 70 kura in 2009. This was an increase, certainly, but over the almost twenty-year period to 2009, only 15.2 per cent of all Māori children were attending kura or other Māori-medium schooling (Waitangi Tribunal, 2010, p. 399). By extrapolating that figure (15.2%) and relating it to hapū or marae communities, we find that a very small pool of competent speakers remains. (This, of course, assumes that those who have a degree of fluency in te reo because of their learning at school and/or university are connected, interested in or know their marae.) Some would say it is unsustainable; it is certainly not where we should be after three decades of language-learning programmes.

A further problem exists. If the pool of Māori who are fluent in their language is getting smaller over time, there are also fewer who are conversant in regional forms of the language. To give an example of the decline in fluency in recent years, Statistics New Zealand stated, 'between 1996 and 2006, the proportion of the Māori population able to converse in Māori decreased from 25.0 percent to 23.7 percent' (2011). The 2013 census presents an even grimmer picture, with the figure dropping to 21.3 per cent.[*] If we look at a longer timeframe from the early colonial period to today, there is a greater decrease of fluent speakers.[†] Although Māori might not have the strong dialectal differences that other languages have, there are idioms, terms and other differences that are unique to regions. But with fewer speakers and fewer learning opportunities for regional

---

[*] In 2001, Statistics New Zealand reported that 130,485 Māori (24.8%) said they could speak Māori conversationally (http://nzdotstat.stats.govt.nz/wbos/Index.aspx); in 2006 only 131,613 Māori (23.7%) could speak te reo conversationally (http://www.stats.govt.nz/Census/2006CensusHomePage/QuickStats/quickstats-about-a-subject/maori/language-ko-te-reo.aspx); and in 2013, according to figures released just as we were going to press, this had dropped further to 125,352 Māori (21.3%), a 4.8% decrease since 2006 (http://stats.govt.nz/Census/2013-census/profile-and-summary-reports/quickstats-about-maori-english/maori-language.aspx). Statistics New Zealand also undertook a survey of the health of the Māori language in 2001. Information can be found at: http://www.stats.govt.nz/browse_for_stats/people_and_communities/maori/2001-survey-on-the-health-of-the-maori-language.aspx. However, Winifred Bauer in a 2008 article in the *Journal of the Linguistic Society of New Zealand* argued that the 2001 and 2006 national census figures on te reo need to be read with caution. Bauer criticised the methodologies used and suggested that they do not accurately capture the state of te reo; that it is much worse than the census figures present.

[†] For further information on the gradual decline of te reo competency and fluency, see, for example, the Māori Language Commission webpage http://www.tetaurawhiri.govt.nz/english/issues_e/hist/.

forms, this uniqueness and key marker of identity will in time become lost. Some Māori fear that much of the distinctive regional language is already lost.

Is Māori to become the language of the marae, the language of ritual occasions only? Will it be a 'fringe' language where it is spoken only spasmodically, and only by a few? Again, many Māori would argue that we are already at that stage.

With problems in reviving our language, where does this leave the marae? Already many marae are seeing fewer and fewer people participating in marae occasions. The 2013 census shows that 110,928 people of Māori descent (18.5 per cent of the Māori population) do not know their iwi. This group is unlikely to know or be involved with their marae. But the marae is the anchor stone of tribal identity, tying every Māori to their wider communities of origin, genealogically connecting the past to the future and journeying us back into a deep Pacific history of common ancestral origins over 3000 years old. It represents one of modern-day New Zealand's unique social and cultural points of difference. Can we afford to lose it? The obvious answer is: no. We cannot afford to lose the distinctiveness of marae. It is integral to Māori identity and it has developed here like nowhere else in the world. If we acknowledge this, it is reasonable to expect that marae throughout the nation should be active, even vibrant, and young Māori, as the next generation of trustees and leaders, should be actively participating in the affairs of their marae community, many with the strength of a regionally based language or te mita o te reo, regional dialect of the Māori language.

Regionally based language and marae are undergoing transformations at levels not seen before. There are marae that are being rejuvenated – fresh coats of paint are brightening up some meeting houses and new dining halls are welcoming guests – and in rituals of encounter, the dialect of elders fluent in te reo – who learnt to speak the local way from their parents and grandparents – continues to reverberate on marae. Treaty of Waitangi settlements are also equipping Māori with the resources needed to enhance marae communities socially, economically and culturally. In addition, emerging potential for cultural leadership is visible amongst some young Māori; this is demonstrated particularly in kura, in te reo competitions and in kapa haka (cultural group) performances. Yet while there are 'busy' marae throughout the country, beneath this concealing bustle it is not hard to find cases where regional language forms or the fine arts of whaikōrero (formal speeches) and karanga (formal ritual calls) are few, or even absent. Although there are many functioning or 'living' marae, they do not tell the complete story of more deep-seated difficulties that marae and language are also having.

The authors in this book provide commentaries on and explore these challenges. We present a range of perspectives from anthropological, sociological, Māori-language and education specialists speaking on what they have seen and found in research that they have carried out, both in communities and in archives. We also bring the views of Māori leaders and emerging leaders who speak candidly about their particular experiences and concerns. These leaders' narratives are first-hand accounts of what is happening in tribal communities in respect of marae and language. Their kōrero or perspectives are woven between longer chapters, some of which are co-written by academics and emerging scholars. Many of the perspectives describe Tai Tokerau or northern experiences that are the focus of work we have just completed under the auspices of the James Henare Māori Research Centre at the University of Auckland. Since its inception in 1992, the centre has focused on the research and development needs of Tai Tokerau hapū (kin groups) and iwi (kin group collectives). Most contributors are either from Te Tai Tokerau or are closely connected to hapū or iwi of the region through research and other work. We think that developments in Te Tai Tokerau reflect those at other marae elsewhere in New Zealand, a view that elders and leaders from other regions have confirmed.

Māori language and marae are in vulnerable states. If this book raises discussion levels about the interconnectedness and fragility of these two things, we will have achieved our purpose.

A Brief Overview

Ngāti Kurī kuia Merimeri Penfold speaks first, laying the challenge for rejuvenating marae and language squarely at the foot of whānau. In giving an unedited account of her upbringing and the influential people early in her life, she also speaks candidly about the predicament she sees her people facing as a result of decades of little leadership in marae and language matters. Her chapter is based on an interview in te reo, which was then translated into English. Her story brings northern te reo to life; it is one of the few examples of published contemporary Tai Tokerau te reo.

Anthropologist Paul Tapsell next traverses an historical journey of the emergence, evolution and then developing crisis of marae. He challenges us to think critically about the state of our marae and discusses also a new approach to bridging disparate communities with marae, through the successful web project 'Māori Maps'.*

Hōne Sadler in the third chapter provides a kaumātua perspective on the state of marae and the effect of the diminishing pool of whaikōrero leadership. His perspective is also expressed in Tai Tokerau te reo with an English translation.

In the fourth chapter, sociolinguist Arapera Ngaha looks at the link between language and identity, focusing particularly on a Northland study that involved many of the authors in this volume. The study examines young Māori perspectives on te reo and cultural knowledge. This information provides a solid grounding for addressing knowledge gaps.

Kevin Robinson, CEO of Te Rūnanga o Te Rarawa, then offers a personal view of what he has seen in his community of Motutī, North Hokianga, over a number of years; namely, the continued migration of people out of Hokianga and its effect on marae. He talks about two entrepreneurial projects – bees and broadband – that are bringing hope and new opportunities for home communities to grow.

In the sixth chapter, educationalist Margie Hōhepa discusses schooling experiences and the role of schools in both Māori-language and cultural knowledge learning. She reflects also on the Tai Tokerau study discussed by Ngaha and later Merata Kawharu and Paratene Tane, as well as international studies on indigenous language regeneration.

---

* Māori Maps was launched in June 2013. Soon afterwards, the 2013 World Summit Awards selected it as a finalist, alongside seven other New Zealand organisations, for showing notable creativity and innovation in information and communication technology.

Kaumātua Fraser Toi reflects in the seventh chapter on the decline of marae leadership since World War II, the changing attitudes and understandings of tikanga, the reasons marae practices have changed and what these circumstances now mean for marae communities.

Sociologist Stephen McTaggart next provides a demographic picture of te reo use. He looks at 2001–06, concentrating in particular on te reo Māori use by young Māori in Te Tai Tokerau. Statistics are important in indicating trends. Among other things, McTaggart's analyses show – along lines of gender, age, region and iwi affiliation, for instance – where the strengths are evident in use of te reo. Additionally, his contribution provides important information for te reo planning and promotion.

Lawyer Kiri Toki in the ninth chapter brings the perspective of one born into the much celebrated cultural renaissance of the 1980s. She notes just how precarious te reo and tikanga remain in its wake, 30 years later, and she calls for re-engagement.

In the tenth chapter anthropologist Merata Kawharu and emerging scholar Paratene Tane look at the value placed on marae and language, comparing kaumātua and young Māori views in Te Tai Tokerau. They explore the development of the website Tewehinui.com as a means to bridge cultural and language knowledge gaps as well as disparate communities. There are also ethical questions around putting customary knowledge on the internet and about the role of kaumātua, marae and schools in this new environment. The authors consider these, and the meaning of taonga in an internet setting.

Another emerging scholar, Pounamu Jade Aikman-Dodd, next provides a personal account of what it means to be Māori while being raised away from home marae communities.

Finally, film-maker Michael Hennessy continues discussion of the ethical questions now facing the team who have created Tewehinui.com. He also looks at interpretations of oral tradition and oral histories as a lead-in to discussing the material on the website.

Addressing the problems that te reo and marae represent to Māori well-being will take much more than a book: it requires a journey of solutions. As Merimeri Penfold said, 'Maranga mai!' This is our contribution to the journey.

Bibliography

Bauer, W., 2008. 'Is the health of Te Reo Māori Improving?' *Journal of the Linguistic Society of New Zealand*, pp. 33–74.
Benton, R. A., 1991. *The Māori language: Dying or reviving?* Wellington: NZCER.
Māori Maps, n.d., http://www.maorimaps.com
——, 2013. 'Journey of Many Thousand Kilometres Puts Marae on the Map'. From: http://www.scoop.co.nz/stories/SC1306/S00002/journey-of-many-thousand-kilometres-puts-marae-on-the-map.htm
Statistics New Zealand, n.d. 'NZ. Stat'. From: http://nzdotstat.stats.govt.nz/wbos/Index.aspx
——, 2002. '2001 Survey on the Health of the Māori Language: Key Statistics'. From: http://www.stats.govt.nz/browse_for_stats/people_and_communities/maori/2001-survey-on-the-health-of-the-maori-language.aspx
——, c. 2007. 'QuickStats about Māori: Language – Ko te Reo'. From: http://www.stats.govt.nz/Census/2006CensusHomePage/QuickStats/quickstats-about-a-subject/maori/language-ko-te-reo.aspx
——, 2011. 'Key Findings on New Zealand's Progress Using a Sustainable Development Approach: 2010 – Speakers of te Reo Māori'. From: http://www.stats.govt.nz/browse_for_stats/environment/sustainable_development/key-findings-2010/preserving-resources.aspx#speakers
Te Taura Whiri i te Reo Māori, n.d. 'History: A History of the Māori Language'. http://www.tetaurawhiri.govt.nz/english/issues_e/hist/
Te Wehi Nui, n.d. From: http://www.tewehinui.com
Waitangi Tribunal, 1986. 'Report of the Waitangi Tribunal on the Te Reo Māori Claim'. Wellington: Department of Justice.
——, 2010. 'Pre-publication. Te Taumata Tuatahi: Te Reo Māori'. Wellington: Printlink.
——, 2012. 'Pre-publication. Matua Rautia: Report on the Kōhanga Reo Claim'. Wellington: The Tribunal.
World Summit Award, 2013. 'Minister Congratulates World Summit Award Finalists'. From: http://www.wsa-awards.org.nz/index.html

MERIMERI PENFOLD (Ngāti Kurī) was born in the Far North. Despite the remoteness of her home from main centres or markets, isolation was not a term that had meaning for her. The seas and gardens provided everything her family needed and in the kūmara-planting season they moved from Te Hāpua to Kapowairua where spring water was plentiful. Her mother, who had eighteen pregnancies and eight surviving children, epitomised strength and courage – attributes Merimeri has demonstrated throughout her life.

Her move to Auckland as a young girl was a profound change. She attended Queen Victoria School for Māori girls and followed this with a short, but intense, education at Faigans College in preparation for university. Merimeri qualified as a teacher and taught in the Far North, the East Coast, central North Island, Rātana Pā and Poroporo. She once took 'the system' on, teaching in te reo Māori (the first language of her pupils), but the school inspectors saw an end to that. She returned to university to complete her B.A., was among the first Māori women to graduate in New Zealand, and lectured at the University of Auckland for many years.

Merimeri has led many endeavours. She was the first Māori woman elected to the University of Auckland Council, and a member of the advisory committee for the seventh edition of the Williams *Dictionary of the Māori Language*. She has also worked on the National Advisory Committee for Māori Education, the Broadcasting Commission, the Māori Unit of the New Zealand Council for Educational Research, and the Māori Women's Welfare League, on which she served as Dominion vice-president from 1970–78. She chaired the management committee of the Te Hapua 42 Land Incorporation from 1976–80 and was intimately involved in the Muriwhenua Land and Fisheries claims in the 1980s. She has translated nine of Shakespeare's sonnets. In 2000 the University of Auckland awarded Merimeri an honorary doctorate.

CHAPTER ONE

KO TE RERE O TE REO

MERIMERI PENFOLD

MEHEMEA KA ORA TE REO MĀORI, KO TE KAWENGA, KEI MUA I te aroaro o ngā kaumātua me ngā whānau. He whakahirahira ngā kōhanga reo, ngā kura Māori, ā, he whakatūnga tā te Pouaka Whakaata Māori, engari ko te take matua o tā tātou mahi ki te whakaora haere i te reo Māori, kei ngā ringaringa o ngā mātua me ngā kaumātua. Mo mātou, kei Te Hiku o Te Ika, kua mate pākaha haere te reo Māori me ōna tikanga mai i te wā e tamariki ana ahau. He tino pākaha tēnei, he mōrearea. Kua pēnei mo ngā tupuranga e toru, anga atu. Kaua mātou e tawhiti te titiro i ō mātou marae ki te kite i ēnei nekeneketanga. Kāore he tino nui ngā whakamāramatanga. He māmā atu i tērā. Kei te whānau, kei te kāinga te tīmatanga me te otinga. Engari kāore ō mātou kāinga e whai tikanga ana ki te whakatinanatia i tētahi wāhi e tautoko ana ki te whakaora haere i te reo Māori, nā te mea kāore ngā

This chapter is based on a filmed kōrero or interview that Michael Hennessy conducted at Pukenui in the Far North as part of the project Te Wehi Nui a Mamao. Merimeri spoke mainly in te reo. Prior to the kōrero, Merata Kawharu and Michael drafted discussion points relating to te reo, marae and Merimeri's upbringing. After the kōrero, subsequent conversations occurred between Merimeri and Merata. Merata compiled the chapter from all of these discussions; Raaniera Te Whata and Mereana Te Whata undertook the English translation which follows.

mātua me ngā kaumātua e āta whai hua ana i te reo Māori me ōna tikanga mo āke tonu atu. Kei te tūmanako ahau, engari e rangirua ana, ā, e uaua ana te wā kei te heke mai.

Ko te Tīmatatanga

Ko Kurahaupō te waka, ko Pōhurihanga te tangata. Ko mātou ngā uri o Pōhurihanga, ko ngā iwi tangata whenua o Te Hiku o Te Ika. He maha ngā kārangaranga maha i konei: Ngāti Murikahara, Puhitīare, Ngāi Takoto, Te Rarawa, Ngāti Kahu, Te Ringamauī, Te Whānau Moana, Patukoraha, me te maha noa atu o ngā kārangaranga maha kei waenganui i a mātou. Koia tō mātou whakapapa i tīmata mai i a Kurahaupō rāua ko Pōhurihanga.

Te Hāpua ki Tāmaki Makaurau

I whānau au ki Te Hāpua i te tau 1920. Iwa tekau mā whā aku tau ināianei! Nā, kei konei tonu au e kapekape ana, e kōrero ana, e aha ana. Heoi anō, e noho ana.

Ka moe tōku whaea i tōku matua i te matenga o tōna wahine tuatahi i te flu i te tau 1918. Rua tekau mā ono ōna tau pea. Ko ngā tau o tāku matua, tata ki 40. Ka moe rāua, ka puta mātou. E hia nei o mātou? Tekau ma rua. E waru o mātou e puta ora mai. Nā, ko mātou katoa i eke ki te waru tau! Kei konei te toenga o mātou. Te kaha o mātou i a mātou e tupu ana, nā te mea, he moumou kai ki konei. He pipi, he ika, he kūmara, koina o ō mātou kai, mo ā mātou oranga. Kātahi te reka o te moana o Pārengarenga. Ko tāku matua, he tangata kaha ki te mahi kūmara. Kāore mātou i hiakai. Kāore mātou i noho pōhara i runga i tana nei mau i a mātou.

I tupu ake mātou i roto i a mātou reo. Engari, ka haere mātou ki te kura, paku noa iho mai te kōrero i a mātou e kōrerotia i te reo Māori. I mau mātou ki te ako i ērā atu momo mea. Ko tēnei ko te wero i aua wā. Ka hoki mātou ki te kāinga, ka puta mai te kōrero a tō mātou matua, 'Kaua koutou e kōrero i tēnā reo, i te reo Pākehā!' Otirā, he tikanga whakatoi mai ki a mātou. Kia mau mātou ki te ako i te reo Māori, ki te reo Pākehā.

I kura au ki te kura o Te Hāpua. Nā, i te wā ka puta mai māua ko Mira Szászy (Petricevich i tērā wā), ka puta māua i te tau 'standard' rima, ono pea. Ka kī tētahi wahine māhita ki a māua, 'Me haere kōrua.' E hiahia ana ia ki te mau i a māua ko Mira ki Ākarana. Ka whakaaro au, 'E, me kite koe i āku mātua. Kāre tēnā whakaaro (kia haere) au; kāre e taea.' He kaha ia ki tana take, ā, me haere māua kura ai ki reira. Ka haere mai tōku whaea, ka mea mai ki ahau i tētahi rā, 'E haere ana koe ki Ākarana?' Ka mea ia, 'He pai koe ki te haere?' Ka kōrero au ki a ia, 'Kāore.' Ahakoa kāore hiahia haere, ka kī tōku whaea, 'E haere ana koe ki Ākarana. Kia kaha. He pai te take mōu.' Nā, ka riro māua ko Mira me te māhita. Engari, nā te māhita i whakahaere ki āna tuahine, tokorua, kua moe tāne, nā rāua māua ko Mira, i tiaki. Pēnā pai.

Ka kī mai te whanaunga o te māhita, 'Āe, mauria mai ngā kōtiro nei, ki a māua e noho ana.' Nā, ka haere māua. Kāore māua i haere ki Kaitāia [ki te kura], i rere tonu māua (mā runga tereina) ki Ākarana. Kātahi anō māua ka noho i te taha o ngā Pākehā nei.

Nā, ko te tīmata tēnei o te Kirihimete. I noho māua ki Tāmaki mai i te Kirihimete atu ki te puarenga o te kura. Kei te mahi kaha tō māua māhita, e mau nei i a māua te rapu karahipi hei tukua māua ki a Kuīni Wikitoria, Queen Victoria School. Ka tata ki te puarenga o te kura ka puta mai te kōrero, 'Haere ki Queen Victoria.' Kua haere mai te karahipi mō māua. I haere mai i raro i te Mihingare, i te kura Mihingare.

Ko tēnei haerenga ki Tāmaki ko tā māua nei wā tuatahi. Pēhea tēnā mō māua? Pēnei ki te kiore! E oma ana, e tirotiro ana! He mea tauhou. He mea tino tauhou. Whitu tekau mā rima ngā tau pea i a au e ngaro atu, nā kua hoki mai au ki konei ki Te Hāpua.

I reira hoki i Tāmaki, ka whakaaro ngā wāhine e tiakina māua, ko wai rāua e pupuri i a māua, tō rāua kūare i te reo, tō rāua kūare i te tikanga Māori. Engari, he pai kē atu, me tukua māua ki Kuini Wikitoria. Kei reira te reo, kei reira ngā tikanga o te ao, me te noho tahi me rātou, ngā kōtiro nō ērā atu rohe. Nō Te Arawa, nō Waikato, nō Whānau a Apanui, nō Ngāpuhi me ērā atu, ngā kōtiro. Ka rongo māua i te reo ki Queen Victoria. Engari kāore te reo e aru mai ki Queen Victoria. Heoi anō, ko mātou katoa e mōhio ana ki te kōrero i te reo. Ka rongo mātou i te reo kē, o tēnā o tēnā.

I a māua e haere ana ki Kuini Wikitoria, kei te āta take haerengia mai te āhuatanga o ngā tikanga e ako i a māua e ngā hunga Pākehā nei. E toru tau pea ka kitea mātou, ko ngā tikanga anō e whāia ana i roto i te kura kia mōhio mātou ki te tiaki whare, ki te horoi kākahu, ki te mahi kai me ērā atu āhuatanga. Ko ērā āhuatanga kua oti mātou i a mātou taenga ki reira ki te kura. Ko ērā ngā tikanga i arumia i raro i te hāhi Mihingare.

Ā muri i tēnā, ka kumea mai māua ki te 'coaching college'. Ko te kaupapa o tērā coaching college, he whiriwhiri tangata e hiahia ana ki te haere ki te whare wānanga. Pēnei hoki ngā kōrero, 'Me haere kōrua ki te kāreti nei. Anei ngā taonga mā kōrua: te reo Pākehā, history, Latin, maths, Māori. Ko ēnei mā kōrua e mau mō te kōtahi tau kia puta kōrua mō te "matric" [matriculation].' Nā wai? Nā ngā rangatira Pākehā ēnei whakatau. 'He iwi mōhio hoki te take haere ngā ahorei o te mātauranga o te whare wānanga.' Heoi anō ka haere māua mo te kōtahi tau ki te coaching college i te 'ferry buildings'. Mutu ake te tau, ka kōrero a Mira, 'Kāre puta te reo Pākehā.' Ka tino pōuri au nō te mea ko tāku wawata, pēnei te kōrero o tōku matua, me pēhea tāku haere kia whakatau. Nā ngā Pākehā nei kia whakatau.

Kātahi ka noho puku me taku pōuri. Ka whakaaro au kua hē aku rangatira ki au. Ka oti ahau, me tuhia au i tētahi reta ki te whare wānanga. I puta au i tāku reta, ka inoi ahau kia whakawātea mai kia tukuna. Nā, ka puta mai te whakaae ana. Kua riro mai taku matriculation. Nā, ka wātea kia haere ngā tauira te huarahi ki te whare wānanga, ki te teachers college, me ērā atu āhuatanga katoa. Pēnā te haere o te kiore o Te Hāpua!

Ko Te Reo Mihi te Marae

Ko Te Reo Mihi o Te Hāpua tāku marae. Ko tērā ingoa ko te ingoa nā Rātana i hua. Ko te marae i mua i tēnā ko Te Hiku o Te Ika. Kāore au i kite i tērā marae. Ko Waiora he marae anō, kei konei kei Ngātaki. Ko Te Reo Mihi kei Te Hāpua. Nā, ko te marae tuatahi o Te Hāpua, ko Te Hiku o Te Ika. Ko Kenana kei raro nei.

I te wā i a au e tamariki ana, ka tupu takoto mai te Hāhi Rātana, i runga i te karanga o Piri Wiri Tua, te kaiwhakaū o te ao Rātana. Ko Piri Wiri Tua tētahi atu ingoa o Tahupōtiki Wiremu Rātana. Ka ngahoro te maha o te iwi Māori ki tana karanga. Ka noho te Hāhi Rātana i waenganui i tēnā marae, i tēnā marae, i tēnā iwi, i tēnā iwi. Nā, pēnā tā mātou nei noho ki konei ki Te Hāpua me te rohe nei.

I te wā ka tū te Hāhi Rātana (i te 1920s), i mua atu i tērā he tangata kaha a Rātana ki te whakapiki te ora ki te tangata. Ka mōhio ia ki te tiaki ki te hunga, ki te rawa kore, ki te māuiui. Koia tēnā te tino meia i a ia. Ka rongo te iwi Māori, ka ngahoro rātou ki a ia. Ka haere kia whakaorangia ō rātou mate. E heke ana ngā tinana. He kaha a Rātana ki te whakapiki te ora. I runga i tērā āhuatanga, kātahi te iwi ka ruatia i a ia, ka kite ia. He tika ināianei, kua ū te rangatira mō te iwi Māori. Nā, ka pērā tana huarahi mai hei tumuaki mō te Hāhi Rātana. Nā, ka whakatūria tāna Hāhi. Ka arumia atu te nuinga o te iwi.

Ka karanga a Piri Wiri Tua, 'Haere mai ki au, he mōrehu.' Kaua e haere mai ki ahau hei Ngāti Kurī, hei Ngāti Porou, hei aha atu. Haere mai ki au he mōrehu.

Te Ao Hurihuri

Ahakoa he whakahirahira te Hāhi Rātana, ki te iwi hei oranga mō te iwi, ka puta te ao hou hoki. He ao hurihuri mo mātou. Ka tahuri atu ngā tāngata i ngā tikanga o te ao tawhito. Ka kitea ahau ināianei i tā mātou nei noho pōhara i Te Hāpua. Ka noho ngoikore ngā āhuatanga ināianei i konei, i Te Hāpua.

Ko tā mātou nei marae ko Waiora, nā riro mai i Te Reo Mihi. Koia kē rā te marae tūturu i roto i Ngāti Kurī. Ehara i te tikanga karanga o te marae Te Reo Mihi o ngā tūpuna. Kāore ngā tūpuna i runga i tērā whare. Kāore he tūpuna.

I a au e tupu ake, kīhai mātou i haere ki ngā marae ki ngā tangi. He mea tauhou tērā. Kīhai mātou nei rā i tukuna haere ki ngā tangi maha. I haere ki ētahi. Engari, kei konā anō te whakaaro e mōhio ana ahau, 'Kaua koutou e haere ki te marae. Hoki koe ki te kura. Hoki koe ki te kāinga.' Ko ērā tū kōrero. Ko ngā tikanga ehara i te tikanga Māori tūturu. Engari e haere nei i raro i te ia o te Hāhi Rātana.

Nā, ka māuiui tētahi o mātou. Kua haere mai ngā āpotoro ki te whakapiki te ora ki a mātou. Nā mātou te haerenga, kua huri mai te pātai ki tōku matua, 'He aha ngā tekoteko kei a koe?' Nō te mea, ka whakaaro ētahi, 'Kei konā te mate o ngā tamariki nei.'

Ka mea atu tōku Pāpā, 'Āe, kei a au. Tukuna ngā taonga ki Rātana Pā.

Whakawāteangia. Ko ēnei ngā mea e pā ana ki te māuiui o ngā tamariki.' He maha ngā taonga nā tāku matua i heke pērā.

I te noho noa iho mātou i ngā tikanga Māori, ngā waiata o ngā kaumātua kuia, ngā tikanga poroporoaki, me te karanga ki te manuhiri. Kua whakakore te reo. Kāore he tangata kaha ki te whaikōrero. Kāore he tino kaha te mau i ngā tikanga i waenganui i ngā tāngata ināianei. Ka noho pōhēhē nei. Koia tēnei tētahi o ngā take, e arumia e ahau ināianei. Nā, ka noho pōhara mātou. Kūare mutunga nei.

Nā, ka hua ki waho atu o tēnei rohe, ka kite, ka rongo i te whakahaere o ngā iwi i runga i ngā marae. Ko ngā whaikōrero, ngā poroporoaki me ērā atu āhuatanga i roto i ngā iwi Māori tūturu, kei te haere tonu. Ka rongo au i te tino rangatira o ngā whaikōrero i waenganui i ētahi atu iwi. Ko ngā whaikōrero kei konei he poto. I ngā rā o mua, he roa ake ngā whaikōrero. Ka huri te ao Māori, te ao o Ngāti Kurī mai rānō, mai i te wā i a au e tamariki ana.

I ngā rā o mua (me ināianei) he rangatira tēnei mea te whaikōrero i roto i ngā hapori Māori. Kei te ora tonu i te rohe o Tūhoe. He reo ātaahua tā rātou me ngā kōrerotanga me ngā whakataukī. Mā ēnei momo āhuatanga kei te tino ātaahua tō rātou reo. Te āhua o te tū o te tangata, te āhua o tō rātou mau kākahu, he ata kitea hoki. Kāore rātou i haere mai i roto i ngā hū omaoma. E mau huiti ana rātou. I whakatūpatongia ngā kaumātua o Te Arawa i ngā rangatahi, 'Me pēnei tō tū i runga i te marae'. Taea e koe te kite i ō rātou hū ātaahua e papai ana. Kāore mātou e tino mahi ana i ēnei mea ki konei. Kāore mātou e tino mōhio ana i ēnei tikanga o te 'tū marae'. Ko te kaupapa, me mau atu te mana kei a koe i te wā ka tū koe ki te kōrero i runga i te marae.

Ahakoa he wā uaua i ēnei wā, ka rapurapu ngā tāngata ki te whaikōrero. Ko tāku manawanui tēnei ināianei kia āta whāngai atu, kia whakaoho ake atu ngā pakeke rā! Me whakaae rātou he tikanga hei aru mā rātou. Engari i a ētahi o rātou e noho nei, pai noa iho te noho kore take. Kāre atu he wawata i tua atu i tēnei i ā rātou ināianei. He uaua, he uaua te arumia ngā tikanga e kōrerotia nei e ahau. Te wawata tērā pea. Tērā pea, ka oho ake tāku iwi.

Te Reo

Ko te rere o te reo mai i a au e tamariki ana ki inaianei: i takoto ngā āhuatanga i waenga i ngā whānau Māori o te motu, ā, ko te haere o te tikanga o ngā kura kia whakakāhore te reo i roto i ngā kura. I reira hoki mātou i whakataetae ana. Ko ngā ture i roto i ngā kura, 'kaua e kōrero i te reo, nā kua arumia, kua tukitukia e ngā māhita. Heoi ano, ko mātou ngā tamariki, ka mau mātou ki te kōrero i te reo. 'Catch us!' Kare mātou i kino. He whakataetae noa iho. Na, kei tō mātou kāinga, ko te karanga i reira, 'kaua kōrero i te reo Pākehā'. Kāre mātou i kawa, kāre mātou i pukuriri. Ko mātou e peke ana, ā, ka patua atu, ā, ka peke ngā kōrero, nā ka puta 'people like me!'

    He pai noa iho te karanga o te kōhanga reo me te kura kaupapa Māori. Engari, me tūpato mātou. Me kore e waihotia te ako i te reo ki ngā māhita anake. Ko te mea nui, ka kōrerotia te reo, kia mōhio tātou katoa.

    Ko tōku matua, whakakāhore te reo Pākehā i tō mātou kāinga. E kore ia e mōhio ki te kōrero Pākehā. Ko tā mātou (ko ngā tamariki) whakarongo i tana reo Pākehā he kata mo mātou! Engari he tangata mōhio ki te kaute kapira i a ia e hoko ana i ana kapia (kauri gum). Ka mōhio ki te reo Pākehā (mō tēnā), arā ko ngā kupu 'pounds', 'shillings' me ērā atu tū momo kupu. Ka noho tokomaha o ngā 'Dallies' (Dalmatians) i waenga i a mātou. He tino mōhio rātou ki te mahi. He kaha hoki ki te ako i te reo Māori. He kata ma mātou nā te mea he pukukata tā rātou whakamātau!

    Ka hoki āku mahara ki te huarahi i ahu mai ahau mai i āku tamarikitanga ki inaianei. I toa ahau, i puta ahau ki te ao mārama, nā te mea, ahakoa kāre ōku mātua i mōhio ki te huarahi o te mātauranga, kuare mai ngā matimati, ka tautoko rāua i tāku haerenga ki tāku huarahi. I puta mai māua ko Mira, nā te āwhina o te hunga Pākehā, āta poipoi i a māua e tamariki ana, puta noa. Ehara i te mea he wahine mōhio māua, kao. Nā te tikanga tiaki a te hunga wahine nei, āta titiro i te huarahi tika, ka whai mātauranga māua. Ko tāku mōhio pērā, mō ngā tamariki katoa o te ao. Mehemea ka tīmata mai te manaaki mai te tamarikitanga, ā, pakeke noa, ka puta. Koia tēnei tāku karanga ki tāku iwi. Kei roto i ō tātou ringaringa te ora me te mate o tā tātou tamariki. Mehemea kāore tātou ngā mātua e pā ana ki ā tātou tamariki mai i te tamarikitanga, kāore ngā tamariki e puta he rangatira. Heoi ano, ka noho. He iwi koretake. Pēnā nō te reo. Pēnā nō te reo.

Me ako ki te kāinga. Kaua e tukuna atu ma wai i kē atu. Mā ngā māhita, mā wai atu, ma wai atu. Tuatahi, koutou me hoki ki te kāinga. Akona te reo, kōrerotia i te reo e koutou ki ngā tamariki. Ma koutou e ako. Pēnei tāku hakahau ki te hunga e aki nei, kia mau i te reo, kia mau i te reo. Kāore anō au kia rongo i a rātou e mea ana, koutou ngā kaumātua, ngā whaea, ngā mātua. Puritia te reo i roto i te kāinga. Akona mai i reira. Moumou taima engari kāore tēnā.

Me tīni / whakarerekē ngā whakaaro. E mōhio ana au he pakeke, engari kei te mōhio koe, me mahia kia tika. Kāore noa iho ngā kupu nahe, engari ko te āhua. He reo rangatira. Me whakaaturia tātou i ētahi o ngā kōrero tawhito o neherā, ngā kōrero i kōrerotia e ngā tūpuna o mua i runga i te marae. Me rongo tātou i ērā. He nui ngā mahi o ngā kaikōrero Māori, kei roto i te reo, kei reirā. Me whakarongo ki ētahi atu o ērā tāngata, ki ērā atu tāonga. Me whakaaturia te hunga e ako tonu ana ki ēnei momo reo kia mahia ai rātou kia whakamaioha rātou, ā, kia matatau, me te ngākau nui ki tā tātou reo. Ehara tēnei te tākoro noiho i ngā māpere. He nui rawa atu i tērā. He wairua kei roto i te whakaakoranga me te reo hoki. Ko te wero mō tātou, mō te Pouaka Whakaata Māori me ētahi atu, kia maumahara i ērā atu mea.

Me whai tangata nō kōnei ki te haere atu ki ētahi atu wāhi ki te ako, e mea nei ahau, ko ngā 'whakakitenga'. Me whakaako i reirā, engari mā tātou e whakakorikori. Ko te kaupapa, me whakamātau atu i tēnei mea te whaikōrero me ētahi atu mea i tērā taumata, whakaakongia, ā, whakahoki mai i ērā mahi ki te kāinga. He rerekē ngā tikanga o tēnā takiwā, o tēnā takiwā. Hei tauira, i roto i Ngāpuhi, e kore koe e mōhio ko wai ngā kaikōrero. Ka noho ngā kaikōrero i waenganui i te iwi. I te wā e rārangitia ana te noho o ngā tangata o tērā tahi ka taea e te tangata ki te mea atu, 'Āe rā, e mōhio ana ahau ki a ia, e mōhio ana ahau ki a ia, e mōhio ana ahau ki a ia'. E taea ana te tirotiro i ēnei kaikōrero, engari kāore e taea i te wā i haere mai a Ngāpuhi. He tākoro tōrangapū i mahia e rātou. He kamakama rātou mō tērā. Kīhai rātou i whakaatungia ko wai ngā kaikōrero, nā reirā ka pupuri tonu ake rātou i tō rātou huanga. He whakangaio katoa hoki ēnei.

He nui te mātauranga kei ngā pukapuka meneti o te Kooti Whenua. He tino nui hoki kia whai huarahi ki ngā wharepukapuka ki te wāhi kei reira ngā meneti mo ngā take whenua. Ahakoa e hopohopo ana ngā kai pānui Māori, me tohutohu te tangata ki tēnā huarahi. Me whakaaturia rātou ki ngā māiatanga. Me whakamahia kia hiahia rātou. He maha hoki ngā huarahi he whakapakari haere i te reo me ōna tikanga. Ehara i te mahi māmā. Engari me mahia.

E tino pono ana tēnei mea te wairua kei roto i te reo, hei tauira, tēnā pea e taea ana ngā ākonga ki te whakatakina tētahi pepeha nō tō rātou kāinga engari kāore rātou i noho ki te kāinga. Nā reirā i ērā atu āhuatanga kei te takiwā noa iho te kōrero. Mēnā ka taea koe te whakamahia te tangata ki te mōhio i ngā waitohu (icons) o ngā takotoranga papa (geography) o ia wāhi, kātahi koe ka whai māramatanga me te mōhio. Kātahi koe ka taea te whakarārangitia haere i ngā kōrero. Hei tauira, e whai tikanga ana i te wā e kōrero atu ana ki tētahi puke. Taea e koe te whakahua hei waitohu, taea e te tangata ki te whakamahia ki roto te whaikōrero me ērā atu āhuatanga o te reo Māori. He tāonga ērā, e whai take ana ki te pupuri, i ngā kōrero Māori kua ākona koe i te takiwā noa iho, kāore e whai kiko, kāore hoki e tino whai māramatanga. Engari he maha hoki ngā huarahi hei whakarangatira i te reo kia ākona e ngā tamariki. He kaha rātou ngā wāhi reke ki te patapatai. I te wā ka mea atu koe, 'he waitohu tēnei', ka mōhio rātou katoa. Horekau e whakauru ana ngā waitohu ki roto i te akomangatanga o te reo Māori o konei, kāore hoki i waenganui i ngā mea pakeke. He maha hoki ngā wāhi i waenganui i a tātou engari kei te arakore ēnei wāhi. E whai tikanga ēnei tāonga, nā reirā me hāngai tonu ki ēnei kaupapa i te wā e ako ana i te reo.

I tata ake nei i tuhi ahau i tētahi ūpoko kōrero e pā ana ki te mahinga o ngā waka pūhoro o ēnei aka pupuri waka i waho i te ture. I whakaatungia ahau, '. . . terā ngā tai o Muriwhenua te hora nei – Te Kokotahi Pārengarenga, Tokerau ki Houhora. He tāonga tuku iho nā ngā tūpuna'. Ohotata ka taea koe te whakamahia i ēnei wāhi, he wāhi whai tikanga ake. Ma tēnei kātahi ka ohorere te tangata ki te mahi i tētahi kaupapa hei tiaki i ēnei wāhi, pērā i ō tātou aka pupuri waka, i ngā wāhi e hao ika ana, ā, ngā wāhi anō kua murua. He huarahi tino rawe ēnei momo kōrero hei whakamahia i te reo. He maha ngā take ka puta mai pērā i ngā āhuatanga tauhokohoko hī ika, te papātanga kai mau ika a rohe, te papa atawhai, te kaupapa here me ētahi atu. E kore koe e taea te whakahāweatia i te kaupapa o te reo mō te whakahua me te whakatika i ngā kaupapa here mai i te ao o te Māori.

Ko tēnei te take me tū tonu ētahi kaupapa i roto i te reo Māori kaua i roto i te reo Pākehā, nā te mea ka ngaro te tino take e whai tikanga ana tētahi kaupapa me te tō rātou wāriu hoki. Taea e te tangata te whakahāweatia i tēnei. I te wā ka mea ahau, 'ngā tai o Muriwhenua', kei te mōhio ngā tāngata i ērā?

Ahakoa he aha te aha me whakatāia ngā kōrero Māori hoki. He tauira anō, 'e hora nei ki Kokotahi Pārengarenga'. Me mōhio te hunga kāinga, ngā kai mau ika me ētahi atu, he aha hoki ērā. 'Ki Tokerau', ko te takutai o Tokerau tata ake ki Houhora. Ko ēnā ngā wāhi e rua. Ko ēnei ngā tai e hora nei i waenganui i a tātou e tūkino ana, e whakakino ana. Ko ēnei ngā tū kupu i roto i te reo Māori. Ko te reo Māori anake e taea ana te hopu i te hā o te ao Māori. Mēnā kei te mōhio ngā tāngata, ko tēnā pū te pātai. Me mahi tātou i tētahi mea mō te mātauranga kore, a, me whakahauhautia ki te ako i ngā wāriu. He huarahi pai te reo Māori ki te mahi i tērā.

Ngā Kōrero o te Whenua

Ka hoki mai ki te kāinga, ka ako i ngā kōrero, i te whakapapa. Kāore i ako ki tētahi atu wāhi. I rongo au i tēnā kōrero mō mātou, mō taku iwi. Nā, i runga i te marae, ka tae mai te manuhiri, ka pātai, 'Ko wai koe?' Nā, 'Ko Kurahaupō, ko Pōhurihanga.' Koia te wā i karawhiu ai i tēnei tū kōrero. Kāhore atu. Kei te matakū Ngāti Kurī ki te kī i tēnā kōrero, engari, he ritenga tūturu. Ka kōrerotia ngā manuhiri ko wai rātou kia mārama ai ngā tāngata katoa te mana ō ia ope, ō ia ope, ā, kia mōhiotia anō hoki he aha te whanaungatanga tōrangapū. Engari kei te matakū a Ngāti Kurī ki te whakaatu ko wai rātou mai ngā ritenga tūturu. Kua ngaro te wairua Māori i waenganui i a mātou. He roa te wā kua tīnei tātou i te ao Māori.

Ka Tū ngā Wāhine i Runga i te Marae

Taea e ahau te kite ka pana ngā wāhine i ngā tāne i roto i ngā tūnga whaikōrero i runga i te marae. Engari i ngā wā o mua, kāore e whakaae mātou te kōrero i runga i te marae. Engari ki a ahau kei te haere mai te wā mō ngā wāhine kia whai tūnga kōrero. Ki tāku nei titiro, kei te pai ake te haere o ngā wāhine i ngā tāne i roto ngā āhuatanga maha! Ka tū tonu ai ngā wāhine i roto i ngā mahi mō te kaikaranga.

Te Wero

I tīmata te ngoikore haere o te marae mo mātou i te kōtahi rau tau ki muri i te wā e tupu ana te mana o te Hāhi Rātana i roto i ō mātou hapori. I haria mai te Hāhi Rātana i te tūmanako hou me te whakapono i te wā e pakeke ana te noho o te iwi Māori mo ō tātou whenua, mo ō tātou hauora hoki. He maha hoki i roto i tā tātou hapori i mate i te wā o te rewharewha i te tau kōtahi mano, iwa rau, kōtahi tekau mā waru. Engari i mau mai te whakapono hou i ngā wāriu hou. I whakaawe pū ake te reo Māori me ngā tikanga o te marae. Kāore tātou kua ora mai i tērā wā. E tukaunga tonu ana mātou i te rangatira kaha i roto i ngā whaikōrero, i ngā waiata, i ngā karanga hoki. Neke atu i te iwa tekau tau kua ngaro haere te reo me ngā mātauranga tawhito.

Ko ēnei āhuatanga, arā ko te tikanga o te marae, kua pōwhiwhi haere. He kuare ētahi o mātou ki te aru i ēnei āhuatanga, ki te whakaputa i ēnei whakaaro i roto i te reo. Kāore whānui te titiro.

Ahakoa koinei āku hakahau, he mahi nui. He wero nui. Ko te wero kia tau ki runga ki ngā pakeke. I te āhua nei, kāore anō kia tau. Kei konā ngā pakeke e titiro ana ki a wai kē atu; teachers, me ā wai atu. He ngāngāra kino tena i waenganui i roto i te iwi Māori. Kāhore ngā pakeke Māori kia kapo kita ai i te take. Ko tāku kōrero ki ngā kaumātua nei, e ngaro ana te whai-kōrero me te tikanga o te whaikōrero. Kei hea koutou?

Ko ēnei ōku whakaaro me tōku āhua mō te whakaako i te reo Māori. Me whakamōhio atu i te rangatiratanga o te reo Māori. Kaua e whakataha i ngā kaumātua, he mahi tā rātou. Pērā hoki mo ngā mātua. Ko te āhua, 'Ma tētahi atu e mahi', kāore kei te tika. E whai tikanga ana te kōhanga reo, te rura me te Pouaka Whakaata Māori. Engari e kore e taea ki te whakaneke te kāinga hei rito mō te whakaako i te reo Māori.

THE DECLINE OF THE LANGUAGE

If te reo is to have a future, the responsibility to provide the environment for Māori to thrive in lies squarely at the foot of elders and families. Kōhanga reo [Māori language preschool learning nests] and Māori schooling are important, and Māori Television also has a role, but the primary responsibility for reviving and rejuvenating the language is with parents and elders. For us in the Far North, te reo [the Māori language] and tikanga [customs] have declined severely ever since I was young. We have a crisis. Over three generations, or more, we have seen an ever increasing deterioration of our language and our customs. We need look no further than our marae to witness the changes. The solutions are not about proposing great or radical interventions. It is more simple than that. They start and end with whānau [family] and the home. But often our homes are not sufficiently equipped to provide the kind of learning and supportive environment that is needed, because parents and elders do not properly value (or are not proficient in) te reo and tikanga in ways that will ensure the sustainability of these things. I do hold out hope but we face an uncertain and difficult future.

Beginnings

Kurahaupō is the canoe. Pōhurihanga is the ancestor. We are the descendants of Pōhurihanga, the people of Te Hiku o te Ika. There are many genealogical connections here: Ngāti Murikahara, Puhitīare, Ngāi Takoto, Te Rarawa, Ngāti Kahu, Te Ringamauī, Te Whānau Moana, Patukoraha, and many other genealogical connections amidst us. Our genealogical connections begin from Kurahaupō and Pōhurihanga.

From Te Hāpua to Auckland

I was born in Te Hāpua in 1920. I am 94 years old now! I am here getting on with things, discussing things, doing what is necessary, living here.

My mother married my father following the death of his first wife who died of influenza in 1918. She was 26 years old and my father was nearly 40. They married and had us. How many of us? Twelve. Eight of us survived. All of us reached eighty years old. Those remaining live here. As we were growing up we grew up strong because of the variety of food here. Pipi, fish, kūmara were our food, for our wellbeing. The seafood from Pārengarenga was delicious. My father worked very hard planting kūmara. We did not want to eat kūmara though! However, through our father's efforts we were not poor.

We were brought up with our Māori language. However, when we went to school we spoke very little Māori. Instead we learnt other, different things. This was the challenge in those days. When we returned home our father said to us, 'Do not speak that language, the English language!' But he was teasing us. He wanted us to learn the Māori language and the English language.

I was educated at Te Hāpua school. When Mira Szászy (known as Petricevich back then) and I completed standard 5 or 6 one female teacher said to us, 'You two should go' [further afield and obtain a good education]. She wanted to take Mira and me to Auckland. I thought, 'You should really see my parents. It's not something that I really want to do; I cannot.' Our teacher was adamant that we should go to Auckland to school. One day my mother came to me and said, 'Are you going to Auckland?' She then asked, 'Is it not good that you go?' I replied, 'No.' Even though I did not want to go, my mother said, 'You are going to Auckland. Be strong. This is a good thing for you.' So Mira, myself and the teacher went to Auckland. The teacher took us to her two sisters, who were married, and they looked after us.

The teacher's sisters said, 'Yes, bring the girls to stay with us.' So then we left. We did not go to Kaitāia [to school], we went straight to Auckland (by train). Both of us stayed with these Pākehā.

This was at the beginning of Christmas. We stayed in Auckland from Christmas through to the beginning of school. Our teacher worked hard to take us around to look for a scholarship so that we may enter Queen Victoria School. Just before school started we received confirmation that we could attend Queen Victoria as scholarships for us had come through. We came under the Anglican school.

This was our first time in Auckland. How was it for us? We were like mice! We were running around looking at everything because everything was new to us. Very new. I was 75 years away from home. I have now returned to Te Hāpua.

When in Auckland, the women who were caring for us pondered which of them would be responsible for us because the women did not speak Māori or know our customs. They decided that it would be better to let us go to Queen Victoria because the Māori language was there, the wisdom of the world was there and the ability to live together with other Māori girls from other areas: from Te Arawa, Waikato, Whānau a Apanui, Ngāpuhi and girls from other places. We heard the Māori language at Queen Victoria but it was not the language that came with us to Queen Victoria. Nevertheless all of us knew how to speak the Māori language. We heard the dialects of different areas.

There was a good reason why we came to Queen Victoria to be taught by these Pākehā. After three years, we realised what the school wanted us to learn – how to keep house, how to wash clothes, how to cook food and those sorts of things; things we already knew how to do before going there. Those were the reasons we came, under the auspices of the Anglican church.

After this we were taken to the 'coaching college'. The purpose of that coaching college was to select those who wanted to go to university. This is what was said, 'Both of you must go to this college. These are the things of value for you both: the English language, history, Latin, maths and Māori. This is what you will both do for one year to enable you both to come through "matric" [matriculation].' Who arranged this? The Pākehā carers [who were looking after us] arranged this. 'Only knowledgeable ones go to university.' Thus both of us went to coaching college at the Ferry Buildings for one year. When that year ended Mira said that she did not pass English. I was very unhappy because my dreams and aspirations, which were the same as my parents' [were in question], and I wondered 'How would I get to university? These Pākehā will help us to gain entrance into university.'

I sat alone in my sadness. I thought that those responsible for us were in the wrong [and that I would not be prepared enough for university either]. I decided that I would write a letter to the University. I sent my letter asking that I be allowed to enter into University. They agreed to it. I got my matriculation, which then makes it possible for students to enter university, to enter teachers training college and all those types of places. That is how it was for the mice of Te Hāpua!

Te Reo Mihi is the Marae

Te Reo Mihi of Te Hāpua is my marae. That name was given by Rātana. The marae before that was Te Hiku o Te Ika. I did not see that marae. Waiora is another marae altogether, here in Ngātaki. Te Reo Mihi is in Te Hāpua. Now the first marae of Te Hāpua was Hiku o Te Ika. Kenana [another marae] is down here.

When I was growing up I was brought up in the Rātana Church at the invitation of Piri Wiri Tua, the person who brought the Rātana Church here. Piri Wiri Tua was also known as Tahupōtiki Wiremu Rātana. Many Māori fell under the influence of the Rātana Church. The Rātana Church became established in this marae and in that marae, and in these people and those people. That is how we live here in Te Hāpua and in this district.

Well before the Rātana Church was established (in the 1920s), Rātana was well known for healing people. He knew how to look after people – the poor and the sick. This is what he was well known for. When the Māori people heard about him they fell under his influence. They went to him to be healed. Their bodies were deteriorating or were sick, but Rātana was able to heal them. In the light of these circumstances, people were drawn to him. It is right that today this learned man has remained strong for the Māori people, hence his calling as leader for the Rātana Church. Thus his Church was established. Many of our people followed him.

Piri Wiri Tua called out, 'Come to me, remnants.' Do not come to me as Ngāti Kurī, as Ngāti Porou or anything else. Come to me as remnants.

The World of Constant Change

Even though the Rātana Church was great – to the people it was their sustenance and also the pathway to the new world – it was also a world of constant change for us. The people turned away from the ways of the past. I now see the poorness of our existence here in Te Hāpua. In Te Hāpua today, our position [or our understanding of customary knowledge, values and practices] is weak [limited].

Waiora, our marae, came from Te Reo Mihi. This is the main marae in Ngāti Kurī. Te Reo Mihi marae does not follow the custom or karanga [call] of our ancestors. Neither does it have our ancestors carved on the house. There are no ancestors.

When I was growing up, we did not really go to the marae to the tangi [funerary rituals]. Attendance at tangi was new to us. We were not allowed to go to many tangi. We did go to some, but there was always the thought which I understood, 'Do not go to the marae. Go back to school. Go home.' Those kinds of statements. These ways were not the traditional ways of Māori. Instead we followed the ways of the Rātana Church.

When one of us got sick, one of the Apostles [church officials or ministers] would come to pray for us to make us well. When we went, the question was put to my father, 'What is troubling or ailing you?' Because some believed, 'That is why the children are sick.' [In other words, it was the treasures of old that were the source of sickness.]

And so my father would say, 'Yes I have them; release the taonga [ancestral treasures] to Rātana Pā. Free them up. These are the reasons why the children are sick.' There were many treasures of my father that were given like that.

If we abandoned or left behind our Māori ways, our customs, the songs of our elders, our farewell speeches, our karanga to our visitors, we would not have our language, there would be no one to speak. There would be no one amidst us today that would really know these customary practices. We sit in a state of bewilderment, hence the reason why I pursue these things now and hence the reason why we remain poor and ignorant to this day.

Outside this district I see and hear that the traditional things are being practised on other marae. Whaikōrero [formal oratory] and formal farewell speeches are still being carried out and are thriving within traditional Māori strongholds. I hear outstanding whaikōrero in other tribes. The formal speeches here are short. In the old days the whaikōrero here were long. The Māori world and the world of Ngāti Kurī have changed since I was a child.

Whaikōrero was (and is) a real feature of the Māori community. Amongst Tuhoe, for example, whaikōrero is still there. They have beautiful language, with references and whakataukī [proverbs]. Their reo is coloured by all those sorts of elements of the language. The way people stand, the way people dress is also notable. They do not come in sandshoes. They put their suits on. And in Te Arawa, the old men warned the young, 'This is how you stand on the marae.' You could see them also with their beautifully polished shoes! These things are not what we really do here. We are not aware of these elements of 'tū marae' [marae protocol]. It is about bringing mana with you when you stand and speak on the marae.

Even though it is difficult today, we are always in search of those who know how to conduct the whaikōrero. Today I believe that we need to nurture and awaken this skill in the older ones. They should agree to a protocol for them to follow. Unfortunately there are some here that just choose to sit and remain idle, without a desire to move beyond this condition. It is of course difficult to pursue the customary practices that I speak of. Perhaps it is only a dream. Perhaps my people will awaken to it.

The Language

The decline of the Māori language from when I was a child to today: Māori families throughout the country have experienced this phenomenon, that is, the supplanting of our Māori language in the schools (hence the reason why we protested). The rule in the schools was, 'Do not speak the Māori language'; therefore, this is what we followed because we would be beaten by the teachers. We were the children who were caught speaking Māori. We did not do anything wrong. We only protested. Now today, at home the call is, 'Do not speak the English language.' We did not harbour any resentment or bitterness. When we were jumping about we would be hit and of course we blurted out in Māori, hence 'people like me' came about.

The purpose of te kōhanga reo and te kura kaupapa Māori is commendable, but we need to be careful. We must never leave the teaching of our

Māori language solely to the teachers. The main thing is that we all speak our language, that we all know our language.

My father prohibited us from speaking English in our home. He could not speak English of course. When we (the children) listened to his English language we laughed, but we had to be careful that he did not catch us. However, he was a very knowledgeable person at counting kauri gum when he was selling it. He knew the English language for the words 'pounds', 'shillings' and other words relating to such transactions. And there were many Dallies [Dalmatians] living amongst us. They knew how to work. They were keen learners of the Māori language. We would laugh at their attempts as they were trying to learn.

I look back at my own journey from when I was young to now. I was strong, I managed to succeed because even though my parents did not know the academic world right through to their fingertips, they supported the path I chose. Mira and I were successful because of the help of the Pākehā people who really supported us when we were young, and beyond. It is not as though we are knowledgeable women, no. It was these women who researched the right path for us that we both became educated. I believe it is like this for all the children of the world: if the support and care is given from an early age and throughout childhood, one will succeed. This is my call to my people, that the life / success and death / failure of our children is in our hands. If we do not nurture our children from a young age, none of our children will produce leadership. Instead, we will remain the same, koretake or useless, poverty stricken. That is how it will be for the Māori language, that is how it will be.

We need to teach our language at home. Do not leave it up to someone else or to the teachers, or whoever else. Firstly you all need to return home to learn the Māori language and speak the Māori language to our children. I myself have not heard anyone say, 'You the elders, whaea, parents, hold onto the Māori language in your homes, teach the Māori language at home.' It seems like a waste of time, but it is not.

We need to change the thinking. I know, it is hard. But it needs to happen. It is more than just the words. It is an attitude. He reo rangatira. [It is a revered language.] We also need to be exposed to some of the really classic pieces spoken by elders such as on the marae. Let us hear them. There are yards of material in the speeches of speakers of the reo. We need to hear more of those people. Listen to these other treasures. Expose learners of the language to that and make them realise, and then they get an appreciation, an awareness and a commitment. It is not playing marbles. Its greater than that. There is wairua [spirit] in the learning and in the language. The challenge for us, for Māori Television and others, is to keep those things in mind.

We also need people from our area to go to other areas to experience what I call 'performances'. Learn from there. But we have to make the move. It is about experiencing whaikōrero and other things at another level, learn from that, and then bring those experiences home. Different areas have different tikanga. In Ngāpuhi, for example, you would not know who were the speakers. The speakers would sit in amongst the people. Sitting on the other side were people lined up, and one could say, 'O yes, I know him, I know him, I know him.' Monitoring of these speakers could happen, but not in the cases when Ngāpuhi came. It was a political game that they played. They were smart about that. They never revealed who the speakers were, and therefore retained advantage. It was all tactics.

The Land Court minute books hold much knowledge too. Access to the libraries where they have all the minutes about land issues is also important. Even though our people are reluctant readers, we need to direct people in that way. Expose them to all the possibilities. Make them curious. There are all sorts of ways of strengthening the reo and tikanga. It is not easy. But it has to be done.

The issue of wairua in language is very real when, for example, learners may be able to recite a pepeha [tribal saying] from their home, but have not had the background or opportunity of being home. The language in those cases is out of context. If, for example – and I would love to do it actually – you can get people to become aware of 'icons', of geography of place, then you can have meaning and understanding. Then you can quote. The words are meaningful, when you are addressing a hill, for example. You can regard it as an icon. And people can use it in whaikōrero and in other elements of the reo. They are treasures, worthwhile hanging on to, instead of only pieces of Māori that you learn to say which are out of context, meaningless and where there is no real understanding. But there are all sorts of ways of enriching the language. And children will take to them. They are curious little things. Once you say 'this is an icon', they all know about it. It is not incorporated into the reo learning here, not even amongst the adults. There are all these things [places] around and they are being ignored. Yet, they have meaning and are, therefore, worthwhile to focus on in the learning of the language.

I wrote an article recently concerning unlawful use of these harbours by trawlers. I made the point, 'Tērā ngā tai o Muriwhenua te hora nei – Te Kokotahi Pārengarenga, Tokerau ki Houhora. He taonga tuku iho nā ngā tūpuna.' Suddenly you can make these places have a significance and people might then be compelled into doing something to protect them, such as in the case of our harbours where trawling occurs and where our waters have been raided. Sayings like this one are a fabulous way of addressing and using the language. All sorts of issues come up, like commercial fishing techniques, the impact on the local fishers, conservation, policy and many others. You cannot underestimate the role of language in helping to address and identify issues from a Māori world view. And that is why some things have to be in Māori, and not in English, otherwise the whole sense of why something is important, what values are important, is lost. People can under-appreciate. When I say 'ngā tai o Muriwhenua', 'the tides of Muriwhenua', do people know what those are? At least, put them in print as well. And 'e hora nei ki Kokotahi Pārengarenga' for example. Local people, fishers and others need to know what those are. 'Ki Tokerau', Tokerau beach, next to Houhora. Those are the two areas. These are the tides spread out amongst us that are being polluted or being abused. Ko ēnei ngā tū kupu i roto i te reo Māori. [These are the kinds of words in the Māori language.] Only te reo Māori can truly capture the essence of a Māori world view. But whether people understand is the question. We have to do something about the lack of understanding and encourage the learning of the values. The language is a good way to do that.

The Stories of the Land

When you return home, you will learn the talk, the whakapapa [genealogy] of home. You never learned all this from somewhere else. I heard this from our people. Thus, on the marae, when the visitors arrive, they ask, 'Who are you?' Then one replies, 'I am from Kurahaupō, ko Pōhurihanga.' This was when this was spoken. Nowhere else. Ngāti Kurī is afraid when such words were spoken, but it is an age-old custom. The visitors will tell us who they are so that everyone will know the mana of each group. The manuhiri will identify themselves and it is important for the identity of each group to be known so that the political relationship can be understood. But Ngāti Kurī are afraid to identify themselves using customary cues. The Māori spirit has been lost amongst us. We have been switched off from the Māori world for a long time.

Māori Women Standing on the Marae

I can see women displacing men in speaking roles on the marae. But, traditionally, we were not allowed to speak on the marae. But I believe the time is coming for women to have a role in speaking. From what I see, they are managing better than men in many cases! Women will always continue to have an important role in fulfilling kaikaranga duties.

The Challenge

The crisis of the marae for us began almost 100 years ago when the Rātana Church began to have influence amongst our communities.

Of course Rātana brought renewed hope and faith, at a time when there was much adversity and difficulty facing our people concerning our lands, and our health also. Many in our community had died in the great flu epidemic of 1918. But new faith brought new values. Te reo and tikanga of our marae were directly affected. We have not recovered since. We are still bereft of strong leadership in whaikōrero, in waiata, in karanga. For more than 90 years we have had a loss of language and a loss of traditional knowledge.

These things, the customs of the marae, they are jumbled. Some of us are not skilled to pursue these things, to bring these thoughts out in the Māori language. There was no planning ahead.

Although these are my opinions, there is a big job before us. A big challenge. This challenge falls on the elders. It seems that it (the challenge) has not landed. They, the elders, are busy looking at someone else, a teacher, others perhaps. This is a very bad problem within the Māori people. The elders have not taken up the subject. My words to the elders: our way of speaking, the customs and speech-making are being lost. Where have you all gone?

These are my thoughts and my attitude about teaching te reo. Drive its significance home. Do not excuse the elders. They have a responsibility. The parents have a responsibility. The attitude 'somebody else can do it' is not right. Kōhanga reo, kura and Māori Television are of course important. But they do not and cannot replace the centrality of the home in learning the language.

PAUL TAPSELL is chair of Māori Studies at the University of Otago. Of Te Arawa and Ngāti Raukawa descent, he has a background in museums and cultural heritage. Having graduated from the University of Oxford in 1998 with a D.Phil. in Museum Ethnography, he has worked as curator of the Rotorua Museum and director Māori at Auckland Museum. In the mid-1990s, he was instrumental in the return of Pukaki, an iconic and important taonga, to Rotorua from the Auckland Museum.

Professor Tapsell's passion is for customary leadership and the potential intersections with today's generation of dislocated indigenous youth, and these are his primary research focus. He is involved in tribal (especially Ngāti Whakaue) and national organisations. Paul is published widely on Māori and indigenous topics and has spearheaded the Māori Maps project.

CHAPTER TWO

TRIBAL MARAE: CRISIS? WHAT CRISIS?

PAUL TAPSELL

I see the legacy of colonisation and the loss Māori suffered: the loss of mana and the right to fully be Māori in your own country. – Piripi Walker, speaking on Radio New Zealand National, 1 August 2010

I GREW UP IN THE RURAL BAY OF PLENTY–WAIKATO REGIONS OF AOTEAROA New Zealand, believing anything north of the Auckland Harbour Bridge was enemy country. Once a year we would visit Uncle Pekamu, Dad's older brother, and his whānau (family) who lived on the lower slopes of the extinct volcano Maungakiekie (One Tree Hill). The journey north would seem to take forever, but to help pass time we 'eye-spied' old pā (terraced villages, now abandoned) from the rear of Dad's car. My uncle's house was a Victorian mansion, with central heating and an impressive view to the northwest: towards enemy country! Uncle Pek and Dad would tease us: 'That's Ngāpuhi country up there boys: they stole our women once upon a time!' Those sorts of comments didn't register much to us youngsters. We were less interested in stories and more interested in exploring the neighbourhood. But we did like the idea of 'enemy country' for seeding further imaginings of battle and war. It seemed to take forever to climb the grassed slopes of Maungakiekie – terrace after steep terrace – until finally we reached a place we could look north, beyond the harbour bridge over the Waitematā. 'Enemy country' we would parrot as we sat on the edge of a large flat area with karaka trees and grazing sheep. We imagined massive palisades protecting us from below, an army of warriors at our command. In our minds we held the high ground and no one could defeat us, not even Ngāpuhi. After winning our battle, we would reluctantly head back to Uncle Pek's home. Later the next day, exhausted boys and dogs were bundled into the rear of the old Ford. We were fast asleep long before the city streets turned to country roads and the old-time pā watched us retreat home, deep into the Waikato.

I still 'eye-spy' the same pā of those backseat days, but now I also include the many pā to the north of Auckland, all the way through 'enemy country' to Te Rerenga Wairua.[*] Although today's marae are not nearly as prominent as their associated pā, marae remain the quintessential focus of tribal Māori identity.[†] But things have radically changed since my childhood, with the unrelenting migration of Māori away from their papakāinga (home marae communities; also often referred to as 'pā' and/or kāinga) to the cities. Can our tribal marae communities survive as they enter their third generation of depopulation? Is there a future for tribal marae given their descendants now live mostly away from their ancestral homes?

This essay has three parts and a discussion. It first looks at the ancient Pacific origins of marae, then traces its historical evolution in Aotearoa. The third part considers the question: are marae in crisis? Utilising a Tai Tokerau-focused case study – Māori Maps Pilot Project – the essay finishes with a discussion on what the future might hold for tribal marae.

Ancient Origins of Marae

In a not so distant past – in human population terms – a community of like-minded people simultaneously developed a unique range of navigational skills in tandem with maritime technology. This enabled them to venture across Pacific seaways in multiple directions, originating from the Asian vicinity of Taiwan over 5000 years ago. Thanks to oral traditions, archaeology, linguistics and genetics we are able to differentiate and physically trace this unique community of mariners from their early

---

[*] The northernmost point of Aotearoa New Zealand.
[†] See Tapsell, 2002 for more comprehensive discussion of marae.

expansion period through to today. As this culture developed so did their reach, culminating in arguably the greatest feat of human exploration (covering one-third of the world), one from which the Māori people proudly descend (Howe, 2006; Irwin, 2006; Kirch, 2000).

But what motivated the distant ancestors of the Māori to leave 'home' some 150 generations ago and to become a distinctive people who genealogically organised their universe to revolve around an oceanic-based marae culture? Past explanations for the peopling of the Pacific centred on a simplistic theory of accidental drift voyaging, promoted by colonial-framed discourse and popularised through school textbooks and imagery up to recent times (for example, Sharp, 1963). Howe (2006) indicates that scholars such as Lewis (1994), Green (1991), Kirch (2000), Finney (2006) and Irwin (2006), among others, have presented overwhelming evidence that indicates the Pacific was populated by deliberate exploration followed by systematic colonisation. The archaeological evidence also indicates that these ancestors were more entrepreneurial than previously credited, suggesting a highly mobile, well-organised trade community who, for more than 5000 years, sought to access new opportunities over the oceanic horizon (Kirch, 2000, pp. 91–95).

Three thousand years before Columbus left his European horizon, the Pacific ancestors of the Māori had already begun navigating into the largest ocean on earth. It appears that trading was a key motivator for the first major expansion of these explorers (Kirch, 2000). They entered the inland seaways of the west Pacific, soon reaching through and beyond the Philippines into the many hundreds of Indonesian and Southeast Asian islands. In due course, an ambitious group emerged out of this coastal trading community, developing new technologies that enabled them to sail east across significant expanses of water (Howe, 2006). Archaeologically they are referred to as the Lapita peoples, after the site in Lapita, New Caledonia, where their pottery was first found.* These relatively isolated lands, including the Bismarck Archipelago off Papua New Guinea and

---

* See Kirch, 2000 for wide-ranging discussion on how this group is part of the Proto-Austronesian class of peoples, which began linking multiple islands in the western Pacific region known today as Near Oceania.

the Solomon Islands, carried large, culturally ancient populations whose ancestors arrived more than 20,000 years ago during the Pleistocene period, when sea levels were much lower due to glaciation.* Evidence of an archaeological, linguistic (for example, Pawley and Ross, 1993) and genetic (for example, Spriggs, 1995) nature suggests the incoming Lapita people were a distinct culture, closely related and trade-oriented. They supplied and linked numerous local populations with gift-exchange items originating hundreds of kilometres away. Although the incoming Lapitas constantly engaged a diversity of ancient communities, they maintained their distinctiveness not just economically,† but also socially and politically.‡ As the generations passed, these people flourished, adapted and asserted themselves culturally throughout Near Oceania. The Lapita culture has long since transformed as it constantly adapted to new challenges precipitated by over 3000 years of relative geographical (oceanic) isolation and shifting resources. Nevertheless, its unique cultural signature§ remains in evidence today, being maintained by island communities throughout the Pacific, including Māori in New Zealand (Kirch, 2000).

The next Pacific expansion was both rapid and influential in the long term. The symbiotic evolution of navigational knowledge and watercraft technology most likely triggered the new wave of exploration into Remote Oceania (for example, Reef and Loyalty Islands, Tikopia, New Caledonia, Vanuatu, Fiji, Tonga and Samoa [Kirch, 2000]). This epoch of expansion is noted for the rapid colonisation of numerous island groups of Remote Oceania along with the many Micronesian archipelagos never before inhabited (Kirch, 2000, p. 167).

Also to emerge from the archaeological record was evidence of a new ritual space, resembling a marae, the further east the ancestors voyaged (Tapsell, 1998, pp. 56–58). During my recent visit to Ra'iatea and Tahiti

---

* See Kirch, 2000, pp. 65–67 for overview concerning population expansion due to very low ocean levels.
† For example, geographic spread of Lapita or Proto-Austronesian pottery and associated patterns and symbolism from Near into Remote Oceania (Kirch, 2000, pp. 85–116).
‡ For example, marriages, commonality of language, custom, shared hierarchical patterns of leadership embedded within landscapes of power (Kirch, 2000).
§ For example, art, language, patterns of settlement, technology, genetic markers.

in the Society Islands, the traditional creation story of 'Marae' was described to me by a tohunga (customary specialist) who explained its layers of meaning as taught by her Tuamotu elders.* The first part of the word, 'ma', refers to the female element. It is represented by, and derives from, 'marama', the moon in a darkened universe. It is also a subtle acknowledgement of Papa tū ā Nuku (Earth Mother), and her life-giving support. The next part, 'ra', denotes the complementary male element. Ra is a reference to the sun (stars) and Ranginui, and its life-giving energy. Combined, mara, marama, maramara are acknowledgements of the complementary duality of the universe's two prime forces, female–Papa and male–Rangi, out of which emerge enlightenment, knowledge and consciousness. Finally, 'e' indicates the idea of 'enabling' something, and providing context. In this case, the context is the complementary nature of ma (women) and ra (men), in an ancestral land- or seascape. Marae, then, is about people and the environment working together – or, in other words, about tangata whenua, people of the land. While from an oral tradition perspective marae refers to people, the archaeological view emphasises that marae is about place. Evidence suggests that the coastal marae of the Pacific was politically hierarchical (Kirch, 1990; 2000), perhaps pragmatically responding to the layering of identity-embedded navigational knowledge and associated power. Pacific anthropologists, historians and oral narrative specialists have begun exploring this likelihood, noting that particular ancient marae appeared to provide earth-bound (Papa tū ā Nuku) reference points by which accurate readings could take place of the celestial (Ranginui) pathways of the sun, moon and stars as the navigators crossed the horizon. Thereafter, such observations – encoded in songs, chants, prayers, narratives and artistic symbolism – became an embodied three-dimensional ocean-star chart by which the tohunga āhurewa (revered navigator) was able to voyage accurately between genealogically important island groups (Di Piazza and Pearthree, 2007; Howe, 2006; Tapsell, 2009).

---

* Co-researcher, Taha Manu-Tahi, 29 April 2012. This tohunga was from the Tuamotu Archipelago, between Tahiti and the Marquesas Islands.

Not unlike Māori tribes today, their ancestors from the eastern Pacific islands also identified themselves by a centralised matua (parent) marae.* These marae came to represent a direct connection between Papa tū ā Nuku (island groups) and a particular zenith star or star pairing within Rangi Nui (the night sky heavens) by which the ancient navigators could fix their relative latitudinal global positioning. This enabled accurate course-plotting between islands.† Given the importance of navigational knowledge to survival and power across generations, it is not surprising that matua marae transformed into reverential or tapu spaces, providing the forum where the deeper layers of navigational knowledge would be accumulated, tested, rehearsed and transmitted.

The further east the evolving maritime culture ventured, the more distinctive and elaborate marae became. The matua marae directly reflected the importance of ancestrally encoded navigational knowledge, undoubtedly in step with technological advances of their ocean-voyaging waka (canoes). By the time the ancestors reached Tawhiti (Tahiti) over 2000 years ago, these marae had transformed into complex, highly ritualised spaces that were set apart from everyday village life. They generally comprised an ātea (basalt plaza) and an āhu (coral slab wall). One particular and very ancient marae complex, Taputapuatea at Opoa on the shores of Ra'iatea, is revered throughout East Polynesia (for example, Tahiti, Marquesas, Aotearoa, Hawai'i, Rapanui and Rarotonga) as the mataamua (eldest) of all marae (Taonui, 2006).‡ Māori, for example, still maintain rituals, narrative, art, song and dance that identify Taputapuatea as an important source of their ancestral identity – spiritual power – and have transferred the name Taputapuatea to places in Aotearoa. Archaeologists have found evidence supporting Taputapuatea as a marae that was recognised throughout the Pacific (Kirch, 2000; Howe, 2006). According

---

* In Hawai'i, marae are also known as heiau.
† See Tapsell, 2009 regarding HMS *Endeavour* journal observations of Tupaea's navigational ability without sextant; Di Piazza and Pearthree, 2007, regarding Tupaea's 1769 spatial-navigational map of the Pacific; and Low in Howe, 2006 for deeper understanding of ancient star-navigation technique.
‡ It is also notable that the islands of Hawai'i, Tahiti and Rarotonga have marae named Taputapuatea.

to archaeologist Yoshiko Sinoto, who reconstructed the wider marae complex known as Tinirau-Hui-Mataitepapa, the āhu of Taputapuatea was uniquely oriented toward the Earth's true north–south axis, while its ātea was positioned facing west and inland toward the setting sun and the mountain named Te Po (Tapsell, 2009; Wiremu Tupaia, pers. comm. 2012). Early writings appear to support traditional accounts of Polynesian navigators and their apprentices journeying to this marae from throughout the equatorial Pacific islands.* The apprentice would return in later life as an elder navigator, but this time with his own new apprentice. All aspects of navigational knowledge would be transferred to the next generation during these epic return voyages from distant home-islands.

Marae never remained static. They underwent continuous transformation and in some cases evolved into elaborate basalt-terraced elevations (for example, the marae named Tai-nui in the Waipu valley and Mahaiatea, both on the coast of the leeward side of Tahiti, which I visited in 2012). These dominant, tapu (spiritually restricted) structures reflected the values associated with land as distinct from ocean resources. Yet throughout this evolution it appears that Taputapuatea remained revered for 1500 years or more as the navigational centre of East Polynesia (Henry, 1912; Kirch, 2000; Tapsell, 2009; Te Rangi Hiroa, 1938). Out of this marae-centred culture, a new oceanic expansion was triggered. By 1000 A.D., Eastern Polynesians had begun embarking on voyages of discovery in multiple directions. They explored into higher and lower latitudes of the Pacific, populating western-based outliers as well as reaching the Americas (Kirch, 2000). As the early kings of England were dealing with marauding Vikings from across the North Sea, the far-flung islands of Pitcairn, Rapanui, Hawai'i, Rarotonga, Te Ika a Māui (Aotearoa) and numerous other Polynesian outliers like Tikopia were being systematically settled (Kirch, 2000). As they discovered, colonised and asserted their authority over the most remote Pacific islands, they also established new navigationally associated marae complexes (āhu and ātea), often naming them after

---

* For examples see Salmond, 1991; 2003; Howe, 2006.

the original Taputapuatea (Taonui, 2006). Today's descendant cultures still revere Taputapuatea as their Vatican-like, metaphysical source of ancestral being and knowledge. For many Māori, Taputapuatea is considered the originating site of wānanga (tribal knowledge) from where their East Polynesian ancestors voyaged all across the Pacific, return-visiting places such as Aotearoa up to 600 years ago.*

Around 1500 A.D., the return-voyaging culture of East Polynesian colonisers and their marae-encoded navigational knowledge came to an abrupt end. Whatever the reasons, the many hundreds of Polynesian outlier-settlements in places such as Hawai'i, Rapanui and Aotearoa became isolated from their originating communities. Yet the marae complexes – also known as papa or pā – remained central to wellbeing, transforming in response to the unique habitats and evolving cultural needs of every island. Marae provided the social, political and economic platform around which communities rebuilt new lives.

Marae Evolution in Aotearoa

Soon after the ancestors of the Māori arrived in Aotearoa, the two elements of the marae, the āhu and ātea, separated into two distinctive, formal institutions (Tapsell, 2002). Although the āhu (or tūāhu) remained a space restricted to the tohunga āhurewa (spiritual specialists descended from navigators), the ātea evolved into a semi-ritualised public leadership space, while still keeping the title of marae (marae ātea). The terraced ancestral pā that are still visible on New Zealand's landscapes were also part of the marae evolution as Māori became more settled. These engineering feats closely mirror the later (post-1000 A.D.) East Polynesian basalt marae and hill sculptures, also called papa, that can still be seen throughout the Society Islands. As generations passed and return voyaging ceased, Māori acclimatised and learned to manage their resources sustainably. The ātea, uniquely adapted to occupy a commanding position within the protection

---

* Wānanga represents a higher school of thought or learning by which all knowledge, beliefs and behaviours of the world are captured in the three baskets of knowledge – see Tapsell, 1998 and Te Rangi Hiroa, 1938 for further discussion.

of the pā, provided both physical and spiritual leadership to its local kin-community or kāinga. In combination the marae ātea complex came to be known as pā-kāinga. Throughout these transformations, the ātea became the exclusive political domain from where the rangatira (kin leaders) exercised social and economic power over surrounding lands, waterways and associated resources.

Meanwhile, the tūāhu remained tapu shrines that were maintained away from pā-kāinga. They were sites where spiritual negotiation between tohunga āhurewa and atua (gods, great ancestral beings) occurred, ensuring the wellbeing and prosperity of the community (Tapsell, 1998).

By the time Tupaea helped navigate the HMS *Endeavour* to Aotearoa in 1769, it appears that there were hundreds of pā-kāinga or marae communities strategically located throughout Aotearoa.* These elaborate, palisade-protected marae locales (Kawharu, 2010) were mostly situated on terraced hilltops, bluffs and promontories. Tupaea declared to Cook that these pā were '... Mories [marae] or places of worship', no doubt because they resembled the basalt-terraced ritual marae or papa of his Ra'iatean/Tahitian homelands. Cook, however, countered that they were '... places of retreat or strongholds' (Beaglehole, 1962, p. 191). Neither was wrong. The dynamic transformations that marae underwent after first arriving in Aotearoa are testament to the continuing agency of Māori leadership up to and beyond the arrival of the *Endeavour*.

Marae adapted to the unique conditions of Aotearoa, setting them apart from the rest of the Pacific. The risks and opportunities of accessing resources within a new land-based environment created tensions between competing kin-communities. Notwithstanding environmental factors (McFadgen, 2007), the marae ātea space developed in response to hundreds of years of such tensions, especially around 1500 A.D. when contact with East Polynesian communities ceased. Hapū became the fundamental social, political and economic kin grouping of Māori society. They developed and maintained their own marae, becoming the politically dynamic

---

* The Māori Maps research project has identified around 800 marae still operating throughout Aotearoa New Zealand, each directly descending from nearby pā-kāinga on which their ancestral communities dwelt at the time of first European contact.

space or place for hapū to ameliorate internal and external tensions. Unlike their Pacific ancestors, the hapū communities of Aotearoa could maintain external kin relationships without having to navigate across ocean expanses. But this did not stop Māori from thinking and behaving like their island-based ancestors. They continued to explore and engage with neighbouring hapū, no doubt contributing to the unique transformations we today associate with marae ātea of Māori communities. With the tapu of knowledge and its spiritual dimensions now contained and maintained in out-of-the-way tūāhu, the ātea transformed into a centralised community space. Ātea provided the forum for leadership to be expressed in rituals of hosting, marriage, gifting, resource-sharing and, on occasion, the life crisis of tangihanga (mourning).

The close proximity of resource-competing hapū also brought a new set of risks. For instance, there was the opportunity for non-mandated interactions between hapū individuals, especially pōtiki (generally younger, more adventurous explorers), sometimes precipitating life-crises (Tapsell and Woods, 2009). The more heritage- or custom-minded kaumātua, kuia (male, female elders) and rangatira needed to be on alert for unsanctioned actions by risk-taking pōtiki (Kawharu, Tapsell and Woods, 2012). Transgressions directly challenged hapū wellbeing and leadership.* Conflict may have arisen, ultimately requiring appropriate marae-prescribed responses.

Today the marae ātea of Māori society remains a prescriptive space that can be transformed into a heightened place of tapu (ancestral restriction) when any visiting group presents itself at the marae or pā entrance. As in former days, local kin assemble to welcome the arriving guests. The engagement proceeds when kaumātua give their signal. In my tribal area of Te Arawa, rituals begin often with a wero (ceremonial challenge) followed by karanga (ritual calls of invitation) offered by host kuia to mark commencement of the pōwhiri (ritual of encounter). Tapu is maintained until the kaumātua have completed the mihimihi (greetings) and waiata

---

* For example, theft, desecration of resources, disturbance of burial sites, inappropriate liaisons with women, wilful injury possibly causing death.

or haka (songs or chants of kin-identification, remembering the dead who might be directly significant to the occasion). Marae are returned to a state of noa (freedom from restriction) at the end of ritual proceedings.

For hundreds of years, the tapu of the marae has been managed by kaumātua and kuia. It is they who prescribe the rules for visitor engagement. On arrival the visitors were (and still are) metaphorically welcomed with honour onto the host's marae as if they had journeyed from another Pacific island. They become the embodiment of shared Pacific ancestry; and may be likened to the arrival of a great voyaging waka (inter-island sailing vessel). At the appropriate moment in the welcome, the visitors, symbolically representing the waka and all it contains – ira atua (spiritual presence), ira tangata (living presence) and kaupapa (reason for visiting) – are ceremonially hauled (tōia mai te waka), pulled (ki te urunga te waka) and then laid (ki te moenga te waka) to rest (ki te takotoranga i takoto ai te waka) on the marae by the tangata whenua (home/local people of the land). The hosting kaumātua and kuia determine the ebb and flow of the ritualised encounter. Taonga (ancestral items of prestige) may be presented, taumau (chiefly marriages) might be negotiated, agreed and/or promised and – more commonly today – gatherings celebrating birthdays, family reunions or other hapū events might take place. Eventually both groups became (re)united under common whakapapa (kinship links) and this would be duly sealed with the sharing of ancestral breath via the hongi (pressing of noses). Immediately thereafter the marae is cleared of tapu. According to my tribal traditions, hākari (ceremonial feast) was in former times laid out upon the marae. Today, food is provided in the neighbouring dining hall. The delicacies provided reflect the mana (prestige, respect) of the visitors. Of course, if at any stage prescribed boundaries were transgressed, it was viewed as an insult, precipitating a new episode of crises requiring utu (payment; reciprocity), which sometimes might remain unbalanced for some years.*

---

* For example, eight generations of spasmodic conflict between hapū of Te Arawa and Mataatua at Maketū in Bay of Plenty (Tapsell, 2006).

It was in the ritually controlled marae context that the first crosscultural encounters between Māori and Europeans occurred, in 1769. One in particular was at Whitianga where Tupaea escorted Cook, Banks and other *Endeavour* crew into a fortified pā-kāinga. Banks notes that the encounter included feasting on dog and the exchange of items (Tapsell, 2009, p. 100). Another recorded encounter was that of du Fresne who entered Te Tai Tokerau only months later. In this case it appears that du Fresne and his landing party transgressed the tapu of a particular site and paid with their lives (Salmond, 1991, p. 395). The many pā sighted and recorded by early European explorers, whalers, traders and missionaries underwent new transformations over the next century in response to a number of externally triggered crises. For instance, epidemics introduced by Europeans underpinned the first major attack on the social, political and economic fabric of Māori tribal society. Oral accounts talk of former great pā being rendered tapu as waves of out-of-control rewharewha (coughing illness) swept through these fortified marae-centred villages. Some pā were so filled with sickness and death they were abandoned and some remain tapu to this day (for example, Weriweri at Ngongotahā in Rotorua and Maungawhau in Tāmaki).

Hapū were barely recovering when a new, but equally deadly, threat jeopardised kin survival. The arrival of firearms challenged marae communities in ways never before experienced. The previously acceptable ritualised practice of hand-to-hand combat between individuals to resolve conflict was thrown into disarray. Death could now be delivered from a distance and by anyone who could load and point a musket. Firearms also reversed the strategic advantage of high-ground pā, exposing their occupants to indefensible attacks by cannon and musket fire. Cultural norms were tipped out as hapū fought for survival. Many of them failed and marae communities suffered radically.

The combination of illness and firearms resulted in near-complete abandonment of traditional hilltop pā, which had previously served and protected occupants for ten or more generations. During times of crisis hapū temporarily realigned as iwi – an inherently unstable grouping of multiple hapū – to, for example, better harvest resources such as in fishing expeditions, more safely enter neighbouring territories, ameliorate major crises, take advantage of any perceived opportunities or counter external threats.* While some hapū aligned with others to take advantage of the new power that muskets provided, by attacking rival hapū, those under attack also regrouped as iwi but took residence in more defensible lowland pā. By the 1830s, a sense of normality began to return in the north (of New Zealand) as the iwi arms race was neutralised and warring groups disbanded. Surviving hapū returned to home territories. Some took up residence in proximity to new resource opportunities, for example, near anchorages, missionary stations and trader homesteads that were on offer as a result of early European interactions. (Missionary stations were also built close to pā following the invitation of rangatira to missionaries to locate themselves nearby.) The marae may have transformed from hilltop pā, but they remained central to community life within unfortified villages, or papakāinga. Elderly hapū leaders were generally content to maintain their pre-Christian beliefs. Nevertheless, they encouraged emerging leaders to enter into strategic relationships with the new arrivals, not least missionaries and traders, in order for the hapū to access all they had to offer from beyond the shores of Aotearoa.

From the 1820s, the Australian gold fields created a demand for cash crops like potatoes, to which entrepreneurially minded Māori leaders such as Hongi Hika, Te Rauparaha and Tuhawaiki were quick to respond. Petrie's (2006) publication, *Chiefs of Industry*, documents the new and emerging entrepreneurial leaders of this transitional period (1820s–50s), especially in the north. In the 1820s, Hongi mobilised a huge labour force, establishing intensive market gardens that stretched all the way from Hokianga right through to Pēwhairangi (Bay of Islands). By the 1830s, produce and goods were being directly exported to and imported from New South Wales using Māori-owned vessels. The 1835 Declaration of Independence and the 1840 Tiriti o Waitangi (Treaty of Waitangi) were strategic in providing accessibility to international trade opportunities. Hapū leaders sought a range of things including secure and unhindered

---

* See Ballara, 1998 for a comprehensive discussion on pre-contact iwi formation as recorded by early-contact historical documentation and Māori Land Court archives and minutes.

access to the Australian marketplace, in order to protect or advance their tino rangatiratanga (chiefly rights of social, political and economic authority over lands, villages and treasured possessions). But soon after signing Te Tiriti (the Māori text of the Treaty), northern leaders such as Hone Heke and Kawiti learned that the Crown had broad intentions to strengthen its authority in New Zealand, directly threatening their own customary power and influence. The northern musket wars of 1845 soon followed, as detailed elsewhere. When peace returned, the northern agricultural industry recovered, contributing to nationwide prosperity (Petrie, 2006). Over the next decade, hapū regained and maintained their sense of economic, social and political independence.

In the mid-1850s, as the Australian goldrush ended, Māori prosperity was challenged by the Crown, which was implementing a colonial agenda designed to legally obfuscate hapū-controlled resources. To the south, it began engaging a hostile strategy to capture control of the fertile lands and resources in the Taranaki, Waikato and Bay of Plenty regions. Māori held large political meetings throughout the central regions of Te Ika a Māui (North Island) to discuss how they should respond. From the 1850s, whare hui (meeting houses) were built primarily to host these many inter-hapū gatherings that would sometimes last weeks or even months as the implications of colonisation were debated. Ultimately, many hapū of the central regions confederated as iwi in preparation to defend their mana, their full right to be Māori in their own country,[*] whether by fighting beside the Crown or against it. On the ensuing battlefields of the Taranaki, Waikato and Bay of Plenty regions, Māori fiercely gave no quarter. But within the legislative chambers of colonial power, the Crown ultimately divided, conquered and ruled. Without exception it alone became the eventual and exclusive winner, divvying up its spoils to itself and incoming British settlers. They deforested Papa tū ā Nuku and reshaped her into farmlands. Hapū struggled to survive and tried to utilise the meagre resources that were 'reserved', if any were reserved at all. Many reserve promises for Māori were broken (Stokes, 1997; Pickens,

---

[*] To borrow from Piripi Walker's quote that opens this essay.

1997; Waitangi Tribunal, 1996; 2003; Ngāti Whātua ō Ōrākei, 2003). Increasingly, papakāinga became isolated from any economic wealth and the previously powerful statements of identity – carved ancestral houses, especially in the central and eastern regions – began to decay, reflecting the hardship of their people.

From the 1860s, papakāinga entered into a state of relative depression compared to their Pākehā neighbours who, by the 1900s, were directly benefiting from hapū estates earlier alienated by various Crown-driven mechanisms.* For Māori across the nation, depression deepened. They were plagued by high infant mortality, tuberculosis and generally poor sanitation as papakāinga became increasingly isolated from the growing Pākehā-controlled hubs of a farming-driven colonial economy. Seasonal flows of cash derived from labouring on local farms, together with county drainage and roadway development schemes, provided some relief. These incomes, however, generally went directly toward supporting whānau units living in homes erected on partitioned lands beyond the papakāinga. The hapū was no longer an economically cohesive unit representing tino rangatiratanga over surrounding ancestral landscapes. Its ability to collectively provide economic wellbeing from surrounding estates had been effectively undermined by its Treaty partner, the Crown. Crown policies and law alienated Māori from their land and resource base. This first began in the 1840s, peaking in the 1860s so that by 1900, Māori were left in control of only 6 million out of 66 million acres (Walker, 1990).

Marae communities suffered as a result of these economic and political upheavals. Ironically, the shared negative experience of colonisation in fact galvanised marae communities and their leadership to seek new solutions. The advent of Māori incorporations refocused rural hapū communities on creating consolidated farming units, bringing the first promise of prosperity in over 60 years. These schemes were set in place by Māori Member of Parliament Sir Apirana Ngata in the 1930s. However, they were hampered by high-interest loans and lack of farming

---

* For example, the Native Land Court and public works legislation. See Kawharu, 1977 and Williams, 1999 for full discussion of the colonial mechanisms of alienation.

skills. Of those schemes that did survive the Great Depression, only a very few provided any significant relief for their rural hapū communities (Kawharu, 1977). The deepening, Crown-perpetuated crisis of intestate deaths resulted in already divided and fractionated hapū-estates becoming so uneconomic that they were easily purchased by outside developers. By the mid-1930s the once tightly populated and close-knit papakāinga had generally fragmented at two levels – within whānau and within hapū. In some cases marae split altogether as whānau walked out to build their own. Nevertheless marae as a central concept prevailed, maintaining a sense of social and political unity in the face of adversity, not least during life-crises such as tangihanga.

As the 1930s Depression eased, Ngata convinced many marae leaders that the upcoming Treaty centenary provided an opportunity for hapū nationwide to unite and demonstrate the importance of the Māori right to equal citizenship under the Treaty. This took two key forms: on the one hand, young Māori men were encouraged to enlist in the war effort and fight on foreign battlefields for their Treaty right to be Māori in their own nation back home (Soutar, 2008; Ngata, 1943). The implications though for marae communities following the war were devastating when many young Māori failed to return. (Northern elder Fraser Toi discusses these issues in more depth in this volume.) On the other hand, Ngata also promoted marae rebuilding programmes. He did this by finding government funds to assist marae committees to rejuvenate, build or upgrade their wharekai (eating halls), whakairo (carvings) and sporting facilities, as tangible demonstrations of Māori citizenship rights in Pākehā-majority New Zealand (Skinner, 2008; Walker, 2001). A major focus of Ngata's nationwide cultural revival effort occurred at the Waitangi Treaty Grounds with the establishment of a 'national marae', which was opened on 6 February 1940 following the gift of land by Lord Bledisloe (the governor-general and the then landowner of the Treaty grounds) to the people of New Zealand.

Communities struggled over a number of decades throughout the nineteenth and early twentieth centuries to maintain their kinship connections, cohesion and their marae. Their existence was fragile; their culture was threatened. Their very survival was imperilled. Some marae decayed and were abandoned, but others triumphed, and some were even built out of the ashes of colonisation. If there was one thing that held communities together, it was their marae. Marae were the focal point for debate, discussion and ritual. They continued to be the embodiment of hapū mana as well as manaaki (hospitality). Marae are expressions of tino rangatiratanga, as represented by the concept 'kāinga' in Article II of Te Tiriti o Waitangi. In its true sense, marae unified while the Crown divided. Marae reminded the living of their past, their heritage and the wider ancestral landscape and, therefore, the reasons for the living to assert and to defend their rangatiratanga. But challenges to rangatiratanga, to the survival and sanctity of marae, continued following World War II. If anything, challenges were only to intensify.

Marae in Crisis

Following the war, Māori moved to the cities in search of better opportunities, not least employment. Marae communities and kāinga directly suffered. The seeds of depopulation can, in fact, be traced back to the nineteenth century, when papakāinga became economically isolated from their lands. But the full effect did not become evident until after World War II.* With war's end, although papakāinga and returning servicemen and women were again united, the vexing issue of relative economic isolation for most marae across Aotearoa remained unresolved. Furthermore, returning soldiers had gained a taste for the wider world. Their female cousins, especially the many who provided labour to the war effort in the cities, had also experienced the liberation of living beyond the kin-controls of their elders. This Māori generation was the first to jump at the opportunity to make a new life in urban centres. The post-World War II economy boomed, resulting in massive urban infrastructural

---

* Returning soldiers were received with great honour by their marae communities, many of which had been rejuvenated under Ngata's scheme. These young men had brought glory to New Zealand and paid a great price to prove Māori carried the right to full citizenship (Ngata, 1943; Soutar, 2008). Statistics from Soutar's book on Māori soldiers show how they suffered a greater casualty rate than any other Allied Force battalion, but they were instrumental in great battles like El Alamein and others.

development (Tapsell, 2011). By the mid-1970s, tens of thousands of Māori had permanently relocated to cities to raise families and provide the industrial backbone – as labourers, drivers, factory hands, nurses, receptionists, foresters, and market gardeners, road workers, railway workers, construction workers and wharf workers – on which modern New Zealand was developed.

In the mid-1970s the United Kingdom's withdrawal from being New Zealand's primary export market precipitated a decade of economic recession. This doubly affected Māori, who were a major contributor to the labour force in rural and urban sectors of the economy. In both cases, marae communities suffered. Unemployment became a new reality for many Māori. Although times were tough economically, Māori could find some kind of refuge in the urban marae-like centres they had built in the 1960s and early 1970s. These centres provided a sense of belonging and a forum and outlet for cultural practices to continue in lieu of home marae. Later in the 1980s, some urban marae centres that were overseen by committees grew into successful pan-Māori organisations, one of which bid successfully for the right to redistribute state-funded benefits directly to Māori living in its urban catchment (Waitangi Tribunal, 1998). Meanwhile, many marae throughout Aotearoa became increasingly impoverished of people and resources, and struggled to pay for utilities in order to keep their facilities operating.

The decline of marae accelerated, especially those that were in remote rural communities. Kōhanga reo (Māori-language preschools) located within marae or tribal community settings also struggled, and many have closed down in the past decade or so. Despite the hardships and difficulties, marae continued to be important to tribal communities. This was particularly evident in the 1987 Ōrākei claim. As explained by Ngāti Whātua ō Ōrākei kaumātua Sir Hugh Kawharu, the restoration of their marae was central to their identity, to their mana; it was a beginning to the hapū recapturing the status of tangata whenua (Kawharu, 1989; 2004). At the 1987 Waitangi Tribunal hearing, Maori Marsden likened the Crown's eviction of the Ōrākei community from their marae as 'he tuporo teretere' – being cast adrift like floating logs (Waitangi Tribunal, 1987). In 1991, following settlement of the claim, the Ōrākei community regained their marae; that is, they finally regained title to lands, most importantly those on which their meeting house and marae stood. Nonetheless, many have missed out on a formative marae education that only elders can provide by action and observation. Fortunately, the emerging 1990s leaders of Ōrākei were able to draw upon the wisdom of the handful of elders who still remembered their former practices and customs prior to 1951, and to maintain the thread of kin accountability – whakapapa – back to the original marae.

The genesis of today's Māori socio-economic statistics can be considered against the backdrop of the brief history that has been canvassed here so far. The 1970s recession completely overwhelmed Māori. Whether they were in isolated rural communities or now living within cities, Māori lacked effective leadership and support networks, as marae once provided. Without the marae, where can Māori turn in order to resecure their social, political and economic wellbeing? As discussed, the unemployment of urban-living Māori emerged during this time. Māori state dependency has created longitudinal consequences for families that have struggled to get 'out of the rut'. As for anyone on unemployment benefits, particularly in long-term unemployment, the psychological effects can be damaging or devastating to a person's sense of self-worth and wellbeing. Māori initiatives, both private and state-led, have not been able to completely address the triggers – stemming from land alienation – of negative Māori statistics (in such areas as health, justice, education and employment).* Of course there are some exceptional and outstanding Māori successes too, not least educational, sporting and commercial attainment. Mainstream media do not always report these successes. Instead, what we do often read or hear are stories about the negative Māori statistics. Successive governments have put considerable

---

* For example: diabetes; heart disease; rheumatic fever; hepatitis; major cancers (lung, breast, cervical, prostate, colon); obesity; mental illness; suicides; teenage pregnancies; gambling and substance addiction; driving without a licence; drunk driving; unregistered vehicles; child abuse; gang recruitment; domestic violence; youth offenders; arrests; petty and violent crime convictions; prison populations; sub-standard literacy; school suspension, expulsion and incompletion rates; examination failures; long-term state tenancies; sub-standard housing; unemployment and low income.

resources into Māori development from a state-defined perspective. In more recent times these initiatives to reverse these statistics have been framed by Māori values and concepts, for example, mana, manaaki, kotahitanga (unity), whānau, whakapapa and ora (wellbeing), with little or no reference to the source of these principles: the marae. In 2012 when addressing high offending rates, low educational achievement, poor health and so on, some government ministries introduced new strategies, promising to more directly engage Māori community providers. It is believed that the community providers who already have successful track records are best placed to deliver marae-aligned wellness programmes to Māori.*

While some Crown agencies appear to be awakening to the role that marae can still play in recovering Māori wellbeing, the contemporary policy approach of historical Treaty settlements is perpetuating a state of crisis for marae. The Crown is focused on settling with 'large natural groupings' or Recognised Iwi Organisations (RIOs) by 2014. While this approach might be argued as necessary from a government perspective (because it would otherwise be difficult, if not impossible, to settle with all claimants, small or large), the approach actually shifts the focus away from local marae to a higher-level, centralised hapū or iwi organisation. The onus is, therefore, on the settlement entity (hapū or iwi organisations) to ensure that marae are properly included in settlement and post-settlement developments. However, difficulties remain. For example, RIOs have set up singular beneficiary lists that cut across the diverse, but inclusive, marae/hapū systems. Instead of being able to belong and remain accountable to each ancestral marae (through different genealogical descent lines), individuals are required by the Crown-led settlement process to be registered only once with their RIO, perhaps choosing just

---

* For example: New Zealand Police (13 Dec 2012): *Turning the Tide: A Whānau Ora Crime and Crash Prevention Strategy*. See http://www.police.govt.nz/featured/new-strategy-aims-turn-tide-maori-victimisation-and-offending; The Ministry of Justice (n.d.) programmes listed under *Achieving Our Targets*. See http://www.justice.govt.nz/justice-sector/better-public-services-reducing-crime/achieving-our-targets; and the Department of Correction's programme for Māori (17 July 2012). See http://www.corrections.govt.nz/news/media-releases/2011_media_releases/corrections_department_wins_maori_language_award2.html.

one marae of affiliation and forgoing any future kin associations with other marae and hapū. Thereafter, RIOs maintain a mandate – one beneficiary, one vote – enabling receipt and consolidation of all settlement assets under one pan-hapū organisation or 'iwi'. What hope is there for marae under such a regime that appears to move descendants further from, rather than closer to, the essence of being Māori: a kin-accountable, tribal identity that is marae-based? Of course there are the alternative arguments in favour of RIOs where, for example, settlement assets can be consolidated into one entity and properly managed, for ultimate distribution to individuals and marae communities. The issues are complex, and experiences between settlement groups vary. The point here, though, is that marae are not represented well, if at all, in Treaty settlement policies and processes. On the one hand, Treaty settlements should provide opportunities to empower marae – the tangible representations of tino rangatiratanga. On the other hand, marae have continued in much the same way as prior to settlement. It may take several more years before we see direct improvement to marae and their communities as a result of Treaty settlements.

Creating Māori Maps

The brief historic overview above provides a context for understanding the plight of many marae communities today. It is beyond the scope of this essay to look in detail into history and its effects on marae. Each of the 803[*] tribal marae in Aotearoa has its own history and experiences. But what can be seen from the discussion is the gradual or cumulative effect of economic, social, political and legal pressures and challenges on marae. Aware of these circumstances, a small team set out to look for a novel way to help reconnect the largely urban diaspora with their home marae communities.

In 2008 the Māori Maps project team began visiting the 188 tribal marae in the northern tribal district, Te Tai Tokerau. It came across

---

[*] As provided on the Māori Maps website.

vibrant marae, but also saw a part of Aotearoa that few see: derelict or abandoned marae. The majority of marae are still in use, but in major need of attention. These were just a few insights into what the team saw of the dozens of papakāinga in Te Tai Tokerau. But this snapshot needs to be contextualised within a deeper, historic frame as presented above.

The aim of the Māori Maps team visits was to geographically record (by GPS – global positioning system) the locations of each marae at the gate, providing a basic overview – Geographic Information System (GIS) data – and to capture high-resolution contemporary images. What is collected is electronically matched to other publicly accessible research material, then managed and safeguarded under a charitable organisation: Te Potiki National Trust, which lists tribal marae of Aotearoa as its beneficiaries.[*]

With two years' practice the team became expert at finding out-of-the-way marae. Sometimes members would see an ancient pā on the skyline: an indication we were getting close. Then affluent Pākehā homes on well-kept farms would seemingly give way to tree-sized gorse weeds escaping through broken fences in all directions. Run-down dwellings began appearing and many times the team had to slow for stock wandering dusty roads as if they owned them. The anticipated marae eventually appeared around the next corner. The team would park in momentary silence, each member observing the ultimate expression of a kin group's mana whenua (exclusive ancestral authority of, over and from surrounding ancestral landscapes). Whare hui were found in various states: some in very good condition, others badly decaying and surrounded by long grass with no community in sight, and no mokopuna (grandchildren). Marae visits during the summer generally provided more positive pictures. Whānau had returned home to assist the few hau kāinga (home people keeping a marae community warm) clean up after another year with limited or no labour to call upon. Tents were pitched in surrounding paddocks as descendants cleaned their marae and the vibrant pulse of a papakāinga returned for a couple of weeks.

---

[*] Visit www.maorimaps.com for full understanding of background, governance and operations of Te Potiki National Trust and its Māori Maps output.

I recall one time as members of the Māori Maps team patiently waited in the summer heat, watching our elders chat at leisure with the home elders beside a marae that we had spent a couple of hours trying to find. Beyond the elders we began noting the wider interaction of young and not so young, cousins meeting cousins. Together they relaxed, played, worked, chatted, helped, argued – these people who normally live apart, elsewhere in an urbanised world. In the shadow of their ancestral marae, beyond any mobile phone reception, the young generation keenly swapped phone numbers, Facebook user names and email addresses. You could feel the mutual need for each other's kinship, to belong to those with whom they shared common traits, behaviours, elders, uncles and aunties reaching beyond their own short, isolated, city-defined lifetimes. We watched a group return from a visit to the urupā (cemetery), holding hands, laughing and giggling, much as their grandparents probably did when they were youthful: a universe of continuity, belonging and being valued had opened up for these young people, who all too soon would depart in different directions. Our team watched that same generation 'hanging out' without a care for the wider world; yet preparing – future-proofing themselves – to begin relating to one another digitally for the coming year after their return to the cities. Like numerous other Māori, they use social networking sites such as Facebook to share and maintain their very special marae-bonded ancestral identity until meeting again next year, regenerating their ancestral selves over another summer.

The team knew then that we were witnessing the new domain into which tribal marae are beginning to transform. Can web-based tools open the new portal for marae to evolve once again in pace with their mokopuna, but still maintain a physical presence, grounding the new digital generation in a tangible marae space/place that has operated without electricity for thousands of years? The marae communities we visited over the summer period seem to suggest this is a way forward. Of course, there will never be a single solution, especially when the history of experiences for marae communities is complex and diverse. But there appears to be some opportunity in the online, networked era within which Māori now live.

Marae in the Future

Prior to East Polynesians arriving in Aotearoa, their marae had continuously evolved and developed in response to more than 2000 years of oceanic exploration and settlement. In Aotearoa the (marae) ātea transformed into a centralised public space, taking on an elevated and terraced profile, or pā, representing mana (ancestral authority) over surrounding whenua. After many generations, these awe-inspiring carved hilltops, volcanic peaks and headlands were abandoned, largely due to crises of introduced illnesses and firearms. Strategies were developed to ensure marae remained the central forum of leadership within reformed lowland papakāinga, staying central to the tribal Māori way of life, for the most part, up to World War II. However, many marae communities struggled under the pressures enforced upon them due to land wars and resulting laws that vastly diminished tribal land estates. And if those pressures were not significant enough, the economic recession of the 1930s – as well as other factors (including the effect of Rātana beliefs on marae culture as Merimeri Penfold discusses in this volume) – has had cumulative, irreversible effects on marae.

Since World War II, further major changes have occurred within marae communities. Perhaps the most significant is that Māori as individuals are no longer culturally, politically or economically dependent on their marae community or papakāinga to survive. This creates a dilemma: hapū and their marae cannot survive without kin support. The marae and their leaders are the primary means for transmitting cultural values and the language that symbolises tribal identity. As discussed in this chapter, and raised elsewhere in this book (see the chapter by Merata Kawharu and Paratene Tane), few kin, particularly taitamariki (young Māori), return to their communities to assist in marae functions. The net effect of limited youth engagement, participation or even simply presence with elders in marae contexts is to reduce the sustainability of community cultural knowledge and values. Questions (and answers) about how to deal with these challenges become critical. For instance, how can marae and their ancestral landscapes continue to be relevant to dispersed communities? What other mechanisms should be utilised by marae to help curb this apparent negative trend? And what roles can other institutions like tribal authorities and schools play to reverse the drift? The challenges of marae are not just about the marae space, however. They are really about people. For today's youth, staying in the home community is generally not seen as an attractive option – despite eagerness among many – when weighed against the employment and other opportunities on offer in cities. But as long as the distinctive baskets of knowledge (ngā kete o te wānanga) and leadership (rangatiratanga) associated with every marae across Aotearoa are protected and maintained, they can meaningfully serve descendants in terms of identity and belonging, wherever they may live in the world.

In comparison to the pre-Native Land Court period, marae today generally lack wider economic, political and social influence. This situation appears not to be improving.* Cultural identity alone will not sustain them. Marae need to provide their descendants with tangible opportunities if they are ever to recover from this crisis. Can marae provide access to resources not available elsewhere? Perhaps the recently established post-Treaty governance entities (PSGEs) can become more inclusive of marae by sharing rights of distribution with associated hapū leadership? Of course there would be variations in what resources are being distributed, to whom and how, and it would be important to identify what role marae might have in the process. In Te Tai Tokerau, upcoming settlements of large or multiple Treaty claims need to keep sight of the centrality of marae. If settlements provide hapū leadership with opportunities to rebuild, strengthen and revive marae as digitally connected centres of descendant wellbeing, the future for Maori looks exciting.

The major question facing many communities is, can tribal marae survive this silent crisis of human resource depletion? Can marae transform themselves again, as in the past, to remain relevant and vital to the new generation of Māori living in mostly distant urban environments? And how can those descendants living away (virtually) reconnect and support their local marae communities who keep the home fires alight?

---

* Due to, for example, aging population, continuing negative migration and no sustained flow of resources on which to rebuild.

The outcomes of the decisions made today, especially about Treaty settlements, language and marae programmes, will have a ripple effect on the living of tomorrow. What will their marae look like when they are elders?

Some of today's youth are reversing my childhood visits to the city: they are returning home to their marae for the holidays and reconnecting. In between receiving 'txts', they might even be 'eye-spying' pā on their journey through 'enemy country' to the safety of their home marae.

Bibliography

Ballara, A., 1998. *Iwi: The Dynamics of Maori Tribal Organisation from c. 1769 to c. 1945*. Wellington: Victoria University Press.

Beaglehole, J. C., ed., 1962. *The Endeavour Journal of Joseph Banks 1768–1771*, vol. I. Sydney: Angus and Robertson.

Department of Corrections, 2011. 'Corrections Department Wins Maori Language Award'. From: http://www.corrections.govt.nz/news/media-releases/2011_media_releases/corrections_department_wins_maori_language_award2.html

Di Piazza, A., and Pearthree, E., 2007. 'A New Reading of Tupaia's Chart'. *Journal of the Polynesian Society*, vol. 116, no. 3, pp. 321–340.

Finney, B., 2006. 'Traditional Navigation'. In: K. R. Howe, ed. *Vaka Moana: Voyages of the Ancestors – The Discovery and Settlement of the Pacific*. Auckland: David Bateman, pp. 156–185.

Green, R., 1991. 'The Lapita Cultural Complex: Current Evidence and Proposed Models'. In: P. Belwood, ed. *Indo–Pacific Prehistory 1990: Proceedings of the 14th Congress of the Indo–Pacific Prehistory Association*, Canberra: Indo–Pacific Prehistory Association, pp. 295–305.

Henry, T., 1912. 'The Tahitian Version of the Names of Ra'iatea and Taputapuatea'. *Journal of the Polynesian Society*, vol. 21, pp. 77–78.

Howe, K. R., ed., 2006. *Vaka Moana: Voyages of the Ancestors – The Discovery and Settlement of the Pacific*. Auckland: David Bateman.

Irwin, G., 2006. 'Voyaging and Settlement'. In: K. R. Howe, ed. *Vaka Moana: Voyages of the Ancestors – The Discovery and Settlement of the Pacific*. Auckland: David Bateman, pp. 54–99.

Kawharu, I. H., 1977. *Maori Land Tenure*. Oxford: Clarendon Press.

——, 1989. 'Mana and the Crown: A Marae at Orakei'. In: I. H. Kawharu, ed. *Waitangi: Maori and Pakeha Perspectives of the Treaty of Waitangi*. Auckland: Oxford University Press, pp. 211–233.

——, 2004. 'Orakei'. In: M. Belgrave, M. Kawharu and D. V. Williams, eds. *Waitangi Revisited: Perspectives on the Treaty of Waitangi*. Melbourne: Oxford University Press, pp. 151–167.

Kawharu, M., Tapsell, P. and Woods, C., 2012. 'Maori Entrepreneurial Behaviour: Lachmannian Insights'. *Journal of Australian Indigenous Issues*, vol. 15, no. 4, pp. 62–75.

Kawharu, M., 2010. 'Environment as Marae Locale'. In: R. Selby, P. Moore, P. and M. Mulholland, eds. *Kaitiaki: Maori and the Environment*. Wellington: Huia, pp. 221–239.

Kirch, P., 1990. 'Monumental Architecture and Power in Polynesian Chiefdoms: A Comparison of Tonga and Hawaii'. *World Archaeology*, vol. 22, no. 2, pp. 206–221.

Kirch, P., 2000. *On the Road of the Winds: An Archaeological History of the Pacific Islands before European Contact*. Berkeley: University of California Press.

Lewis, D., 1994. *We the Navigators: The Ancient Art of Landfinding in the Pacific*. Hawai'i: University of Hawaii Press.

Low, S., 2006. 'Nainoa Thompson's Path to Knowledge: How Hokule'a's Navigator Finds His Way'. In: K. R. Howe, ed. *Vaka Moana: Voyages of the Ancestors – The Discovery and Settlement of the Pacific*. Auckland: David Bateman, pp. 186–197.

Māori Maps, n.d., http://www.maorimaps.com

McFadgen, B., 2007. *Hostile Shores: Catastrophic Events in Prehistoric New Zealand and Their Impact on Maori Coastal Communities*, Auckland: Auckland University Press.

Ministry of Justice, n.d. 'Achieving Our Targets'. From: http://www.justice.govt.nz/justice-sector/better-public-services-reducing-crime/achieving-our-targets

New Zealand Police, 2012. 'Turning the Tide: A Whanau Ora Crime and Crash Prevention Strategy'. From: http://www.police.govt.nz/featured/new-strategy-aims-turn-tide-maori-victimisation-and-offending

Ngata, A. T., 1943. *The Price of Citizenship*. Wellington: Whitcombe and Tombs.

Ngāti Whātua ō Ōrākei, 2003. 'Wai 388 Treaty Claim: Tamaki Makaurau'. Auckland: Ngāti Whātua ō Ōrākei Māori Trust Board.

Pawley, A. and Ross, M., 1993. 'Austronesian Historical Linguistics and Culture History'. *Annual Review of Anthropology*, vol. 22, pp. 425–459.

Petrie, H., 2006. *Chiefs of Industry: Maori Tribal Enterprise in Early Colonial New Zealand*. Auckland: Auckland University Press.

Pickens, K., 1997. 'The Wellington Tenths 1873–1896: A Report Commissioned by the Waitangi Tribunal'. Wellington: The Tribunal.

Salmond, A., 2003. *The Trial of the Cannibal Dog: The Remarkable Story of Captain Cook's Encounters in the South Seas*. Newhaven: Yale University Press.

——, 1991. *Two Worlds: First Meetings between Maori and Europeans, 1642–1772*. Auckland: Viking.

Sharp, A., 1963. *Ancient Voyagers in Polynesia*. Auckland: Paul's Book Arcade.

Skinner, D., 2008. *The Carver and the Artist: Maori Art in the Twentieth Century*. Auckland: Auckland University Press.

Soutar, M., 2008. *Nga Tama Toa: The Price of Citizenship – C Company 28 (Maori) Battalion 1939–1945*. Auckland: David Bateman.

Spriggs, M., 1995. 'The Lapita Culture and Austronesian Prehistory in Oceania'. In: P. Bellwood, J. Fox and D. Tryon, eds. *The Austronesians: Historical and Comparative Perspective*s. Canberra: Department of Anthropology, pp. 119–142.

Stokes, E., 1997. *The Allocation of Reserves for Maori in the Tauranga Confiscated Lands*. Waikato: Waikato University Press.

Taonui, R., 2006. 'Polynesian Oral Traditions'. In: K. R. Howe, ed. *Vaka Moana: Voyages of the Ancestors – The Discovery and Settlement of the Pacific*. Auckland: David Bateman, pp. 22–53.

Tapsell, P. and Woods. C., 2009. 'A Spiral of Innovation Framework for Social

Entrepreneurship: Social Innovation at the Generational Divide'. In: J. Goldstein, J. K. Hazy and J. Silberstang, eds. *Complexity Science and Social Entrepreneurship: Adding Social Value through Systems Thinking*. Litchfield Park: ISCE Publishing, pp. 471–486.

Tapsell, P., 1998. 'Taonga: A Tribal Response to Museums'. D.Phil. thesis, Oxford University, Oxford.

——, 2002. 'Marae Identity in Urban Aotearoa New Zealand'. In: J. Moddell, ed. *Moral Communities. Special Issue of Pacific Studies*, vol. 25, nos 1/2 – March/June. Hawai'i: Brigham Young University, pp. 141–171.

——, 2006. 'Te Arawa'. In: Ministry of Culture and Heritage, ed. *Māori Peoples of New Zealand: Ngā Iwi o Aotearoa*. Wellington: David Bateman and the Ministry for Culture and Heritage, pp. 219–225.

——, 2009. 'Footprints in the Sand: Banks's Maori Collection, Cook's First Voyage 1768–71'. In: M. Hetherington and H. Morphy, eds. *Discovering Cook's Collections*. Canberra: NMA Press, pp. 92–111.

——, 2011. 'Aroha Mai: Whose Museum?' In: J. Marstine, ed. *The Routledge Companion to Museum Ethics: Redefining Ethics for the Twenty-First-Century Museum*. London: Routledge, pp. 85–111.

Te Rangi Hiroa/Buck, P., 1938. *Vikings of the Sunrise*. New York: J. B. Lippincott Company.

Tupaia, W., pers. comm., Taputapuatea, Opoa, 25 April 2011.

Waitangi Tribunal, 1987. 'Report of the Waitangi Tribunal on the Orakei Claim'. Wellington: The Tribunal.

——, 1996. 'The Taranaki Report: Kaupapa Tuatahi (Wai 143): Muru me te Raupatu – The Muru and Raupatu of the Taranaki Land and People'. Wellington: GP Publications.

——, 1998. 'Te Whānau o Waipareira Report'. Wellington: GP Publications.

——, 2003. Te Whanganui a Tara me Ona Takiwa: Report on the Wellington District. Wellington: Legislation Direct.

Walker, R. J., 1990. *Ka Whawhai Tonu Matou: Struggle Without End*. Auckland: Penguin.

——, 2001. *He Tipua: The Life and Times of Sir Apirana Ngata*. Auckland: Viking.

Williams, D. V., 1999. *Te Kooti Tango Whenua: The Native Land Court 1864–1909*. Wellington: Huia Publishers.

HŌNE SADLER (Ngāti Moerewa, Ngāti Rangi and Ngāi Tawake ki Te Waoku) has a Master of Matauranga Māori degree from Te Wānanga o Raukawa. He was brought up in Tautoro, south west of Kaikohe. Hōne attended Tautoro Māori School and after his family shifted to Kaikohe, he attended Kaikohe Māori School and then Kaikohe Primary School, completing his compulsory education at Northland College in 1967.

He graduated from North Shore Teachers' College, beginning his teaching career in 1970. He taught in the primary and secondary services before moving to the tertiary sector, where he began at Northland Polytechnic. He is now a senior lecturer in the Māori Studies Department at the University of Auckland.

Hōne is a fluent native speaker of te reo and has been steeped in tikanga Ngāpuhi and Ngāpuhi histories and hakapapa, with mentoring by his parents and his uncles. He has been involved with the Tiriti o Waitangi claims for about 40 years. He was chosen, along with Patu Hohepa, Erima Henare, Hirini Henare and Rima Edwards, by Ngāpuhi to lay the foundations for the opening of the Ngāpuhi early hearings of Te Paparahi o Te Raki, the WAI 1040 claim.

CHAPTER THREE

TE MEMEHA HAERE O NGĀ KAIKŌRERO TOHUNGA KI RUNGA I NGĀ MARAE

HŌNE SADLER

KO RAUNGAITI HAERE TE NOHO O NGĀ TAUMATA KŌRERO KI RUNGA i ngā marae o Ngāpuhi i te mimiti o ngā puna pupuri kōrero, pupuri tikanga hoki. Me tōku hakapae e pērā katoa ana ki runga i ngā marae puta i te motu whānui. Erangi, he waimārie kē ētahi o ngā marae nā te mea e kaha tonu ana ō rātou taumata i te whai tohunga ki te tuku mihi hakatau hei pōwhiri manuhiri, e mau tonu ana ki ngā kaupapa tika, kia noho ora tonu ngā tikanga tuku iho o ngā mātua, tūpuna.

Ko te nuinga o ngā kaumātua e pupuri ana i te mauri o ngā marae i ēnei wā tonu, ko rātou hoki te hunga kātahi anō kia hoki mai ki te kāinga, e hia kē tau e ngaro ana ki roto i ngā ngahere raima, ki ngā tāone nunui. I hakarērea e rātou ngā kāinga tupu i te tamatānetanga, ā, ka haere ki te rapu mahi, oranga hoki mō rātou me ō rātou whānau, tamariki anō rā hoki. Nā ka tae ki te kaumātuatanga, ka mutu te mahi, ka pā mai te tō o te kāinga ka kore e taea te karo, ā, ka hakatika ka hoki.

He tauhou hoki rātou ki te noho i ngā taumata. Kāhore anō kia pakari ai ō rātou reo. Kāhore e tino mōhio ana ki ngā mahi hakahaere o te marae. Nā, ko ngā taimahatanga ko utaina ki runga i ō rātou pokowhiwhi hei amo mō te iwi, hapū me te whānau. Koia ēnei ko te nuinga o ngā tūmomo tāngata e mau ana i ngā kawenga mō ō tātou marae. Ehara i te mea ko te aha, erangi koia ēnei ko ngā nekenekenga o te wā. Ko rukuhia e rātou ngā wai hōhonu, ko ētahi ko ngā kanohi nahe e puta ana i te wai, ko te nuinga e kaha ana, e hakamomori ana, kia kaua e torongi.

I konā kē ngā tohu e hakaatu ana i tēnei āhuatanga i roto i ngā tau e whitu ngahuru, e waru ngahuru atu ki te iwa ngahuru. Erangi i aua wā horekau kē he āwangawanga, he mānukanuka raini i te mea e ora tonu ana ō tātou mātua. Ko rātou kē te hunga e mau ana i ngā kawenga mō te ora tonu o te reo. E māeneene tonu ana te oro o te reo ki ngā wāhi katoa o te hunga e mau tonu ana ki te reo, ki ngā kāinga, ki ngā marae, ki ngā huihuinga whānau, hapū me te iwi.

Hoi, ka tae ki ngā tau o te waru ngahuru, ka matemate ngā mātua, ka hakarērea mai ngā kawenga ki te hakatupuranga o muri mai. Kāhore nei kia tino pakari, ā, ka pā mai te mokemoke.

He aha rā tētahi rautaki hei hakaora mai i tō tātou reo kia kaua rā e ngaro? I te mea, ki te ngaro te reo ka memeha ngā taumata kōrero ki ō tātou marae. Ko puta te kōrero a Tā Himi Hēnare e pēnei ana:

'Ko te reo te tāhūhū o te mana Māori.'

Ki te ngaro tō tātou reo, ko ō tātou ao ā-iwi, ao Māori, ka ngaro, ko ō tātou tikanga katoa ka ngaro, ka ngaro katoa tātou te iwi.

Ko te tino hua i puta i ngā rangahau me te rīpoata o Te Paepae Motuhake[*] e mea ana ko te huarahi hakaora mai i tō tātou reo kei roto i ngā ringaringa o te whānau. Me tīmata ki roto i ō tātou kāinga te hakaora mai i tō tātou reo. Atia te hakapautanga o te hia miriona tāra i ngā tau ki muri hei hakaora mai i tō tātou reo, i roto i ngā tirohanga e memeha haere tonu ana te reo.

Nā reira, kia kaha nei tātou ki te tautoko i tēnei tono, i te mea ki te kore te reo e kōrerongia ki roto i ō tātou kāinga ka memeha. Ka memeha ki roto i ō tātou kāinga ka memeha ki runga i ō tātou marae.

---

[*] Te Paepae Motuhake, 'Te Reo Mauriora: Te Arotakenga o te Rāngai Reo Māori me te Rautaki Reo Māori', 2011, p. 47.

THE DEARTH OF COMPETENT SPEAKERS ON THE MARAE

The diminishing pool of skilled speakers – accomplished experts who are also the receptacles of customs and etiquette – means Ngāpuhi marae are becoming bereft. I also suspect that this may be so for marae throughout the land. But some marae are fortunate because they still have depth within their ranks: experts who are able to perform the duties of speeches of welcome for their visitors and still adhere to correct ritual, to enable the etiquette of our ancestors to remain authentic.

The majority of the elders today, who are the caretakers of the life force of our marae, are those who have just recently returned home, after many years spent in the concrete jungles, in the large cities. They left their ancestral homes of their youth to seek work as sustenance for themselves, their families and also their children. Now that they have reached their elder years, they have finished work. The strong draw to return home, which cannot be evaded, comes – and then they return home.

They are strangers to the speakers' bench. Their language has not yet attained the appropriate level. They do not really know the machinations of the marae. Despite that, the burden is placed upon their shoulders for them to carry for their iwi, hapū and family. This is the calibre of the majority of people who carry the responsibility for our marae. These are the signs of the times. They have immersed themselves into the deep end and some are just able to keep their eyes above water and the majority strive hard and endeavour at all costs to stay afloat and not drown.

The portents were there in the 1970s, 1980s and 1990s, signalling what might be. But in those times there were no worries or misgivings because our parents were still there. They were the ones who carried the responsibilities for the ongoing security and health of te reo. The lilting sounds of te reo were heard in all places of those who still spoke it, in their homes, on the marae, at family, hapū and iwi gatherings.

Suddenly, the 1980s were upon us: the demise of our parents began and the responsibility was now left to the coming generation. They were not well prepared, and then loneliness set in.

What then is a strategy that will ensure the revival of our language so that it may not be lost? For if the language is lost, the speaking benches on our marae may disappear. Sir James Henare said:

'The language is the overarching essence of Māori authority.'

If our language is lost, then the world views of our iwi (ao ā-iwi), our Māori world, will be lost; all our customs and etiquette will be lost and we as a people will be lost.

The principal finding of the research in the Paepae Motuhake report[*] is that the revival of our language is in the hands of the family. Let us begin in our homes to revive our language. Despite the expenditure of millions of dollars over the past years to revive our language, investigation shows the continued demise of the language.

So, therefore, let us vigorously support this call, because if the language is not spoken in our homes it will wane. If it wanes in our homes, it will die on our marae.

---

[*] Te Paepae Motuhake, 'Te Reo Mauriora: Review of the Māori Language Sector and the Māori Language Strategy', 2011, p. 47. Te Paepae Motuhake was an independent panel appointed in 2010 to report to the Minister of Māori Affairs.

ARAPERA NGAHA is of Ngāpuhi and Te Arawa descent and is a senior lecturer in the Department of Māori Studies at the University of Auckland. Her teaching covers aspects of te reo Māori and contemporary issues as they relate to Te Tiriti o Waitangi. Her research is primarily concerned with regenerating and revitalising te reo. The link between te reo and Māori identity is a particular interest, as is working with communities to seek out the best strategies for engaging our people in language learning. Arapera also has a strong interest in ethics and how they are addressed in research within Māori communities.

CHAPTER FOUR

TE REO MĀORI AND MĀORI IDENTITY: WHAT'S IN A MAUNGA?

ARAPERA NGAHA

LANGUAGE IS MORE THAN THE WORDS THAT ARE COMMUNICATED from one to another. Language helps to present our identity in diverse ways: through our relationships with others, through the engagement in and with aspects of our culture, and through the way we use language in our day-to-day interactions. In this chapter I look at how young Māori participants in one particular research project, Te Wehi Nui a Mamao, use language to express their Māori identity. Almost 500 Māori taitamariki (youth) completed surveys in which they were asked about their language behaviours, their linguistic environment as well as their understanding of local and regional cultural knowledge. A number of those aged sixteen and over also participated in focus group discussions, which explored issues concerning the use of te reo, cultural identity and their aspirations for the future. The survey data is analysed using both quantitative and qualitative methods and the results are discussed alongside data from other research in this field. Central to these analyses is an exploration of how strong the link is between te reo and Māori identity.

Part of the rationale for this study is the concern that not only is te reo Māori still in a vulnerable state, despite the ongoing efforts of te reo revitalisation programmes, but that it is in crisis – the crisis being that if we do not take strong steps now to ensure that te reo is sustained long term, then it too will go 'the way of the moa' (Hohepa, 2000) and, like so many other indigenous languages, die out! By first investigating the levels of both language and cultural knowledge among taitamariki we felt that we might then be able to address knowledge gaps, and develop a web 2.0 resource that will provide opportunities for promoting, and supporting regional language and knowledge. The website (Tewehinui.com) is discussed elsewhere in this volume by Kawharu and Tane and by Hennessy.

This investigation begins with a brief consideration of some of the literature on language and identity, followed by an overview of the methodology undertaken to gather the data used in this study. The speaking ability of the young Māori participants is addressed and followed by discussion of community supports for te reo learning. The qualitative data from the surveys is then examined for evidence that links te reo with Māori identity. Direct quotes, where they are used, are referenced with the assigned number (in brackets) of the survey document from which the quote is taken. Discussions on the findings of this study show that there are clear signs that use of te reo is very limited. However, expressions of Māori identity are still evident in the linguistic choices made by these young people and in their understandings and use of tikanga and mātauranga Māori.

The international literature on the relationship between language and identity posits three theoretical positions that could be useful to these discussions. The first raised here is the post-modern tradition that suggests that language is not essential to identity (Nash, 1987; Edwards, 1996; Song, 2003). Nash (1987) says that language is mutable over time and, therefore, a person can still identify as being Greek, Tongan, Chinese or Māori and not speak the language. The second position, the essentialist tradition, tends to be supported by the Māori literature. Essentialism suggests that identity and language are inextricably linked (Durie, 1997; Fishman, 1999; Ngaha, 2005) therefore te reo is all-important to understanding who we are as Māori. Census data shows that less than a quarter

(23.7 per cent), of the total Māori population say they can speak Māori (Statistics NZ, 2007), which appears to belie this essentialist position. If te reo and Māori identity are so inextricably linked, then those who identify as Māori ought to be speakers of the language, and if the language is under threat then it could be argued that so too is the distinctiveness of our Māori identity (Gee, Stephens, Higgins and Liu, 2003). The Waitangi Tribunal Report (2010) goes so far as to say, 'Without it [te reo], Māori identity would be fundamentally undermined, as would the very existence of Māori as a distinguishable people' (2010, p. 48).

The third relevant position, ethnolinguistic vitality theory (Giles and Johnson, 1987), further suggests that if Māori are to retain a collective identity that places language at the centre, then three elements must be present in order to maintain and develop the language. Firstly the numbers of speakers of the language must be sufficient to maintain a population of speakers and intergenerational transmission of language is necessary to provide that support. The second and third elements required are institutional support such as that provided by government, and recognition or elevated status of the language. Goodwill and support must also be forthcoming from the wider community (Giles, Bourhis and Taylor, 1977; Giles and Johnson, 1987; Fishman, 2001). The numbers and fluency of speakers who can demonstrate both regional and cultural knowledge must be consistently maintained at high levels to ensure the ongoing vitality of te reo and Māori identity.

The latest research on the health of te reo shows the growth and development of te reo Māori is not strong and this clearly signals a crisis. In their studies with Māori youth, Borell (2005) and Ormond (2004) both suggest that te reo is not a priority for our taitamariki. Their research found that Māori youth have different priorities, in terms of identity, to those of their parents and grandparents and may express themselves as Māori in ways that do not always include use of te reo. Although they still strongly identify as Māori they are also more likely to prioritise markers of identity that position them in the locality where they live, ahead of traditional Māori markers of identity (Borell, 2005 cited in Ngaha, 2011, p. 16). This chapter investigates what markers of identity appear to be important for this particular group of young Māori.

Background to the Database

As part of the overall Te Wehi Nui a Mamao project, it was important to know more about what taitamariki today know about their own regional reo, about their own iwi (tribe) and hapū (sub-tribe) stories and regional tikanga. Some of this knowledge is learned through intergenerational sharing of stories with other whānau and hapū members, kuia and kaumātua (elders). Sometimes the stories are illustrated and learned through whakataukī (proverbs); through pepeha (tribal sayings), waiata (songs) and mōteatea (songs of lament), and sometimes through written accounts. The research team felt that if any gaps in the knowledge of this cohort could be found then the website could be tailored to present the appropriate regional cultural information in ways that would firstly attract the attention of taitamariki and their community, and then address their learning needs. Local kaumātua from the study region were also asked what they considered the gaps in learning were and how they might be addressed. The internet is a medium easily accessible and familiar to most young people. Tewehinui.com offers a way of learning about and hearing their regional dialect and their own traditional stories. It complements the more traditional methods of iwi and hapū learning that are based within marae, hapū and whānau settings.

The survey used in this study required little in the way of free writing and instead posed questions and offered prescribed responses. Respondents were invited simply to 'tick the box' for the response that they agreed with or that was the closest match to their views. They were then asked to assess their own ability to read, understand and speak Māori. Further questions identified whether they lived with a speaker of te reo in the home; who that person might have been, the frequency with which the respondent heard te reo and in what kinds of places they were most likely to hear te reo spoken. These questions gave a brief overview of the linguistic environment that has helped shape each respondent's language behaviours. Knowledge of cultural context was also explored through questions that asked respondents to name places of specific interest to iwi and hapū in each region. These included the names of marae, maunga (mountains), awa (rivers), urupā (cemeteries), waiata and pepeha (tribal descriptors) or whakataukī (proverbial sayings) of paticular regions. At several points along the way respondents were offered the opportunity to comment on particular questions and these narrative comments have helped to add colour and depth to the empirical data. Students from two kura kaupapa Māori (Māori-medium primary schools) and six mainstream high schools took part in the surveys along with several young people who were no longer at school, who were working or were students engaged in tertiary study. The respondents ranged in age from 10 up to 22 years of age.

Te Reo: So What's the Problem?

The history of the decline of te reo has been well documented. Recognition of that decline became most evident when the results from the first national survey of the state of te reo, undertaken in the 1970s, were made known (Benton, 1997). This major piece of research, referred to in this chapter as the New Zealand Council for Educational Research (NZCER) survey, indicated that only a very few Māori communities still had te reo as the lingua franca and remained as places of intergenerational language transfer. These communities were in geographically isolated rural areas, which it was felt contributed greatly to their ability to retain the language and their traditional customary practices. However, as a result of urbanisation, greater engagement with the non-Māori speaking population and reduced contact with the home community, the language shift from Māori to English has accelerated rapidly to a point where the shift and attrition of te reo in the rural community is now comparable to that for whānau Māori living in urban settings. The geographic isolation of rural Māori communities can no longer be expected to support the retention of te reo (Ngaha, 2001).

The results of the NZCER survey were one of the catalysts for the revival of te reo Māori in the 1970s; that revival was also part of a wider Māori cultural renaissance. Other initiatives at the time saw Māori push for justice and redress for the loss of their language, the loss of lands and the loss of autonomy, through the actions of the Crown. The Waitangi Tribunal was established in 1975 to enquire into Māori grievances against the Crown. A case was made to the Waitangi Tribunal in 1986 for the restoration of the status of the language, for the right to learn and use te reo in all domains and for government support to foster the language.* In 1987 the Māori Language Act was passed. This act requires the government to actively promote and nurture te reo Māori, and affirms it as an official language of New Zealand. It was in this context that the NZCER survey findings facilitated a push for support, within the education arena, for Māori-medium education. The first kōhanga reo (Māori-medium preschool) opened in Wainuiomata in 1981 and the first kura kaupapa Māori, Te Kura Kaupapa Māori o Hoani Waititi in Glen Eden, West Auckland, followed in 1985. (Hōhepa, this volume, covers the growth and development of Māori-medium schooling in more detail.)

Since that first major survey of te reo, Te Puni Kōkiri (Ministry of Māori Development) and Te Taura Whiri i te Reo Māori (The Māori Language Commission) have worked with Statistics New Zealand to observe the health of te reo through surveys and examination of census data over time. These studies, Te Puni Kōkiri 2002; 2003; 2004; 2008; and Te Puni Kōkiri and Te Taura Whiri i te Reo Māori, 2003, have maintained an overview of the growth and development of te reo and the findings have helped to ensure resources and programmes are targeted to best meet the needs for te reo growth and development. However, as census data shows (Waitangi Tribunal, 2010), te reo Māori is still very much in an endangered state and some suggest a state of crisis.

Results of the Survey

The survey respondents were asked to assess how well they could speak Māori, read Māori and understand Māori, rating their ability on a Likert scale from 1 to 5. A rating of 5 (excellent), describes highly developed fluency. A rating of 4 (above average) suggests that, with assistance, respondents may be able to produce sustained conversational fluency and a rating of 3 (average) suggests that respondents may be able to engage in short conversations in te reo. At a rating of 2, below average fluency,

---

* See Te Reo Maori Claim (WAI 11) 1989.

respondents can only articulate short sentences or phrases in Māori and a rating of 1 (not at all) suggests they are absolute novices with te reo.

Self-assessment is highly subjective and has its critics. Claiming a high level of competence also requires a great deal of confidence and for many Māori, who through their tikanga are encouraged to be humble, it may be doubly difficult to do so. For these reasons one must read these assessments with caution and remember that they are simply one way to assess language competence. There are other measures, such as the accurate and appropriate delivery of mihimihi (formal ritual language used in greetings and salutations), waiata, mōteatea and/or pepeha and whakataukī. These forms of fluency are considered later in this chapter.

Table 4.1 below illustrates the self-assessed te reo ability results for all the respondents. Those who rated their ability as 5 were almost all current students in kura kaupapa who had also been engaged in Māori-medium education from kōhanga reo onwards – see Hōhepa (this volume), Table 6.3.

Table 4.1: Self-assessment of te reo ability, by percentage of total respondents

	Speak Māori (n = 483)	Read Māori (n = 489)	Understand Māori (n = 485)
Excellent	10	20	13
Above average	12	15	13
Average	30	30	32
Below average	37	24	35
Not at all	11	11	7
Total	100%	100%	100%

The shaded area illustrates the higher levels of fluency and includes some first-language speakers of te reo. For these fluent speakers, the rates of speaking (22 per cent) and understanding te reo (26 per cent) in this study group are less than that of reading te reo (35 per cent), and as expected, there are more who say they can understand te reo than say they can speak Māori. As noted earlier, having confidence in one's ability is a major factor in being able to claim te reo fluency.

Te Puni Kōkiri's report on the health of te reo in Te Tai Tokerau notes that the demographics changed markedly between the census of 2001 and that of 2006. The older generations who were most likely to be fluent speakers are declining, and the Māori population is largely young; the median age in 2006 was 22 years (Te Puni Kōkiri, 2008). Consequently, there has been a drop in the language rate from 2001 to 2006; down 1 per cent for those up to 14 years of age and a 3 per cent drop for those aged 15 and over. The percentage of under 14-year-olds with speaking ability in Te Tai Tokerau in 2001 was 22 per cent (the same percentage as in this study). In 2006 it was 21 per cent while the national rate was only 18 per cent.

When the figures from the Te Wehi Nui a Mamao study were broken down by age, 18 per cent of those who were under 14 years of age rated their speaking skills as excellent, or above average. Almost half (48 per cent) of these students attended kura kaupapa Māori. Although 22 per cent of the total research group rated their speaking skills as above average to excellent, this is not nearly a strong enough indicator to promote and carry sustainable levels of language regeneration. The ongoing challenge is to find ways to help lift the levels of fluency of those in the lower levels and thereby lift the overall language rate. The next step in this study looked at the supports or influences that were present in the linguistic environment for this cohort that encourage learning te reo and promote positive language behaviours.

Being around the language and hearing the language being spoken in everyday contexts is paramount for assisting language learning and for promoting positive language attitudes. The next two charts show places where respondents noted they heard te reo spoken most frequently. Figure 4.1 breaks down the places or the language domains where these participants stated they heard te reo being spoken and Figure 4.2 focuses on the language of the home.

The language domains in this survey were those considered important in previous studies that addressed language maintenance and the use of te reo (Boyce, 1992; Ngaha, 2001; 2005; Benton, *et al.*, 2002). Most domains were initially identified in the NZCER survey of the 1970s. In Figure 4.1 they are shown in order from the highest to lowest percentage of respondents who noted these as places where they heard te reo spoken.

Figure 4.1: Places where te reo is heard most frequently, by percentage of total responses

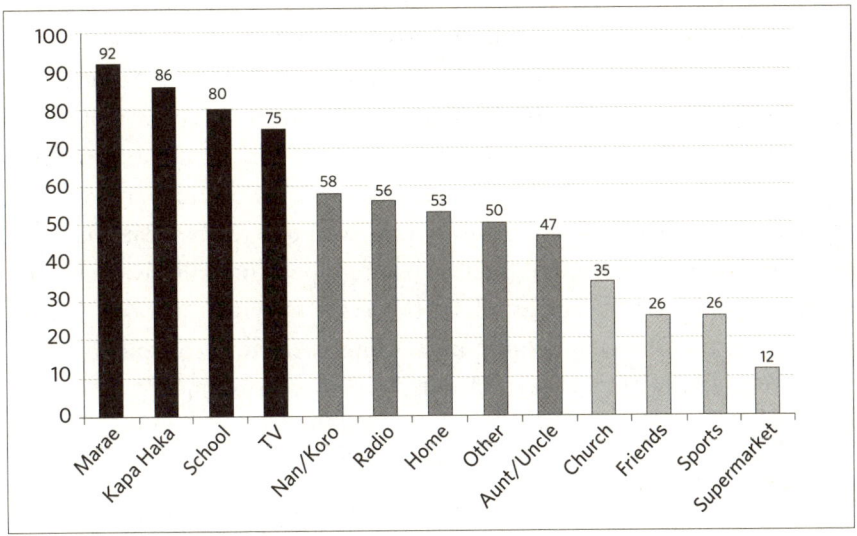

These responses fall into three broad areas which I have considered as Māori-friendly spaces, whānau-friendly spaces and public spaces, each distinguished by a different shade in the graph. As expected, 'Māori-friendly' places were those where tikanga and te reo are practised regularly, such as marae and kura kaupapa Māori. These spaces rated from 75 to 92 per cent for frequency of hearing te reo. The second band of language domains relates primarily to whānau-oriented places and spaces; these rated from 47 to 58 per cent. The more public places, such as sporting venues and supermarkets, are where respondents are least likely to hear Māori spoken: 12 to 35 per cent.

Ninety-two per cent of the study group rated marae as places where they heard te reo spoken and 86 per cent rated kapa haka (Māori dance and performance) events and activities in the same way. School and the medium of television also form part of that high-frequency exposure. It is encouraging to note that even though the majority of participants in this study were in mainstream schooling (84 per cent), 80 per cent of respondents noted 'school' as a domain where te reo was heard. This suggests that people speak Māori, give directions in Māori and/or use

Māori in activities at school, albeit outside the classroom. The television channels or programmes watched were not stated, but it is likely that their responses reflect viewing of the two Māori Television channels. The use of lexical items in te reo is minimal on mainstream television (de Bres, 2006).

The whānau domain is extremely important for survival of the language as it is there that opportunity for intergenerational language transfer is strongest. Grandparents' homes, the current home and homes of close relatives (aunts and/or uncles) are rated by around half the taitamariki (53 per cent) as places where the opportunity for hearing te reo is great. Of those 53 per cent, 64 per cent rated their own te reo speaking skills from average to high fluency. Such ratings affirm the value of having good language supports in the home and community. What is particularly encouraging is that the hearing of te reo that students reported in grandparents' homes was at a higher percentage than they reported for their current home. This signals that grandparents and kaumātua still have an important part to play in the revival of language and culture.

A significant finding in this work is that the position of the home as a domain where te reo is heard has shifted quite dramatically from earlier research; the NZCER study and that of the author (Ngaha, 2001). In both these studies the language of home, marae and religious activity occupied the first three positions, where te reo could 'always be heard' (Ngaha, 2001, p. 176). Those studies differ from this one in that they involved Māori of all ages, but it is still a major concern that the domain of 'home' where te reo is heard most – grandparents' homes – is here positioned fifth, with the current home and other whānau homes even lower.

In the more public and social spaces, primarily English-speaking domains, it is not surprising that low ratings are recorded because these are the areas where speakers of te reo are more likely to mix with non-speakers. However, the low percentage for hearing te reo in the domain of 'church' reflects wider social change as well as the Māori societal change that has contributed to the decline in te reo usage. In the NZCER study of the 1970s, Benton considered this domain one of very high reo use, and one where ritual reo was the norm. In Ngaha (2001) the domain of religious activity (which included prayers in the home; saying grace before meals; prayers for the sick; daily family prayers and tapu-lifting ceremonies) was in third highest position, after home and marae domains. Almost a decade on, the present study rates church at 35 per cent, which is tenth out of thirteen domains. Although this may appear to signal a dramatic shift in te reo use, this positioning may more likely reflect the much reduced contact that contemporary Māori society has with church and religious activity.

This study indicates a number of unknowns about te reo that is heard in the home, and these could be explored further. For example, nothing is known about the frequency or language type of the day-to-day dialogue in te reo. Who speaks te reo the most, in what contexts, to whom, what is said and how reciprocal is the interaction likely to be? Are the adult speakers within the home first-language speakers of te reo or second language (L2) speakers, and if L2 speakers, how fluent are they? These factors all significantly affect language transmission. The optimal uptake is achieved when young people are immersed in the language all day, every day, in all situations – and when they are learning from first-language speakers (Boyce, 1992; Ngaha, 2001).

Figure 4.2 categorises the participants' own homes according to the language heard there, English only or at least some Māori. In the homes where some Māori was heard, the generational make-up is also shown.

More than half these young people (51 per cent) said they lived in homes where some degree of te reo was heard: 24 per cent of those homes were parent and child generation homes, 19 per cent were three-generational (including grandparent generation) and 8 per cent were homes where the only adults in the household were grandparents. In all the homes where Māori was heard, there was at least one adult speaker of te reo, and sometimes other children in the home also spoke Māori. But as noted above there are still a number of unknowns about the home language, particularly regarding the quality of te reo spoken, the frequency of dialogue in te reo and who speaks te reo.

For those who recorded high levels of fluency, 32 per cent lived in three-generational homes and 37 per cent in two-generational homes, and all these homes had adults who spoke Māori. The remainder of those with high fluency (31 per cent) noted that they learned te reo in school and had no adult speakers of te reo at home. It is also more likely that those who live in homes with te reo would also go to places where it is heard, since the language is part of their everyday lives and normal practice. Being in close proximity to the language in a variety of contexts aids the intergenerational transmission of language.

Figure 4.2: Participants' own homes, by language heard and by generational type

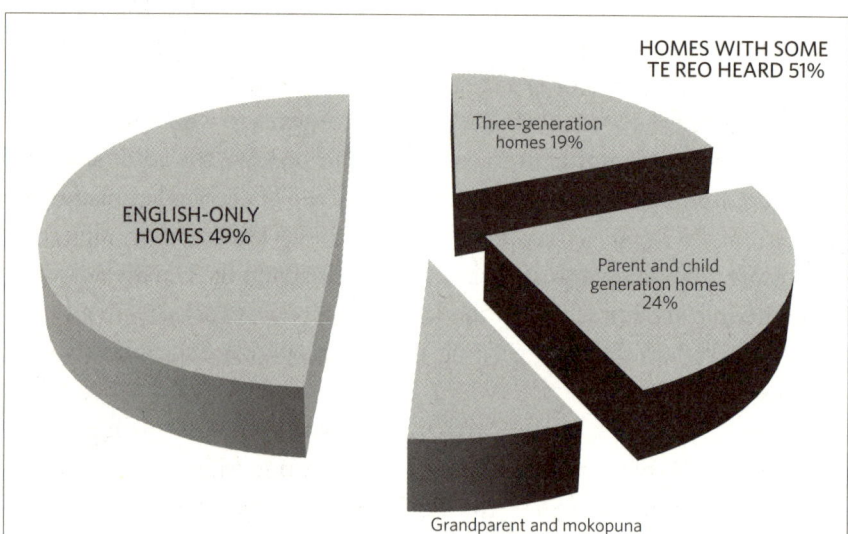

It is significant that more than half the survey respondents (54 per cent) had attended kōhanga reo. It is also significant that 64 per cent of those who had attended bilingual classes within mainstream schools had attended kōhanga reo and 75 per cent of those enrolled in kura kaupapa Māori had also attended kōhanga reo (see Hōhepa, this volume). This suggests that early contact with te reo at preschool level has been conducive to building the foundations for speaking and thinking in Māori. That early exposure to the language, cultural symbols and icons such as those found in pepeha and waiata has also ensured a solid base in cultural knowledge. When this is supported by the language of home, it reinforces and strengthens both language and identity.

Expressions of Identity

Expressions of identity do not rely solely on the use of the indigenous language. They are sometimes seen in the choice of language used, in the practice of customs and traditions, or even in the content and context of discussion. These applications can make strong links with Māori identity, even when the language spoken is English. To search out such expressions, I looked first at the 'open' questions in the survey to see how many were recorded in te reo, or used any Māori at all.

The four open questions drew 304 comments overall. The first open question asked for comments on the type of school attended – mainstream, bilingual or kura kaupapa – and received 26 per cent of the total responses. The second question asked 'Why marae are important to you' and more than half the comments (57 per cent) responded to this question. Its high rate of response also reflects the importance of marae to Māori, and Kawharu and Tāne in this volume explore these responses further. The third question sought general comments on the survey (drawing 15 per cent of responses) and the final question invited comments about how respondents might support marae and tribal affairs later in life, or might help retain their iwi and hapū identity when, and if, they no longer lived close to their tribal homeland (this two-pronged question drew 2 per cent of responses).

Figure 4.3 (overleaf) shows the percentage of responses made in English, those made only in Māori, in formulaic (or ritual) Māori and a mixture of Māori and English.

Those respondents who were fluent in te reo had the choice of recording their responses in Māori or in English, and those who wrote only in Māori did so in well-constructed sentences in te reo (8 per cent); all of these were written by students currently attending kura kaupapa Māori.

> 'He pai ōku tau katoa i te wā i haere au ki te kohanga reo, me te pai hoki o te kura kaupapa.' [All the years I spent at kōhanga reo were great, and likewise my time at kura kaupapa.] (001)

> '. . . Nā te mea tērā te wāhi o tōku tupuna.' [. . . Because that is the place where my ancestor belonged.] (003)

'Ka hono ai te whānau ka whakatinanahia ngā mahi o ngā tupuna. Ka ako i nga tikanga Māori.' [The extended family is united through engaging in the ancient practices of the ancestors, in the learning of Māori traditional customary practices.] (005)

Figure 4.3: Type of language used, by percentage of all comments received

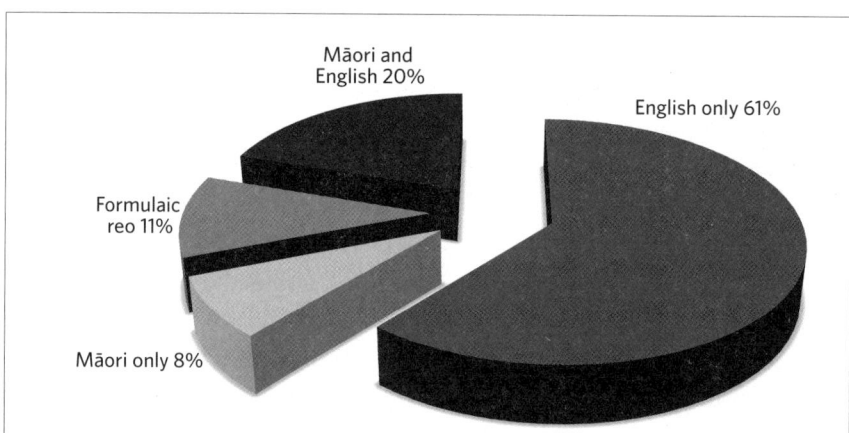

The majority of responses (61 per cent) were in English only. Then there were those who mixed codes and switched Māori phrases or words within English sentences. Sometimes 'formulaic' Māori language was inserted into the English sentence. Examples of formulaic reo are where particular prose is predetermined, is widespread and reasonably well known in the Māori world. They are used in common sayings, in pepeha, whakataukī and in ritual greetings. The following are some examples from the students' responses:

'. . . ko tōku tūrangawaewae'* [. . . My place to stand] (008)

'. . . I would be lost pērā i te moa ngaro noa'† [. . . just like the moa lost forever] (017)

---

* Tūrangawaewae is literally translated as 'a place to stand'; however the meaning is much deeper than simply a 'space': it is whakapapa and tikanga that create the platform for that 'place'.
† The moa was a bird native to this land that was hunted to extinction. This particular phrase is often used as an analogy for the loss of te reo Māori and the loss of Māori identity.

'Kia ora' and 'ka pai' are both forms of salutations frequently used in this study and inserted into the English responses. Where simple phrases or words only were inserted into the English text, these were most often the names of schools, place names or Māori words that are used frequently in the mainstream vernacular, moving into New Zealand English (NZE) and recorded in the Orsman *Dictionary of New Zealand English*. Code mixing was common in this study group and Macalister (2005) suggests that it is precisely that inclusion of Māori which makes NZE distinctive. Code mixing in this way also allows those with low-level skills in te reo to engage with the language in ways that do not require fluency, and it allows them to exhibit and assert their Māori identity.

> '... my whānau only visit the marae in the Hokianga.' (388)
>
> '... koretake [useless] mainstream ...' [a comment made about a previous school] (492)
>
> '... fundraising for maybe the upkeep of the marae, the urupā [cemetery] ...' (501)

In a tally of the Māori words used in these comments, excluding full sentences in Māori and proper nouns, the most commonly used words were 'whānau' and 'marae'. It is not significant that the word 'marae' was used so much given the nature of this particular study, but both these words can be found in the Orsman dictionary, signalling their high rate of usage in NZE. What is significant though is the frequent use of other Māori words less likely to be known or used in mainstream NZE. Examples of these words were hākari (celebratory feast), tūpāpaku (corpse), hā (breath), mauri (life force) and whānau pani (bereaved family). The use of these terms suggests an understanding of the value placed on important rituals or customary practices which are crucial for sustaining the identity and mana of marae communities. It signals knowledge and understanding from within the culture, within the Māori world.

These comments illustrate further how a Māori world view is expressed by taitamariki in this study. The Māori words express how they feel about their marae and are examples where the full meaning in the target language, te reo – not the translation – is desired (see also the Kawharu and Tāne chapter for further examples).

> '... I can feel the mauri and the peace come upon everyone...'* (099)

> '... that is where the hā comes from...'† (188)

When translating from one language into another there is always room for misinterpretation, particularly when the words concerned convey concepts rather than real world entities, and so code mixing in this way reduces the room for error and possible offence (Holmes, 2005). Translations most often require a more in-depth and lengthy explanation, conveying context in a way that is not always possible in one-word translations (Biggs, 1989; Mutu, 2001). They also illustrate concepts that are understood by those who derive from and live within a Māori world, and which are not always, nor easily, understood by those outside the culture. One can only surmise that for these respondents, an English translation or equivalent does not give an adequate interpretation.

And then there are the examples where a Māori word is used when the English would do just as well, but using te reo provides an emphasis not conveyed by the English alone:

> 'we should do more kōrero Māori [speaking Māori]' (492).

This comment is just one example that shows positive attitudes towards te reo, and the desire for more opportunity to utilise and practise speaking Māori. That same sentiment was repeated many times in the course of this study, in the comments section as well as in the group discussions. The use of te reo through code mixing not only offers opportunity to assert Māori identity as noted earlier, but might also be viewed as a political statement that reaffirms and aligns the individual with their community, their identity as Māori, albeit without fluency in te reo (Bell, *et al.*, 2000; Ngaha, 2001).

---

* Mauri as defined by Marsden (2003) is life force which 'generates, regenerates and upholds creation ... the bonding element that holds the fabric of the universe'.
† Hā is the breath of life, for all that it means to be Māori.

The content of these comments were for the most part not unusual or surprising, but there were two expressions of Māori identity of a contemporary nature which offered further insights into taitamariki considerations around their identity. Borell's (2005) study, noted earlier, suggested that more localised identifiers were more important. Terms such as 'Rewa hard' and 'South Side' are descriptors of the suburb of Manurewa and the South Auckland region respectively and were terms used regularly by the taitamariki in her study, who lived in these suburbs (Borell, 2005, p. 66).

In this study 'Māori side' (219) is an expression used in the same way. It highlights positive aspects of being Māori and has been made popular through its use in the children's television programme *Pukana*. *Pukana* features young presenters speaking predominantly in te reo and engaging with children in everyday fun activities. 'Mean Māori Mean' (129, 216) was also used in some surveys, mirroring the phrase used in the sports and entertainment show *Hyundai CODE* on Māori Television. This show highlights Māori achievement, particularly in the sports arena. It is extremely popular among Māori youth because it reflects life choices (in the sports domain) that they can relate to and many aspire to enter into, and it also encourages them to emulate the 'star' personalities who appear on the programme. The expressions 'Mean Māori Mean' and 'Māori side' are both used to express the view that being Māori is fun and that it's 'cool' to be Māori.

The power of the media, especially television, to influence youth in positive ways is evident in this study group's survey data. One person said that they would 'like to promote te reo me ōna tikanga preferably through kapa haka and waiata Māori'* (491) because these are activities that interest taitamariki. In the group discussions with students, music through waiata and kapa haka was talked about often, in very positive ways – and music is inherent in many celebratory occasions within the Māori world. Kapa haka and waiata Māori are strong illustrations of te reo in practice. These activities provide opportunity to showcase Māori language, culture and

---

* 'Te reo me ōna tikanga' means, essentially, 'the language and associated customs'.

Māori identity; they are empowering for our youth and they promote positive attitudes to the wider community. Activity-based learning such as this is not new and has proven to be a useful tool in learning not only language, but also the cultural value system.

Cultural Markers of Māori Identity

Markers or indicators of Māori cultural identity such as whakataukī and pepeha are significant carriers of cultural histories (Mutu, 2001; Carter, 2004; Ngaha, 2005; Kawharu, 2008). In this study there was ample evidence that familiarity with these cultural symbols was widespread and not confined to those students with a background in Māori-medium education, although they were more likely to know and express these idioms of identity.

The survey respondents were asked to name particular cultural elements and their responses are illustrated in Table 4.2. Each element is listed from the best-known item to the least known according to the survey responses. These are in no way intended to show one element is more valuable or valued than any other, but simply to show which elements were better or less known to this group of young people. Hōhepa's chapter (Table 6.4) uses the same data, but differentiates between the responses of two groups, those who attended Māori-medium schools and those who did not.

Iwi, marae and hapū rate highly in this table. Having that level of knowledge about where you belong, or come from, is one level of cultural identification. It is basic and important. Knowing these few elements is the beginning of knowing and understanding your place in the world: the Māori world. Pepeha, incorporating any of the markers listed in Table 4.2, provide a deeper level of knowledge. They describe an iwi or hapū's traditional geographical boundaries by naming specific features such as mountains, mountain ranges, rivers and waterways, and might also refer to the chieftainship in the region and local marae. Knowing the various elements of pepeha signals a level of understanding of local identity through Māori knowledge systems, expressed in Māori ways and always in te reo. But more important than simply being able to name each of these elements is to know the stories that lie behind each of those names and therefore the cultural principles that guide behaviour, explain the association of ancestors with places, or identify important trusteeship principles in respect of particular places, and so on.

Table 4.2: Particular cultural markers and symbols, by respondents' ability to name

Cultural markers	N	Percentage
Iwi	433	86
Marae	391	78
Hapū	345	69
Maunga	315	63
Awa	298	59
Tupuna	169	34
Wharenui	150	30
Wharekai	81	16

In this study, it is clear from their talk about marae that most of the respondents spend very little time engaged in wānanga (learning opportunities) or in hui (various gatherings) at their own marae where this cultural knowledge is traditionally imparted. Being able to access the cultural background is, therefore, limited by access to Māori-friendly domains such as marae, whānau and school activities where this talk usually takes place.

Cultural knowledge was also demonstrated in the respondents' ability to write down waiata, pepeha or whakataukī and Māori phrases that they knew. More than 58 per cent of respondents were able to name waiata they knew, and 77 per cent were able to write down common Māori phrases, or pepeha and whakataukī. The phrases were all very well known, but two in particular clearly illustrated the dialect belonging to Te Tai Tokerau: 'Ae marika!' and 'Meinga, meinga!'* The waiata were predominantly from Te Tai Tokerau; they were about tupuna or landmarks from the region.

---

* 'Ae marika' is an exclamation that can range in meaning from a very positive affirmation ('Yes indeed!') to a sense of wonder ('Well I never!') to mild disbelief ('You don't say!'). 'Meinga, meinga' is an exclamation that expresses a sense of disbelief ('You don't say!').

But where waiata from other iwi traditions were recorded, these were recounted by respondents who had whakapapa links to those iwi. This demonstrates that these young people could also discern those elements of identity that linked with their own particular region of origin through whakapapa. It is especially significant that those who recorded pepeha and whakataukī were able to do so with a high degree of accuracy.

Te Reo in Crisis, and One Way Forward

One of the main concerns elders of the study region had was that our taitamariki are not often present in the whare (meeting house) when iwi and hapū stories are recounted, and as noted earlier the students' data supports that position. Transfer of that knowledge, which is integral to knowing who they are, can no longer be taken for granted. The language can also be a barrier. In this study, the self-assessment of language ability (see Table 4.1) suggests that only 26 per cent of respondents could understand the stories if they were recounted in te reo, which is the traditional medium for transferring knowledge of this type. In earlier times the whole community was involved in marae events, but that is no longer the case, as can be seen by the frequency of marae attendance reported by these taitamariki and what they see their roles being on the marae (see Kawharu and Tane, this volume).

This investigation shows that on a broad level, cultural knowledge among the young people in this study is varied. Where their education is in the medium of te reo, where they live in homes with speakers of te reo and are in close proximity to their marae, these young people are much more likely to know the reo and to have the cultural knowledge that aids understandings about their identity. None of this is new nor is it surprising. What is significant though is that waiata and pepeha and the cultural elements within these, which are all strong signifiers of Māori identity, are better known by these students than conversational Māori.

These findings strongly indicate that our language, te reo Māori, is at crisis point. Although our young people are engaging in te reo through activities such as kapa haka and in learning basic cultural knowledge through symbols of identity such as marae, pepeha and whakataukī, there is little in the findings to suggest that many are extending their language skills and abilities beyond the kura kaupapa classrooms and kapa haka stage. These domains alone are not enough for te reo to survive. Numbers enrolled in kōhanga reo and kura kaupapa have fluctuated over recent years. In 2009, 25,349 Māori students were in Māori-medium education: only 15.2 per cent of all Māori school students and 6.5 per cent less than were enrolled in 2004 when numbers in Māori-medium education were at their highest, 27,127 (Waitangi Tribunal, 2010). It is imperative that other avenues are pursued to ensure greater opportunities for expanding te reo and cultural knowledge among taitamariki Māori and their communities. Community engagement is necessary to reinforce te reo and cultural supports outside the school domain.

Positive cultural identity and security are important for Māori youth to participate and succeed in contemporary New Zealand society. The web 2.0 resource Tewehinui.com is a new opportunity for accessing cultural knowledge that provides the touchstones for identity formation. Those touchstones are the reo, the stories and histories of each region as recounted in waiata, in whakataukī, in pepeha and by the elders from within each community. It is important that whenever possible they are presented both in te reo and in English to ensure broad accessibility. But it is also imperative that the dialect and vocabulary of regional language is preserved. We believe that Tewehinui.com, as a source of information easily accessible by everyone, will encourage the growth and development of te reo, in particular for people who, like that 30 per cent in this study, rate their speaking skills in te reo as average.

The subtitle of this chapter asks the question, 'what's in a maunga?' The maunga is, I suggest, representative of all that traditional and regional knowledge about who we are. For too many of our taitamariki these are still unknown. Unless our taitamariki can access that knowledge in ways that are meaningful for them, the crisis of language and identity loss will continue. The touchstones to their identity and their language will remain at a distance, and the ability for many to achieve their potential for success in contemporary Aotearoa will continue to be out of reach.

Bibliography

Bell, A., Davis, K. M. *et al.*, 2000. 'Languages of the Manukau Region: A Pilot Study of Use, Maintenance and Educational Dimensions of Languages in South Auckland'. Report to the Woolf Fisher Research Centre, University of Auckland, Auckland. Manukau: Manukau Institute of Technology.

Benton, N., Forer, P., and Hopa, N. with Henare, A., Johnstone, W., Ngaha, A., Rawiri, A., 2002. 'Well-being and Disparity in Tamaki Makaurau: Nga Whakaaro o te Iwi', Auckland: James Henare Māori Research Centre.

Benton, R., 1997. 'The Māori Language: Dying or Reviving?' Working paper prepared for the East–West Center Alumni-in-Residence Working Paper Series. Wellington: New Zealand Council for Education and Research.

Biggs, B. 1989. 'Humpty Dumpty and the Treaty of Waitangi'. In: I. H. Kawharu, ed. *Waitangi: Māori and Pakeha Perspectives of the Treaty of Waitangi*. Auckland: Oxford University Press.

Borell, B., 2005. 'Livin in the City Ain't So Bad: Cultural Diversity of South Auckland Rangatahi'. Unpublished M.A. thesis, Massey University, Palmerston North.

Boyce, M., 1992. 'Māori Language in Porirua: A Study of Reported Proficiency, Patterns of Use, and Attitudes'. Unpublished M.A. thesis, Victoria University, Wellington.

Carter, L. J., 2004. 'Whakapapa and the State: Some Case Studies on the Impact of Central Government on Traditionally Organised Māori Groups'. Unpublished Ph.D. thesis, University of Auckland, Auckland.

de Bres, J., 2006. 'Māori Lexical Items in Mainstream TV News in New Zealand. *New Zealand English Journal*, vol. 20, no. 17, pp. 17–34.

Durie, A., 1997. 'Te Aka Matua: Keeping a Māori Identity'. In: P. T. Whaiti, M. McCarthy, and A. Durie, eds. *Mai i Rangiātea: Māori Wellbeing and Development*. Auckland: Bridget Williams Books, pp. 142–62.

Edwards, J., 1996. 'Symbolic Ethnicity and Language'. In: J. Hutchinson and A. D. Smith, eds. *Ethnicity*. New York: Oxford University Press.

Fishman, J. A., 1999. *Handbook of Language and Ethnic Identity*. New York: Oxford University Press.

——, 2001. *Can Threatened Languages Be Saved? Reversing Language Shift Revisited – A 21st Century Perspective*. Clevedon: Multilingual Matters.

Gee, S., Stephens M., Higgins R. and Liu J., 2003. 'Toku Reo, Toku Mana! Toku Reo, Toku Tuakiri! Toku Reo, Toku Mauri Ora'. *He Pukenga Kōrero: A Journal of Māori Studies*, vol. 7 (2), pp. 16–24.

Giles, H., Bourhis, R. and Taylor, D., 1977. 'Towards a Theory of Language in Ethnic Group Relations'. In: H. Giles, ed. *Language, Ethnicity and Intergroup Relations*. London: Academic Press, pp. 307–348.

Giles, H. and Johnson, P., 1987. 'Ethnolinguistic Identity Theory: A Social Psychological Approach to Language Maintenance'. *International Journal of the Sociology of Language*, vol. 68, pp. 69–99.

Hohepa, P., 2000. 'Towards 2030 A.D. Māori Language Regeneration Strategies, Government, People'. *He Pukenga Kōrero: A Journal of Māori Studies*, vol. 5, no. 2, pp. 10–15.

Holmes, J., 2005. 'Using Māori English in New Zealand'. *International Journal of Sociology of Language*, vol. 172, pp. 91–115.

Kawharu, M., 2008. *Tāhuhu Kōrero: The Sayings of Taitokerau*. Auckland: Auckland University Press.

Macalister, J., 2005. *A Dictionary of Māori Words in New Zealand English*. Melbourne: Oxford University Press.

Marsden, M., 2003. 'God, Man and the Universe'. In: T. A. C. Royal, ed. *The Woven Universe; Selected Writings of Rev. Māori Marsden*. Masterton: The Estate of Rev. Māori Marsden.

Mutu, M., 2001. 'Ko Pūwheke te Maunga – Pūwheke is the Mountain: Māori Language and Māori Ethnic Identity – Reaffirming Identity Through Language Revitalisation'. *He Pukenga Korero: A Journal of Māori Studies*, vol. 6, no. 2, pp. 1–8.

Nash, M., 1987. *The Cauldron of Ethnicity in the Modern World*. Chicago: University of Chicago Press.

Ngaha, A., 2001. 'He Wāhi Tare: A Sociolinguistic Study of te Reo o Ngāpuhi, Language Proficiency and Patterns of Language Use'. Unpublished M.A. thesis, University of Auckland, Auckland.

——, 2005. 'Language and Identity in the Māori Community: Without te Reo, Who Am I?' In: J. Holmes, M. Maclagan, P. Kerswill and M. Paviour-Smith, eds. *Researching Language Use and Language Users*. From: http://www.nzlingsoc.org/documents/Ngaha.pdf, pp. 29–49.

——, 2011. 'Te Reo, A Language for Māori Alone? An Investigation into the Relationship between the Māori Language and Māori Identity'. Unpublished Ph.D. thesis, University of Auckland, Auckland.

Ormond, A., 2004. 'The Voices and Silences of Young Māori People: A World of Impossibility'. Unpublished Ph.D. thesis, University of Auckland, Auckland.

Orsman, E. and Orsman, H. 1994. *The New Zealand English Dictionary: Dictionary of New Zealand Words and Phrases*. Auckland: New House Publishing.

Song, M., 2003. *Choosing Ethnic Identity*, Massachusetts: Blackwell Publishing.

Statistics New Zealand, 2007. 'QuickStats about Māori: Census 2006 / Tatauranga 2006'. Wellington: Statistics NZ.

Te Puni Kōkiri, 2002. 'Survey of Attitudes Towards and Beliefs and Values about the Māori Language: He Rangahau i ngā Whakapono me ngā Uara Hoki mō te Reo Māori'. Wellington: Ministry of Māori Development.

——, 2003. 'He Reo e Kōrerotia Ana – He Reo Ka Ora: A Shared Vision for the

Future of te Reo Māori'. Wellington: Ministry of Māori Development.
——, 2004. 'Te Reo Māori i te Hāpori: Māori Language in the Community'. Wellington: Ministry of Māori Development.
——, 2008. 'Te Oranga o te Reo Māori i te Rohe o Te Taitokerau: The Health of Te Reo Māori in Northland'. Wellington: Ministry of Māori Development.
Te Puni Kōkiri and Te Taura Whiri i te Reo Māori, 2003. 'Te Rautaki Reo Māori; The Māori Language Strategy'. Wellington: Ministry of Māori Development.
Waitangi Tribunal, 1989. 'Te Reo Maori Claim WAI 11'. Wellington: The Tribunal.
——, 2010. 'Pre-publication Waitangi Tribunal Report: WAI 262 te Reo Māori'. Wellington: The Tribunal.

KEVIN ROBINSON (Te Rarawa) has been the chief executive officer for Te Rūnanga o Te Rarawa for eighteen years and leads a team that now numbers 60. He has worked on many boards and committees, including as a director to the Northland District Health Board; a member of a group developing customary fisheries regulations; an iwi representative on the National Paepae Taumata Māori group, which helped to negotiate and formulate the customary fisheries regulations; a member of Te Kotahitanga o Te Taitokerau Resource Management Committee; and a member of Te Tai Tokerau health alliance. Kevin chairs the Panguru–Motutī Forestry Trust, and is an active whānau member of the marae komiti at Motutī from where he hails. If his work with, and for, Te Rarawa doesn't keep him busy enough, he is also a grandfather of five and a great-grandfather of one.

CHAPTER FIVE

MOTUTĪ ROAD: AT THE END OF THE ROAD, OR JUST THE BEGINNING?

KEVIN ROBINSON

MOTUTĪ ROAD IS A DEAD-END ROAD IN THE HEART OF NORTH Hokianga. Twelve years ago, perhaps fifteen, despite its remoteness, we had quite a number of whānau living there. A big bus would come down and pick the children up in the mornings and take them to school. The bus would come to Motutī Road empty, and leave full. Now, we have a small school bus, perhaps a fifteen-seater. It comes in the mornings and goes out with perhaps two or three tamariki. And that's on a good day.

Once thriving, many Te Rarawa communities in Hokianga have now only a glimmer of their former prosperity. This snapshot of Motutī Road is not an uncommon picture. It reflects a reality that, unfortunately, is experienced by others throughout Hokianga, and I suspect also in other similarly remote Māori communities nationwide. Motutī Road shows also

---

This chapter, like that of Merimeri Penfold in this volume, began as a kōrero between Kevin and Merata Kawharu – a less formal undertaking than Merimeri's, as it was a single collaboration rather than part of the Te Wehi Nui a Mamao collection of oral histories (see Michael Hennessy, this volume). Merata wrote up these notes from the kōrero.

the changing demographics. Where we had a relatively youthful community, our community is now aging. Its members are not of child-bearing age. The ones that are, have moved away, to the towns and to the cities. Now we would have perhaps twenty people on Motutī Road. But twelve to fifteen years ago, the community was between eighty and a hundred people.

The magnetism of cities attracted people from other Te Rarawa communities even earlier – many years earlier. It was in the 1930s that my grandparents moved away to Auckland, taking their children with them. And so they walked off the farms basically at that time, and they either on-leased them or just left. Of course a lot of them have been incurring rates since then, many of which have never been paid. Now you have beneficiaries of that whenua who tātai (genealogically connect) to that whenua and are born with a 'number' over their heads and they do not even know it. They do not even know they have land interests.

What does this all mean for our communities? If the rural–urban drift that we often talked about as occurring in the post-war period is still happening, and still emptying out our communities, what does that mean for our marae? What place will our marae have in the lives of our children and grandchildren, especially those urban-based descendants? How can we reverse the trends?

A fundamental principle for Te Rarawa is that the marae represents the backbone of our identity as a people and who we are in relation to our lands. Our marae cannot survive without our children. The children and their families provide the main support for marae. The ones that remain at home still do that of course, but the numbers are very small. For instance, those who carry out the formal roles on the marae, the elders, are few in number. We have a limited number who fulfil marae responsibilities for not just one marae, but a number, and for throughout Te Rarawa. Just recently, for example, our kaikaranga from Motutī went to Panguru to assist the local people in hosting visitors to a tangi as there was otherwise insufficient local support. The burden is on the shoulders of just a few. Sometimes kaumātua will be attending tangi days on end, one after the other. It is tiring for anyone to attend tangi for hours at a time. To fulfil the duties of manaaki manuhiri (looking after guests) through whaikōrero (formal speeches) or karanga (formal calls of welcome), which sometimes go through to the late afternoons or evenings, it is even more tiring. And yet the key people who undertake these roles are those 60 years or older. It is a lot to ask of them. These circumstances are the reality in Hokianga. Most of Te Rarawa live away from the tribal rohe.

In recent times, a major contributor to a decline in marae communities has been government policy that on the one hand provides social welfare to those who cannot find employment, but on the other hand places a cap on welfare – especially to long-term unemployed. Those who have not been able to work for one reason or another now need to find employment or training. The rural regions of Te Rarawa are not employment havens, and in many regions, there are no training programmes or facilities. We then see people being forced to move away to Kaitāia, Whangārei or further afield. Whole families move. School rolls drop. The number of teachers who can be employed also drops. Marae communities weaken.

The biggest loss, though, concerns the cultural investment in our children. The children are no longer around our kaumātua and kuia listening to and seeing the tikanga, the reo, the mita (regional style) and the stories that are told on our marae. And so now we have the group who are living outside Motutī missing out on that experience as they grow up. They know where they are from, and they come back, but those are short visits and infrequent. Others may have been brought up 'on the marae' first before moving away and they will have the values instilled within them, but in many cases, when they grow up, their children will not have that. Their world is completely different. Of course that brings positive things too, perhaps better access to a wider range of things that city life offers, but the cities do not provide the cultural sustenance of home marae.

These basic circumstances are characteristic of all of our marae throughout Te Rarawa, in one form or another. I suspect similar patterns are found to one extent or another throughout iwi beyond Tai Tokerau as well.

For the few who remain in marae communities, to ease the load particularly on the elders, we have built housing immediately adjacent to the marae. At my marae, we have kaumātua living there, and a kuia who is also the treasurer for the marae committee, and a kaikaranga (female leader who performs the customary calls of welcome to guests) who is the marae committee secretary. Her children are very supportive of marae functions as well. In these three cases, it was a government programme that provided funding to build the homes. The housing was a joint arrangement with the Far North District Council, the Northland Regional Council and Te Rūnanga o Te Rarawa. Following the success of the housing programme, then, we have been able to have our marae resource people on hand. Perhaps ironically, what we have is one arm of the government contributing to the decline in marae communities; another arm trying to patch up the problem.

Faced with these socio-cultural difficulties, the Rūnanga is engaging in innovative ways to curb the problems and revive our Te Rarawa marae. By establishing a broadband network, where the Rūnanga is a partner, we aim to have all Te Rarawa marae 'fibred'. Ultimately also, rural homes will have access to broadband. Many Māori own their own businesses, and it is hoped that broadband will be an incentive for them to return home and run their businesses from the Hokianga. But also those who live away, whether elsewhere in New Zealand or overseas, may have an opportunity to connect to their marae websites, and perhaps even stream into marae hui or to the funeral day of a tangi, for instance.

Another major Te Rarawa initiative has seen the establishment of a bee school in Kaitāia. Over a 12-month period students learn everything to do with bees. Much land here in the Far North is covered in mānuka, and much of that land is Māori-owned. The Far North has the highest levels of UMF, or Unique Manuka Factor, in New Zealand, enabling medical-grade honey to be produced. The returns on ordinary 'bush' honey are great, but with medical-grade mānuka honey, they are substantial after only three or four years. Bee business is a major opportunity to utilise resources growing freely on otherwise non-productive, or under-productive, Māori-owned land.

In a completely different vein, Te Rūnanga is developing a te reo programme as well to shape a future that promotes the language, and the regional variations of the language, as central to the lives of Te Rarawa descendants. This includes, for instance, developing a language programme as part of school curriculum. We are bringing together key people in the community, principals and members of school boards of trustees to help develop the language programme. This is but one idea among many as we face the future following the settlement of our historical Treaty claims on 28 October 2012.

Hokianga has much on its horizon. The Motutī bus might one day again be full. A dead end on Motutī Road? I don't think so.

MARGIE KAHUKURA HŌHEPA (Te Māhurehure, Ngāpuhi) is an associate professor and the Associate Dean – Māori – of the Faculty of Education, University of Waikato. Margie began her career in education as a primary school teacher in Te Tai Tokerau. As a parent she has also been a board of trustees member in a Tai Tokerau secondary school.

Margie's field of research is Māori education and is framed by kaupapa Māori. Much of her work revolves around Māori-medium schooling. Recent study has focused on the development of Ngā Whanaketanga Rumaki Māori (Māori-medium equivalent of national standards), Māori educational leadership, schooling improvement in Māori-medium settings and Māori-medium initial teacher education. She takes a very personal interest in this type of schooling as a grandmother of mokopuna attending kōhanga reo and kura.

CHAPTER SIX

TE REO MĀORI AND SCHOOLING

MARGIE HŌHEPA

THE USE OF AN INDIGENOUS LANGUAGE HAS BEEN ACKNOWLEDGED as a basic right (Skutnabb-Kangas, 2007). The reality for many indigenous minority peoples, however, is that the realisation of this right has been seriously undermined through colonisation. For Māori the impact of colonisation is highly evident or, more to the point, audible in the limited use of te reo Māori as a medium of socialisation and communication between successive generations of whānau (family), hapū (sub-tribe) and iwi (tribe). When a language is not able to be used to any great extent, it is not just the language that may be lost. Important stores of cultural knowledge may also be at risk.

Associated with language rights are questions of access to cultural knowledge and values indexed by that language. Language is key to the perpetuation of a culture, its knowledge and its value systems (McCarty, 2007; Littlebear, 1999). When a language is in danger of disappearing, the systems of knowledge carried by that language are also at risk. Within Māori society, whānau, hapū and iwi are fundamental to the guardianship of cultural knowledge and values as well as to their transmission to future generations and guardians. These levels of familial and relational organisation help to identify, protect and provide access to localised Māori cultural knowledge and values. Support by wider social institutions and systems has a critical impact on guardianship and on the transmission of knowledge to children and youth.

Processes of colonisation have involved schooling systems as a significant tool in attempts to eradicate indigenous language, culture and knowledge from children and also from their communities (Baker, 2006; Rau, 2008; Simon and Smith, 2001). What role then might schools now play to help ensure that indigenous language and culture survives, in ways that are meaningful, culturally located and productive? What school-related factors might be involved in ensuring that an indigenous cultural knowledge and language are successfully imparted to youth and thus created and recreated across generations?

This chapter focuses on relationships between schooling experiences and Māori language and cultural knowledge among Te Tai Tokerau youth today. 'Mai i Tāmaki ki te Rerenga Wairua, te tai hoe tamatāne, te tai hoe tamawahine te rohe o Tai Tokerau' is a saying sometimes used to denote Te Tai Tokerau. It describes Te Tai Tokerau as bounded by the east and west coasts between Te Reinga as the northern-most marker and the greater Auckland area as the southernmost (albeit highly contested) boundary. Other descriptions of Te Tai Tokerau, as Aotearoa New Zealand's northernmost region, generally identify it as stretching from the North Cape, marginally north of Cape Reinga, to Kaipara on the west and Mangawhai on the east.

The chapter begins by discussing key theories and approaches to indigenous language regeneration. It explores views of the role schooling may play in regeneration. In various parts of the world, including Aotearoa New Zealand, schooling has been repositioned as now being able to actively support the regeneration of indigenous languages and cultures. This contrasts with a history that included the banning of Māori language from schools.

Māori-medium schooling in Aotearoa New Zealand, with Māori the language of instruction for at least part of each day, has become a key context for te reo Māori regeneration among students. It also supports language regeneration in students' homes and across their family members (Royal Tangaere, 1997; Hohepa, 2006). This chapter examines the degree to which such educational experiences are available to children and youth growing up in Te Tai Tokerau. It discusses relationships between schooling experiences and Māori language and cultural knowledge, as reported by 500 Te Tai Tokerau Māori youth who participated in the Te Wehi Nui a Mamao research project. Additionally it looks at implications that Māori-medium education sites have in supporting the development of hapū- and iwi-related language and cultural knowledge. Information the project collected from Te Tai Tokerau youth indicates that schooling through te reo makes a difference not only to their competency in te reo Māori, but also to their levels of hapū and iwi knowledge.

Indigenous Language Regeneration

Sociolinguistics has been responsible for much research and theoretical energy in developing understandings of language regeneration. Fishman (1991) provides a comprehensive discussion of intervention efforts into language loss under the heading of 'Reversing Language Shift' (RLS). He deals with 'theory and practice of assistance to speech communities whose native languages are threatened because their intergenerational continuity is proceeding negatively, with fewer and fewer users' (1991, p. xii).

A major claim is that such language shift cannot be reversed at a societal level if it is not reversed at the family and local community levels. In order to affect a language shift, 'small-scale social life' must be focused on and it is here – in 'the qualitative emphases of daily informal life . . . always the most difficult arenas in which to intervene' (Fishman, 1991, p. 8) – that the nurturing of a threatened language needs to occur. His major argument is that:

> [t]he priorities at various points in the RLS struggle must vary but they must, nevertheless, derive from a single, integrated theory of language-in-society processes that places intergenerational mother tongue transmission at the very center and that makes sure to defend that center before setting out to conquer societal processes that are more distant, dubious and tenuous vis-à-vis such transmission. (Fishman, 1991, p. 6)

The fostering of intergenerational mother tongue is viewed as a cultural right and societal resource that requires commitment at institutional and at governmental levels. Fishman, however, is critical of efforts to reverse language loss through controlling the institutional language of education, mass media or government without sufficiently safeguarding the intimate, intergenerational language transmission context. He is referring to the transmission of language across generations in families and communities. This is a significant point in relation to our project, given that we focused on elders and youth in particular and on strategies (such as Māori-medium education) and learning tools (such as web 2.0 resources) which might effectively support the transmission of cultural knowledge and language to a younger generation.

Fishman (1991) has developed a 'Graded International Disruption Scale for Threatened Languages' as a guide to understanding the extent to which a language is endangered. It also provides a plan of action for prioritised intervention in language loss (Baker, 2006). The scale is based on the premise that intervention at one stage will be futile unless earlier stages are at least partly addressed, and that actions at each stage are accompanied by awareness of how they contribute to intergenerational transmission and continuity of a language. There are eight stages in the scale. Stage 8 is the worst-case scenario, with perhaps only a handful of (usually elderly) fluent speakers remaining. Stage 7 is when a language may be used by older members of a culture but not by its younger members. Intergenerational transmission and use at communities exists at stage 6; literacy in the language exists at stage 5. At stage 4 compulsory education is available in the threatened language. Stage 3 includes the language being used in less specialised work areas that involve interaction with majority language speakers. Stage 2 focuses on the availability of lower government services and mass media in the language, and stage 1 involves some use of the language in higher education, central government and national media (Fishman, 1991).

In efforts to reverse language loss, Fishman advocates a diglossic existence (in which distinct forms of the language are used in different settings or domains) for cultural communities whose language has little political power in the public and institutional levels of society. He recommends that their community language remain bounded in their socio-cultural traditions, values, beliefs and practices. If these traditions are still extensively practised in modern life, in the sense that they occur regularly in day-to-day lives and across a range of contexts, then concentrating efforts in this way may be fruitful. Indeed, it has been argued that te reo Māori was protected from total loss much in this manner. Language activities of the marae, of tangi (funerals) and hui (meetings), practices of karanga (ceremonial ritual call), whaikōrero (formal oration), waiata (song) and karakia (incantation), were some of the mechanisms that kept Māori language in Māori earshot (Smith, 1989). Diglossia is considered by Fishman to be a point on a language shift continuum that, as an initial stage of reversal, provides boundaries that can protect a language.

Alternatively, Chrisp (1997) proposes that diglossia, rather than being considered an early point in language revitalisation, be utilised to develop a theoretical framework for Māori revitalisation. He argues that work from such a framework can identify Māori-language domains and English-language domains, and can develop mechanisms to help expand Māori language within Māori-language domains.

Aotearoa New Zealand has instances of diglossic approaches to the use of te reo Māori: for instance, only Māori language being used in Māori cultural contexts such as pōwhiri (welcomes). In addition, te reo is increasingly included in domains that have tended to be seen as English language, such as television and education. The potential of public, non-traditional contexts such as educational institutions either to take over socialising functions, or to help regenerate socialising functions of personal contexts such as those of whānau (Urlich Cloher and Hohepa, 1996), is increasingly being recognised and realised. Indeed, taking over and replacing the socialising and enculturating functions and practices of families was the implicit and explicit agenda of various types of schooling (for example, boarding schools) set up for 'native' children in many parts of the world. It is somehow fitting that schooling is now being used to help regenerate and reinforce those functions.

What is being increasingly recognised is that for an indigenous people, their indigenous language 'must survive in order to bridge the traditional and modern worlds that the people carry within themselves and confront in their daily lives' (Fogwill, 1994, p. 235). Māori have seen the cost when a new language such as English is imposed on them with purported intentions of providing access to benefits of a changing world, but has the effect of restricting growth and development of their indigenous language.

The goal of language regeneration is not to return simplistically to the 'traditional way' but to ensure that traditions live on, in meaningful and contextualised ways, alongside language and culture. It is also well established that learning in a mother tongue can provide a greater likelihood of academic success (Baker, 2006). There is evidence that this is the case for an indigenous language that is not necessarily the first language of students, including Māori language. In Aotearoa New Zealand, the National Certificate of Educational Achievement (NCEA) results indicate that Māori students taught through te reo Māori are more likely to gain national secondary school qualifications than Māori students taught through the English language (Murray, 2007). Children who do well academically have better employment opportunities, have greater potential to becoming meaningful participants in community affairs, and enjoy many other benefits.

Living languages are modern languages. Although inextricably linked to a traditional past, they are in the present – they contain and provide meaning in the day-to-day lives of their people. So-called traditional beliefs, values and practices of a culture that are carried by a language are part of a people's lives now, today and every day. The goal of language regeneration is to ensure that language and the culture it indexes are a vital part of a people's wellbeing and healthy existence.

The Role of Schooling in Language and Cultural Regeneration

There are claims that schools are not, or cannot be, a critical factor in the regeneration of a language (Chrisp, 1997; Fishman, 1991; Jacques, 1991). The main thrust of the argument is that schools cannot be expected to take a significant responsibility for ensuring that a child becomes a competent speaker of a particular language. This seems rather ironic given that schooling has played a pivotal role in language shifts experienced by many indigenous minority groups around the world. Church- and state-administered schools have been key players in severe disruptions to the socialisation of indigenous culture and language, as was the case for Māori (Simon and Smith, 2001).

Schooling played a significant role in the decline of many indigenous languages at the latter end of the twentieth century. In the 1980s many children who came out of kōhanga reo (Māori-language preschool; 'kōhanga' literally meaning 'nest') as Māori-language speakers and entered into English-medium primary schooling very quickly stopped speaking Māori (Sharples, 1989). Schooling can still be a factor in language shift to English among the small numbers of young Māori speakers.

Many indigenous groups in danger of language and culture loss, however, also view schooling as a major means of regeneration (Keegan, 1991). Crystal (2000) also identifies a strong presence of an endangered language in the educational system as an important strategy for avoiding language death. There are well-publicised cases of language regeneration in which immersion schooling has played a critical part, such as in the cases of the Hebrew and Welsh languages (Nahir, 1988; Baker and Jones, 2000). The role of schooling can be seen as a tool used to help support the (re)transformation of a language and a culture back into the lives of a people.

Aotearoa New Zealand is often identified as a leading nation, internationally, for educational programmes focused on language regeneration from early childhood through compulsory schooling to tertiary levels. Māori-medium education programmes in early childhood involve children five years and under. Early childhood Māori-language programmes (from high to total immersion) that the Ministry of Education has licensed include: the previously mentioned kōhanga reo that operate under the auspices of Te Kōhanga Reo National Trust; puna reo (another Māori immersion preschool; 'puna' literally meaning 'spring'); and ngā puna kōhungahunga (spring of infants – play groups, some of which operate in te reo Māori only). There are also bilingual early childhood programmes that provide anywhere between 12 to 80 per cent Māori-language immersion.

Compulsory schooling spans children and young people from approximately five to eighteen years old. For this age range there are school programmes in the state system that deliver either all or some of the curriculum through te reo Maori. These programmes include kura kaupapa Māori (immersion schools with an explicit Māori philosophical base) and kura-ā-iwi (immersion schools that adhere to tikanga, or conventions and dialect of an identified iwi). Within largely English-medium schools there are also other immersion (rumaki) and bilingual (reo rua) units and classrooms within largely English-medium schools. At the tertiary level this country has three legislatively recognised whare wānanga (Māori institutions of higher learning), which provide Māori- and English-medium programmes and qualifications.

How significant are such educational opportunities in supporting Māori children and youth to become knowledgeable members, linguistically and culturally, of Māori society? When we consider the proportions of Māori children in early childhood education and educational settings that are providing substantive learning opportunities in te reo Māori, the picture is not at all rosy.

'Ngā Haeata Mātauranga – Annual Report on Māori Education, 2008/09' indicates that just under 30 per cent of all early childhood education provisions were Māori-medium. Just over 12 per cent of these provided high to total immersion programmes; the remaining 18 per cent provided bilingual programmes for at least 12 per cent of the time (Ministry of Education, 2010).

In the 1980s and early 1990s, kōhanga reo numbers increased quickly from one pilot in 1982 to over 800 programmes catering for 14,000 children by 1993. Since then there has been a steady decline in both the number of kōhanga and the number of children attending. By 2009 there were only 464 kōhanga reo. Enrolments in kōhanga dropped 25 per cent from 14,027 in 1993 to 10,600 in 2004, then to 9165 in 2008, with a slight rise in 2009 to 9288 (Ministry of Education, 2009). In 2009 there were another eleven licensed services (such as puna reo) that provided high immersion programmes for 296 children. By far the majority of 36,118 Māori children in early childhood education (approximately 91 per cent of all Māori preschoolers) attended English-medium programmes.

Primary and secondary schooling with Māori as the medium of instruction is helping only around 21 per cent of Māori students to have some degree of learning experience as speakers of te reo Māori (Ministry of Education, 2010). The amount of Māori language that children in these schools may experience, however, varies greatly depending on the level of immersion they are in, which spans the following levels:

- level 1: (81 per cent to 100 per cent immersion) – maintenance programmes in which Māori is the principal language of communication and instruction, and the principal curriculum is taught entirely in Māori;
- level 2: (51 per cent to 80 per cent immersion) – development programmes in which Māori is the language of communication and instruction for most of the time;
- level 3: (31 per cent to 50 per cent immersion) – emerging programmes in which English is the main language of communication and instruction;
- level 4: (12 per cent to 30 per cent immersion) – essentially English-medium programmes that incorporate between 3 and 7.5 hours a week of teaching in Māori.

(Ministry of Education, n.d.)

While there are over 2500 schools for primary- and secondary-aged students in Aotearoa New Zealand, only 394 offer Māori immersion or bilingual programmes. Out of 28,171 students enrolled in Māori-medium education in 2009, only 11,634 were enrolled in level 1 classroom settings. Nearly the same number of children were enrolled in level 3 and 4 classrooms (11,376 children). What this means is that only about 40 per cent of children in Māori-medium settings, that is around 8 per cent of all Māori children, are getting any substantive Māori-language experiences in school settings. However, there is evidence of educational and cultural benefits for the minority of Māori children who have access to Māori-medium education.

In addition to learning through the medium of te reo Māori, opportunities to learn Māori language and cultural knowledge can also be accessed by studying te reo Māori as a separate subject. This occurs in both English- and Māori-medium secondary school programmes. In 2009, 13,670 Māori students were learning te reo Māori as a separate subject for three or more hours per week.

While raising Māori achievement is a concern of all schools, for Māori-medium schooling provisions such as kura kaupapa Māori, it is not the only concern. For the most part, Māori concerned about the fate of te reo Māori me ōna tikanga (Māori language and culture) drove the initiation and development of Māori-medium schooling in the 1980s. Simply delivering official state curriculum through the medium of Māori was not considered enough to ensure that Māori language and culture continued. Māori-medium schooling programmes are, or should be, critically concerned with the teaching of Māori cultural knowledge. Even though there are kura, including kura-ā-iwi, that focus on language and knowledge of particular tribes, there is little other than anecdotal evidence about how programmes help to regenerate and strengthen regional forms of Māori language and knowledge. There is much potential to examine as well as support this important facet of identity inside schooling.

The extent that Māori-medium schooling sites are able to focus on specific tribal language and knowledge, as opposed to more universal or 'standardised' forms of Māori language and cultural knowledge, can depend on a number of factors. These factors include where the sites are located, the level of iwi involvement and support in schooling in their respective rohe (region) and schools' and teachers' levels of interest and knowledge in regional language and heritage.

Iwi groups have developed strategic education plans that explicitly address what their young people should know in terms of their iwi identity; see, for example, Ngāti Kahungunu Cultural Standards Project (Ngāti Kahungunu, n.d.). The Ministry of Education has entered into education partnerships with a number of iwi, including one in Te Tai Tokerau called Te Putahitanga Mātauranga (Hohepa, *et al.*, 2004), which operated from 1999 to the mid-2000s. The iwi partner aimed to have a strong focus on Māori dialects and knowledge of Tai Tokerau iwi incorporated into work with schools. Although this was not fully realised by the end of the partnership, one project that was developed was Te R.I.T.O. Māori. This provided isolated rural mainstream schools with teachers of te reo Māori who assisted with professional development and mentoring to build school capacity for delivering te reo programmes.

The ministry reported that in 2009 there were active partnerships and relationships with 32 iwi (Ministry of Education, 2010). These often include a focus on ensuring that educational programmes and school curriculum within a given iwi rohe include iwi cultural knowledge, language and identity. An evaluation of one such partnership involving Ngāti Porou, 'Whaia te Iti Kahurangi', found a change in the reported use of Ngāti Porou dialect during the first few years, with 62 per cent of the principals and teachers believing there was more use of te reo o Ngāti Porou in their schools (Wylie and Arago-Kemp, 2004).

Nationally, the education sector's involvement in Māori language and cultural regeneration has an impact on only a small proportion of Māori children and youth. What is less clear is how such involvement is affecting levels of knowledge of language and culture among the young at tribal and regional levels. Of specific interest in this chapter is the schooling of young Tai Tokerau iwi members. To what extent are early childhood education and school contexts able to support rohe-based language and cultural regeneration and maintenance?

Schooling in Te Tai Tokerau: The Historical Context

From the first contacts between Māori and non-Māori in Te Tai Tokerau in the late eighteenth century and indeed for some time afterwards, Māori was the major language of communication for economic, cultural and religious exchange (Jenkins, 1991). The ascendancy of Māori language, measured by the number of Māori-language speakers (both Māori and non-Māori), continued during the early colonisation of Te Tai Tokerau and the formation of 'New Zealand' as a colony in 1840.

Following the introduction of Western forms of print literacy in the early nineteenth century, many Māori developed reading and writing skills in Māori. Early written observations document individuals from Te Tai Tokerau being taught to read and write in English as well as te reo Māori (Jenkins, 1991; Simon, 1998). Māori also considered mastery of literacy skills a desirable way of accessing and understanding the unfamiliar technology, skills and knowledge that they were being exposed to and were eager to use (Jackson, 1975). Jenkins (1991) discusses Ngāpuhi leader Hongi Hika's involvement in the development of the orthography for written Māori and the implications this also had for access to muskets. Additionally, there are accounts from the 1830s that Māori in the Hokianga region could read (Yate 1833 cited in Jackson, 1975, p. 33) as well as write (Marsden 1837 cited in Haami, 2004, p. 20).

Tracing back to the first introduction of non-Māori educational institutions in this country, Te Tai Tokerau has the longest history of contact and participation with Western styles of schooling. Māori relationships with schools began in this country in 1816 at Rangihoua in Pēwhairangi, Bay of Islands, with the establishment of the first Church Missionary Society mission school. The school folded after two years due to low numbers of students, an early indication perhaps that schooling in Te Tai Tokerau would have problems (Simon, 1998).

Schooling was perceived by missionaries and later by colonial governments as an effective means of 'civilising' and assimilating Māori into Christian or British ways of life. Missionaries who established the first schools opted to teach Māori students to read and write in Māori only. This made a lot of practical and pedagogical sense given Māori was the language of the students. There were, however, other reasons for restricting Māori access to instruction in English. The missionaries wanted to keep Māori away from negative influences of secular Pākehā society. Until the introduction of the native schools system in 1867, much of the printed Māori corpus was religious in nature. By controlling the language of instruction and the production of printed Māori-language texts, missionaries took charge over the knowledge and information Māori could potentially access through print. Alongside missionary-controlled printing, publications issued by the government and Māori emerged in the nineteenth century (Curnow, Hopa and McRae, 2002). The Māori-language newspapers, in particular, illustrate the extent to which Māori were gaining control over reading and writing in Māori as well as their reactions to issues and challenges of the time.

The transition from Māori as the major medium of formal instruction in schools to English-only instruction accompanied a series of legislative ordinances and acts. The Education Ordinance of 1847 enabled mission schools to access subsidies, providing that among other things they gave instruction in the English language. The 1867 Native Schools

Act established a national state-controlled system of schools for Māori children. Māori contributed land as well as to the cost of buildings and staff. The schools did not receive state funding unless instruction was through English 'as far as practicable' (Simon, 1998). The 1877 Education Act paved the way for non-Māori children to be provided with free, secular and compulsory education. Schooling was not compulsory for Māori until 1894 (Simon, 1994; 1998).

The Native Schools Code of 1880 allowed for some Māori to be used with young children, but only as a means to help them learn English. By 1903 official attitudes to the use of Māori had largely reversed and its use in school contexts was strongly disfavoured (Simon, 1998). The era of the native schools system raised issues about the place of Māori language, knowledge and practices in schools. Periods of virtual exclusion were followed by controlled and selected inclusion of Māori culture, mainly aspects of material culture and performing arts (Simon and Smith, 2001). English-medium education was to remain the status quo through to the closing of native schools in 1969 and to continue into the 1970s. This had a hugely detrimental effect on the levels of Māori language and cultural knowledge in several generations of young Māori.

By the 1970s the state of te reo was considered so critical that both Māori and non-Māori believed there was little chance of reversing the trend of language loss. A Māori-language survey in the 1970s found that only 17.9 per cent of mainly older Māori were fluent speakers of the language (R. A. Benton, 1978). Ngaha in this volume discusses the survey findings pertaining to Te Tai Tokerau in more detail. However, some key links made between those findings and schooling are relevant to this discussion. The survey found an inverse relationship between levels of formal schooling and expressed preferences for te reo Māori. That is, the longer a survey respondent had remained in formal schooling, the less likely they used te reo. There were also indications that more children were punished in Te Tai Tokerau for using Māori in schools, and these punishments occurred over a longer period of time, than further south in the North Island (N. Benton, 1989).

The tenuous position of te reo Māori in the 1970s provided an impetus for its re-introduction as a medium of instruction in compulsory schooling. Motatau in the Bay of Islands was considered as a possibility for the programme in 1973–74, when the Māori Unit of the New Zealand Council for Educational Research examined the feasibility of Māori bilingual schooling at a district high school. The first bilingual school programme, however, began in 1977 in the Bay of Plenty settlement of Ruātoki, where a large proportion of school entrants still spoke Māori as their first language.

The next significant development was the previously mentioned kōhanga reo (Hohepa, *et al.*, 1992). Years of subtle and not so subtle discouragement of Māori-language use both in and out of the home, coupled with beliefs that a good grounding in English helped constitute 'good educational experiences before beginning school' (Royal Tangaere, 1997, p. 6), helped to undermine intergenerational language transmission, so important for the viability of a language and cultural knowledge. Kōhanga reo was seen as an important development to address this, as a programme focused on early childhood that brought young children and native speakers from the grandparent generation together in a Māori-medium learning environment. This was closely followed by kura kaupapa Māori, initially a Māori-driven, Māori-funded schooling system in the mid-1980s, which was officially recognised as a state schooling option in the 1989 Education Act.

In 1988, 170 years after the first school at Rangihoua closed, Te Tai Tokerau was again host to an historic Māori educational 'moment': the Matawaia Declaration. This called for an independent Māori education authority, in the form of a fully autonomous statutory body, as a means of Māori control over Māori philosophies and practices in education from preschool through to adulthood. The Hui Reo Rua o Aotearoa adopted the declaration at Matawaia Marae in January 1988. Although the overarching goal of this document has not been fully realised, developments such as kōhanga reo for early childhood, kura kaupapa Māori for compulsory schooling and wānanga in the tertiary sector can be seen to reflect its intent. The declaration reflected the heavy dissatisfaction some Māori felt with the inadequate ways in which the education sector and the then Department of Education were addressing Māori education, particularly in relation to te reo Māori me ōna tikanga. This historical moment indicates continued concern felt in Te Tai Tokerau about how Māori as a people might best relate to the education system that has developed in this country, and about the place of Māori language and culture in education to best meet the needs of Māori children and their communities.

Education and Schooling in Te Tai Tokerau Today

The national education system in Aotearoa New Zealand spans non-compulsory early childhood and compulsory primary and secondary schooling.

The Tai Tokerau region has one of the lowest rates of Māori participation in early childhood education. In 2009, when information was being collected from youth for the Te Wehi Nui a Mamao research project (see the chapter by Ngaha), national participation rates were 95 per cent across all children and 91 per cent for Māori children (Ministry of Social Development, 2010). However, in some areas of Te Tai Tokerau only about 75 per cent of Māori preschool-age children attend early childhood education programmes. In 2009 just over 2586 Māori children were enrolled in licensed early childhood services in the Northland Regional Council area, which spans the Far North, Kaipara and Whangārei (Ministry of Education, 2013). The number of high-immersion early-education settings such as kōhanga has been dropping over the years; for instance, in 2006 there were nearly 60 services offering high immersion programmes, compared with 48 services in 2009 (only three years later), 46 of which were kōhanga reo settings.

In 2009, only 737 Māori children were in the 48 services with high (level 1) immersion in te reo Māori, including 666 children enrolled in kōhanga reo. The majority, 1729 Māori children, were in 41 services providing bilingual programmes of lower (levels 2–4) immersion. The remaining few attended English-medium services.

The same year, compulsory schooling had just under 14,000 Māori students enrolled in at least 115 state schools in the Northland Regional Council area 2012 (Ministry of Education, n.d.[b]). Of these schools, approximately 33 provided secondary schooling. There were nine kura

kaupapa Māori, catering for 744 students (Ministry of Education, n.d.[c]).*
In total, 1073 students were enrolled in level 1 Māori immersion classrooms and a further 752 in level 2 classrooms. Again these numbers reflect a drop, albeit slight, compared with numbers in 2006, when there were 1251 Māori students in level 1 immersion and 797 in level 2 immersion programmes.

Te Wehi Nui a Mamao Research and Schooling

Te Wehi Nui a Mamao researchers' data collection methods with the youth participants from various schools in Te Tai Tokerau (described in more detail in the chapter by Ngaha) sought a range of information. A written survey asked young Māori to report on their knowledge relating to their tribe, to Māori language, and to their preschool and school experiences. This section of the chapter examines their responses about their schooling in relation to their personal ratings of Māori-language abilities; and their knowledge pertaining to their local marae, hapū and iwi.

The eight schools attended by youth who participated in the study are relatively small; half have under 200 students. Only one, which is a secondary school, has (just) over 500 students – nationally the average secondary school roll is about 1000 students. All eight schools have a large proportion of Māori students, if not a predominantly Māori roll. The size and make up of these schools reflect the generally small, rural or provincial characteristics of Tai Tokerau communities and settlements. Five schools offer primary through to secondary school programmes. Three offer only secondary schooling. Four of the schools (including the three secondary schools) are located in provincial townships and four are in rural areas. All schools are located in communities with identified iwi and functioning iwi marae, to which many of the students belong.

A range of teaching programmes is delivered in the eight schools. Three schools teach in English, with te reo Māori taught only as a

---

* This figure does not include all kura kaupapa Māori in the region as of 2009, as some were awaiting full state-school status at the time.

curriculum area. Two schools are kura kaupapa Māori, which deliver nearly all teaching through te reo. The three remaining schools provide both Māori- and English-medium classroom programmes.

Survey responses reflect a diversity of preschool and school experiences and corresponding differences in marae, hapū and iwi-related knowledge. Just over half of the participants had exposure to kōhanga reo and thus learning through Māori language during their preschool years. In comparison, only 30 per cent of the participants reported Māori-medium learning experiences in their compulsory schooling years, either in bilingual or in kura kaupapa Māori settings. Participants who attended kura kaupapa Māori were more likely to have attended kōhanga reo than their peers who experienced bilingual schooling.

Not surprisingly, Māori-medium educational experiences related to the degree to which youth participants were able to provide information relating to their marae, hapū and iwi. Students who reported having attended Māori-medium schooling provided more information than their peers who had only attended English-medium schools. However, a proportion of participants who had not experienced Māori-medium settings were also able to provide such information, as discussed below.

Te Kōhanga Reo

As noted above, over half (54 per cent; 268 out of 493 who responded to the question) of the youth reported that they had attended kōhanga reo as preschoolers. Participants in this group were more likely to perceive their competency at speaking, reading and understanding Māori as 'above average' to 'excellent' than those who had not attended kōhanga, as shown in Table 6.1, overleaf.

These results were not unexpected. What is of interest is that a proportion (albeit small) of participants who had not attended kōhanga also rated their ability in speaking, reading and writing te reo Māori as above average to excellent. This group may reflect the impact of later, school-based opportunities to learn Māori language. Table 6.2 presents the percentages of students who were able to provide information relating to their marae and rohe, in descending order, by kōhanga reo attendance and non-attendance. In every instance, differences favour kōhanga reo attendees.

Table 6.1: Self-report of te reo Māori competencies as 'excellent' or 'above average', by kōhanga attendance and non-attendance

Te reo Māori ability (n = 493)	Percentage of participants who attended kōhanga (n = 268)		Percentage of participants who did not attend kōhanga (n = 225)	
	excellent	above average	excellent	above average
Speaking Māori	15	14	3.5	7
Reading Māori	29	20	8	10
Understanding Māori	20	17	3.5	4

Table 6.2: Provision of information relating to marae and rohe, by kōhanga reo attendance and non-attendance

Local knowledge (n = 493)	Percentage of participants who attended kōhanga (n = 268)	Percentage of participants who did not attend kōhanga (n = 225)
Named (at least one) iwi	92	80
Named (at least one) marae	88	67
Provided (at least one) common local Māori phrase	83	71
Named (at least one) hapū	81	56
Named (at least one) awa	70	49
Provided (at least one) waiata	68	48
Attended iwi/hapū hui	52	31
Named (at least one) tupuna	44	22
Named (at least one) wharenui	39	26
Named (at least one) urupā	39	21
Named (at least one) maunga	20	9

The positive relationship between kōhanga reo attendance, self-reported te reo Māori competencies and levels of local knowledge suggests that early opportunities to learn through the medium of Māori are linked to knowledge about the local hapū, iwi and geographical area. This relationship should not be unexpected as the curriculum of kōhanga reo generally includes culturally located teaching such as children's pepeha (tribal sayings or proverbs), which may contain information about hapū, iwi, marae, waka, awa and so on (Royal Tangaere, 1997). When this kind of learning occurs within hapū and iwi boundaries it can arguably be made more relevant and salient by opportunities to see and experience directly the cultural landmarks and buildings referred to in the pepeha.

Of note, 56–80 per cent of kōhanga reo non-attendees were able to name iwi, hapū and marae. Others were also able to provide more specific information about their marae. Although this survey information does not enable us to examine this in depth, Ngaha (this volume) identifies marae, kapa haka and school – in that order – as the three most likely places participants reported hearing Māori. It might be reasonable to infer that these contexts might provide access not only to Māori language, but also to Māori knowledge regarding local hapū and iwi.

Continued learning in Māori-medium educational settings when children move to compulsory schooling can also be expected to support the development of local language, hapū, iwi and culturally significant geographical knowledge. To what extent are participants' educational experiences providing ongoing access to such learning opportunities?

Māori-medium Schooling Experience

A large proportion of participants who reported that they attended kōhanga reo were in Māori-medium school settings at the time they were surveyed. As noted above, this was more likely to be the case for kura kaupapa Māori students, 75 per cent of whom had attended kōhanga. In comparison, 64 per cent of those in bilingual classes had attended kōhanga reo.

In addition, participants attending kura kaupapa Māori were more likely to perceive themselves as excellent at speaking, reading and understanding Māori, as shown in Table 6.3 (see also Ngaha, this volume, Table 4.1).

Table 6.3: Self-report of te reo Māori competencies as 'excellent' or 'above average', by Māori-medium schooling attendance and non-attendance

Māori-language ability (n = 494)	Percentage of participants who have attended Māori-medium schooling (n = 149)		Percentage of participants who have not attended Māori-medium schooling (n = 345)	
	excellent	above average	excellent	above average
Speaking Māori	26	21	3	7
Reading Māori	40	21	11	13
Understanding Māori	31	24	4	8

While we collected self-reports on Māori-language fluency, the fluency levels of written responses in Māori provide supportive evidence about the positive influence Māori-medium schooling has (see Ngaha, this volume). With regard to identifying common local Māori phrases, there was not a great deal of difference between the proportion of those who had attended Māori-medium schooling (79 per cent) and the proportion who had not (77 per cent).

Table 6.4: Provision of information relating to marae and rohe, by Māori-medium schooling

Local knowledge (n = 494)	Percentage of participants who have attended Māori-medium schooling (n = 149)	Percentage of participants who have not attended Māori-medium schooling (n = 345)
Named (at least one) iwi	93	84
Named (at least one) marae	86	74
Named (at least one) hapū	82	64
Named (at least one) maunga	78	57
Provided (at least one) waiata	78	51
Named (at least one) awa	74	54
Attended iwi/hapū hui	54	38
Named (at least one) tupuna	50	27
Named (at least one) urupā	41	26
Named (at least one) wharenui	39	26

Photography was an important component of the Māori Maps and Te Wehi Nui projects discussed elsewhere in this book. The following small but poignant collection of Tai Tokerau photographs by Krzysztof Pfeiffer, taken for these and other projects, showcases a selection of sites from the urban-centred Ngāti Whātua ō Ōrākei marae in the south, to pā like Pouērua and marae in Pēwhairangi, the Bay of Islands and Hokianga, and on to Te Oneroa a Tōhē, Ninety Mile Beach, in the Far North. Beyond the buildings – the whare tupuna (ancestral meeting houses), the whare kai (dining halls), the whare karakia (the churches) and the kōhanga reo (Māori-language preschool) – are vast ancestral landscapes within which marae are located. Encompassing all that we see – the mountains and pā, the waterways and forests – these landscapes also map cultural footprints that extend under cities and their concrete walls.

Marae are vibrant centres of communities. As hubs of connection and re-connection, they are vital to local hapū members who keep their marae working every day and to hapū members who return when they can. These photographs show a changing reality. Many communities have built new marae in other places, many have left their tūrangawaewae (homelands) altogether. The falling-down whare, the long grass, show what was and what sometimes now is. But other marae in Tai Tokerau function as they always have – and vibrancy goes beyond the buildings. People regroup and regather, the hau kāinga (local communities) bring manuhiri (visitors) into their embrace. In remaining and providing manaakitanga (hospitality) despite economic hardships or the outflow of people, these hapū show a determination to keep marae sustainable into the future. And seeing children at marae – climbing trees, peering through meeting-house windows or even on tea-towel duty – hints at a future. In their ever-changing world, marae will continue to provide a haven more important than ever.

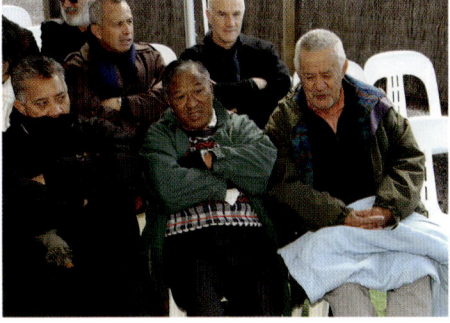

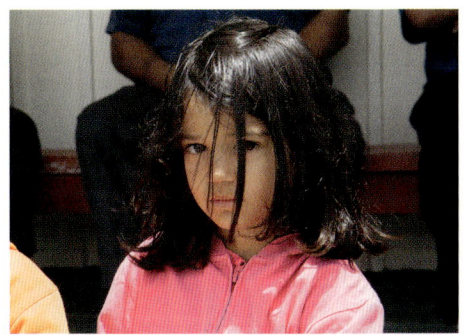

Schooling: A Support and a Challenge

Some, not unexpected, relationships emerged between youth responses to questions relating to schooling experiences, te reo Māori abilities and their familiarity and knowledge of their marae.

A greater proportion of participants who reported Māori-medium educational experiences were able to provide information reflecting knowledge relating to their marae, hapū and iwi. Access to Māori-medium education gives Māori children and youth a direct opportunity to learn Māori language and cultural knowledge. In many Māori-medium education sites, such as kura involved in this study, borders between 'school' and 'whānau, hapū and iwi communities' are likely to range from being blurred to being hardly in existence. By their very nature, many Māori-medium schooling contexts source their teachers and Māori language and cultural knowledge from their communities. Granted, this is important, but it alone will not be enough to ensure regional language and values are transferred to young Māori. Other resources are important too. The development of the Te Wehi Nui a Mamao web 2.0 resource (discussed in this volume by Kawharu and Tane, also by Hennessy) has also drawn directly from community knowledge banks and thus can provide further support and extension to teaching programmes that may already be richly imbued with local knowledge relating to Māori language, marae, hapū and so on.

Given the relationships found between Māori-medium schooling experience, te reo and iwi-based knowledge, there are implications – for Tai Tokerau youth, their whānau, hapū and also iwi – should there be a continuation of the 2006–10 downward trend in high-immersion preschool and compulsory school provisions. Indications are that there have been slight increases in enrolments in high-immersion provisions in the Northland Regional Council area since 2009. In 2012, 735 Māori children were enrolled in kōhanga reo and 1202 Māori students in level 1 immersion school settings. However, by far the majority of Māori students in Te Tai Tokerau do not attend such a service and do not experience the benefits of Māori-medium education to develop local Māori language and knowledge. As discussed elsewhere in this volume, Māori communities and their schools that we worked with in Te Tai Tokerau, if not also those elsewhere, face significant challenges.

There are some other positives. The survey findings do indicate that, at least in Te Tai Tokerau, English-medium schooling can help to develop Māori students' knowledge about Māori language and their hapū and iwi, even though they may develop less depth and breadth of language and tribal knowledge than those who experience Māori-medium schooling. While Māori language and culture have yet to become compulsory areas of the New Zealand Curriculum, one of the principles of the New Zealand Curriculum for English-medium schooling is that 'All students have the opportunity to acquire knowledge of te reo me ōna tikanga [the language and associated customs]' (Ministry of Education, 2007, p. 9). The web 2.0 resource in this case is seen as potentially doing more than just supporting the development of Māori language and culture programmes in schools, but also ensuring that they reflect valued knowledge from local hapū and iwi, and in some instances helping to drive the development of localised curriculum so that it includes and values local Māori knowledge. Clearly there is a long way to go, but if communities (including schools) and government are alert to the downward trends and respond to them now, by building on existing programmes and developing new initiatives, language and culture have a chance to grow and to be vital in communities once again.

Bibliography

Baker, C., 2006. *Foundations of Bilingual Education and Bilingualism*, 4th edn. Clevedon: Multilingual Matters.

Baker C. and Jones, M. P., 2000. 'Welsh Language Education: A Strategy for Revitalisation'. In: C. H. Williams, ed. *Language Revitalisation: Policy and Planning*. Cardiff: University of Wales Press, pp. 116–137.

Benton, N., 1989. 'Education, Language Decline and Language Revitalisation: The Case of Maori in New Zealand', *Language and Education*, vol. 3, no. 2, pp. 65–82.

Benton, R. A., 1978. *Can Māori Language Survive?* Te Wāhanga Māori Occasional Paper no. 2. Wellington: New Zealand Council of Educational Research.

Chrisp, S., 1997. 'Diglossia: A Theoretical Framework for the Revitalisation of the Māori Language'. *He Pukenga Kōrero*, vol. 2, no. 2, pp. 35–42.

Crystal, D., 2000. *Language Death*. Cambridge: Cambridge University Press.
Curnow, J., Hopa, N., and McRae, J., 2002. *Rere Atu, Taku Manu! Discovering History, Language and Politics in the Māori-language Newspapers*. Auckland: Auckland University Press.
Fishman, J., 1991. *Reversing Language Shift*, Clevedon: Multilingual Matters.
Fogwill, L., 1994. 'Literacy: A Critical Element in the Survival of Aboriginal Languages'. In: Jean-Paul Hautecoeur, ed. *Alpha 94: Literacy and Cultural Development Strategies in Rural Areas*. Ontario: Ministry of Education, pp. 229–247.
Haami, B., 2004. *Putea Whakairo Māori and the Written Word*, Wellington: Ministry of Culture and Heritage in association with Huia Publishers.
Hohepa, M., 2006. 'Biliterate Practices in the Home: Supporting Indigenous Language Regeneration'. *Journal of Language, Identity and Education*, vol. 5, no. 4, pp. 293–301.
Hohepa, M. K. and Jenkins, K. E. H., with Mane, J., Sherman-Godinet, D., and Toi, S., 2004. 'The Evaluation of Te Putahitanga Mātauranga'. Wellington: Ministry of Education.
Hohepa, M., Smith, L., Smith, G., and McNaughton, S., 1992. 'Te Kohanga Reo Hei Tikanga Ako i te Reo Maori: Te Kohanga Reo as a Context for Language Learning'. *Educational Psychology*, vol. 12, nos 3 & 4, pp. 337–346.
Jackson, M., 1975. 'Literacy, Communications and Social Change'. In: I. H. Kawharu, ed. *Conflict and Compromise: Essays on the Māori Since Colonisation*. Wellington: A. H. Reed and A. W. Reed.
Jacques, K., 1991. 'Community Context of Bilingual Education: A Study of Six South Island Primary School Programmes'. Unpublished Ph.D. thesis, University of Canterbury, Christchurch.
Jenkins, K. E. H., 1991. 'Te Ihi, te Mana, te Wehi o te Ao Tuhi: Maori Print Literacy from 1814–1855 – Literacy, Power and Colonisation'. Unpublished M.A. thesis, University of Auckland, Auckland.
Keegan, P., 1991. 'The Benefits of Immersion Education: A Review of the New Zealand and Overseas Literature'. Wellington: New Zealand Council for Educational Research.
Littlebear, R. E., 1999. 'Some Rare and Radical Ideas for Keeping Indigenous Languages Alive'. In: J. Reyhner, G. Cantoni, R. St Clair and E. Parsons Yazzie, eds. *Revitalising Indigenous Languages*. Flagstaff: Northern Arizona University Press, Flagstaff, pp. 1–5.
McCarty, T., 2007. 'Revitalising Indigenous Languages in Homogenising Times'. *Comparative Education*, vol. 39, pp. 147–163.
Ministry of Education, n.d. 'Primary Teachers Collective Agreement', Schedule 1. From: http://www.minedu.govt.nz/NZEducation/EducationPolicies/SchoolEmployment/TeachersPrincipals/PrimaryTeachers/CollectiveAgreement/Schedule1.aspx

——, n.d.[b] 'Number of Students by Māori Language Immersion Level and Regional Council 2004–2012'. From: http://www.educationcounts.govt.nz/statistics/maori_education/schooling/6040

——, n.d.[c]. "Kura Kaupapa Māori and Kura Teina'. From. http://www.educationcounts.govt.nz/indicators/data/quality-education-provider/3792

——, 2007. 'The New Zealand Curriculum for English-medium Teaching and Learning in Years 1–13'. Wellington: Learning Media.

——, 2008. 'Ka Hikitia – Managing for Success: The Māori Education Strategy 2008–2012'. Ministry of Education, Wellington, 2009 updated version. From: http://www.minedu.govt.nz/theMinistry/PolicyAndStrategy/KaHikitia/PublicationsAndResources-EnglishLanguageVersions.aspx

——, 2009. 'Education Report: Annual Census of Early Childhood Education Services'. From: http://www.educationcounts.govt.nz/statistics/ece/ece_staff_return/licensed_services_and_licence-exempt_groups/34821

——, 2010. 'Ngā Haeata Mātauranga – Annual Report on Māori Education, 2008/09'. From: http://www.educationcounts.govt.nz/publications/series/5851/75954/4

——, 2013. 'Māori in ECE'. Excel file. From: http://www.educationcounts.govt.nz/statistics/ece2/mori-in-ece

Ministry of Social Development, 2010. 'The Social Report: Te Pūrongo Oranga Tangata 2010'. From: http://www.socialreport.msd.govt.nz/knowledge-skills/participation-early-childhood-education.html

Murray, S., 2007. 'Achievement at Maori Immersion and Bilingual Schools: Update for 2005 Results'. Wellington: Ministry of Education.

Nahir, M., 1988. 'Language Planning and Language Acquisition: The "Great Leap" in the Hebrew Revival'. In: C. B. Paulston, ed. *International Handbook of Bilingualism and Bilingual Education*. New York: Greenwood Press.

Ngāti Kahungunu Iwi Inc., n.d. 'Te Pae Huarewa – Ngāti Kahungunu Cultural Standards'. From: http://www.kahungunu.iwi.nz/sections/homepage/KahungunuCulturalStandards.htm

Rau, C., 2008. 'Assessment in Indigenous Language Programmes'. In: E. Shohamy and H. Hornberger, eds. *Encyclopedia of Language and Education, Language Testing and Assessment*, vol. 7, 2nd edn. New York: Springer Science+Business Media LLC, pp. 319–330.

Royal Tangaere, A., 1997. *Te Puawaitanga o te Reo Māori: Ka Hua te Hā o te Pōtiki i Roto i te Whānau – Ko Tēnei te Tāhuhu o te Kōhanga Reo*. Wellington: New Zealand Council for Educational Research.

Sharples, P., 1989. 'Kura Kaupapa Maori: Recommendations for Policy'. *Access*, vol. 8, no. 1, pp. 28–36.

Simon, J. A., 1994. 'Historical Perspectives on Schooling'. In: E. Coxon, K. Jenkins, J. Marshall and L. Massey, eds. *The Politics of Learning and Teaching in Aotearoa–New Zealand*. Palmerston North: Dunmore Press, pp. 34–81.

———, ed., 1998. *Ngā Kura Māori: The New Zealand Native Schools System, 1867–1969*. Auckland: Auckland University Press.

Simon, J. A. and Smith, L. T., 2001. *A Civilising Mission? Perceptions and Representations of the New Zealand Native Schools System*. Auckland: Auckland University Press.

Skutnabb-Kangas, T., 2007. 'Human Rights and Language Policy in Education'. In: S. May and N. H. Hornberger, eds. *Encyclopedia of Language and Education*, vol. 1, Springer, pp. 107–119.

Smith, L. T., 1989. 'Te Reo Maori: Maori Language and the Struggle to Survive'. *Access*, vol. 8, no. 1, pp. 3–9.

———, 1999. *Decolonising Methodologies: Research and Indigenous Peoples*. London: Zed Books.

Urlich Cloher, D. and Hohepa, M., 1996. 'Te Tū a te Kōhanga Reo i Waenga i te Whānau me te Tikanga Poipoi Tamariki: Māori Families, Child Socialisation and the Role of the Kōhanga Reo'. *He Pukenga Kōrero*, vol. 1, no. 2, pp. 33–41.

Wylie, C. and Arago-Kemp, V., 2004. 'Whaia te Iti Kahurangi: NZCER Evaluation'. Wellington: New Zealand Council of Educational Research. From: http://www.educationcounts.govt.nz/publications/schooling/5447

FRASER TOI

Roharoha te maunga,
Waiarohia te awa,
Hokianga te moana,
Ngātokimatawhaorua te waka,
Kupe te tupuna,
Ngāpuhi te iwi,
Ngāti Korokoro te hapū,
Kokohuia te marae,
Te Whakarongotai te whare nui,
Toi Kai Rākau te tangata.

Whakatipu mai au i raro o ēnei tātai pepeha, ki te tonga o Hokianga-whakapau-karakia, i raro hoki i ngā tohutohutanga me ngā akoranga o ōku mātua ko Piwai rāua ko Kare Te Aroha Toi. Tōku rā whānau ko te 25 Hōngongoi 1941. Kātahi ka huaina taku ingoa e ōku mātua ko Apirana Fraser Toi. Muri mai i tā rāua wehenga atu ki te ao wairua, ka tau mai te tūranga kaumātua ki runga i ahau, kia pupuritia te mana o tō mātou marae, me te mana hoki o taku whānau me taku whānau whānui. Ngā akoranga katoa i whiwhi mai ahau mai rāua ōku mātua, e mau tonu ana i tēnei wā tonu, hei arataki i ahau i runga i ōku hīkoikoiranga maha puta noa i te motu. Nā reira, kore rawa e motu ngā mihi aroha ki a rāua, arā, ki a koutou katoa o te wāhi ngaro. Moe mai i roto i ngā ringa atawhai o te Ariki, moe mai, moe mai, haere oti rā.

I grew up in South Hokianga-whakapau-karakia with these genealogical sayings and with the wisdom and teachings of my parents Piwai and Kare Te Aroha Toi. I was born on 25 July 1941. I was named by my parents Apirana Fraser Toi. After they died, the responsibility of being an elder fell to me, to protect and to hold on to the authority of our marae, our family and wider community. Everything I learnt derives from my parents and I still hold on to these things today as guides for everything I do throughout the country. Therefore, my acknowledgement to them, and to all of you who have passed on, never severs. Rest in peace in the embracing arms of God, sleep, farewell.

CHAPTER SEVEN

AUĒ, TAUKIRI Ē: THE CHANGING FACE OF MARAE

FRASER TOI

IT WAS PROBABLY ONCE INCONCEIVABLE THAT TŪTURU TIKANGA MĀORI – creations so skilfully formulated by our tūpuna (ancestors) as a lasting form of law and order and a code of conduct – could one day be tampered with, or even compromised. Surely a cultural heritage of total respect and acceptance towards tikanga (custom) would stand the test of time, no matter what challenges Māori people faced. But we are now in a quandary. Can tikanga in fact continue uncompromised? And if not, then at what cost? One may ponder these ideas when the importance of tikanga is considered in light of it being central to the identity and future of a people and their culture.

Our tūpuna maintain or assert their authority and chiefly status upon the succeeding generations when tikanga that they shaped continue to be followed as guides. Their infinite knowledge and wisdom of worldly, environmental and spiritual matters, plus their understanding of the significance of tikanga in guiding survival, remains important. But when it comes to how tikanga is now practised on our marae, there are questions – particularly amongst kaumātua (elders) – about the kinds of changes that are happening and whether they are acceptable, or not.

Unravelling the Decades

In the post-war period of the 1940s and 1950s, tūturu tikanga Māori and tikanga marae were alive and well with an abundance of kaumātua and kuia (female elders) at every marae throughout Ngāpuhi and more generally throughout Te Tai Tokerau.

The recognised tuakana/teina tikanga (elder or more senior individuals having responsibility towards, and presiding in whakapapa [genealogical] terms over, their younger siblings or relatives) was in operation, with everyone including the kuia knowing instinctively their designated positions and the duties required of them.

From near and far, kaumātua converged during hui tangihanga (funeral gatherings), ready to 'do battle' and to showcase their artistry of debate and counter-debate in the whaikōrero (formal speech-making) between the hosts and the visitors.

Seated around the wharenui (ancestral meeting house or inner marae), through the thick blue haze of their non-stop tobacco smoking, they conducted their business. The kaikaranga kuia and the tupoupou kuia (who, in the first instance, perform ceremonial calls of welcome or response, and in the second prepare the deceased for lying in the wharenui then watch over it) all assumed their positions of responsibility.

Although some of their topics for discussion were community-based, the kaumātua would relish in their specialities of kōrero hītori, whakapapa and tono tupāpāku. They were loath to divulge too much from their personal kete kōrero, so those listening would regard the opportunity to learn something new as a welcome addition to their kete mātauranga.[*]

On the arrival of manuhiri,[†] the kaikōrero or speaker holding the floor at that time would commonly pause his address with the utterance 'Pito

---

[*] Kōrero hītori: renditions of historical stories; tono tupāpāku: the claiming of rights or interests in relation to the deceased, based on genealogy and ūkaipō (birth place); kete kōrero: kits of knowledge held privately; kete mātauranga: kits of worldly knowledge.
[†] Guests. Manuhiri or manuwhiri comes from 'manu' meaning 'bird' and 'whiri' meaning 'to plait', and refers to the gathering of chiefly leaders and kaumātua who can be likened to special or prized birds such as the huia or toroa (albatross). As guests, they assemble at the entrance or gate to the marae and wait to be called into the marae and join with the tangata whenua; hence manuwhiri, or the idea of weaving or plaiting into one group.

kōrero hakahokia': 'I will continue in due course'. This tikanga is still in operation today. Once they completed their tangi and harirū (greetings; literally meaning 'how do you do') of the pae mate or mourners only – unlike the protocol of today where they harirū right around the whare – the kaikōrero regained his feet and delivered the mihi whakatau (official speech of welcome) to the manuhiri in accordance with tikanga marae. After all formalities were completed, the speakers returned to the subject that was under discussion before the arrival of the manuhiri, and resumed debate with the usual, or expected, vigour. This continued each day and into the night until the end of the hui.

> Auē – taukiri ē
> Kei hea wa tāua rangatira mo āpōpō
> Kua riro, kua riro, kua riro atu i a tātou
> Kei te mura o te ahi rātou e hingahinga nei ē
> Kei tāwāhi e whawhai ana i tētahi pakanga nui
> ia rangi āio te noho o te ao katoa
> Auē – taukiri ē.*

Throughout Aotearoa in the 1950s and 1960s, this tangi mōteatea (lament) resonated around the walls of every marae as the grieving kaumātua and kuia, along with the members of their whānau, hapū and iwi, counted the senseless loss of loved ones in World War II. In due course, each marae discussed the implications of this. They settled on the only logical solution: to promote the younger and, therefore, 'second tier' men- and women-folk of home, as replacements for a generation lost. The required intensity and expectations of such position did not suit most of them, and their deficiencies and lack of experience were exposed. Given the feelings of inadequacy that many of these younger people had about fulfilling

---

* A translation of this tangi mōteatea or lament does not convey the subtleties embedded in the language, but the following gives a sense of the meaning: How tragic – and we cry in pain / Where are our leaders of tomorrow? / They have all been taken, taken, taken away from us / They have been felled at the front lines on active duty ['te mura o te ahi' means 'the heat of the fire'] / Fighting the great war overseas / So that the world can live in peace.

the customary roles expected of them, marae witnessed their deliberate non-attendance at, or non-support of, hui tangihanga. This alone had a prolonged and devastating effect on most marae, not only in the post-war period, but also in the decades to follow. The position and authority of te reo kaumātua (the speaking elders) was changing, and changing for the worse.

The situation was compounded by the Department of Education's controversial 'proclamation',[*] lasting from the 1930s to the 1950s, to ban te reo Māori within schools, plus the mass exodus of the people to the cities for employment following the war. So the outlook for marae communities was grim. These factors – the loss of leaders from the war, government education policy and urban migration – all contributed to a new breach in tikanga practices, and in what was regarded by most as a system of resolute endurance.

Changing Roles and Protocols

From the 1960s to the 1970s, in an unprecedented attempt to reduce the obvious deterioration of marae-based cultural leadership, the elderly female leaders of the marae – kuia and whaea – sat alongside the few remaining future tāne (male) leaders. They did this in an advisory role, offering support and encouragement to them. Female leadership has always had an important place in marae. Perhaps their voices of authority had been in some respects suppressed or not properly acknowledged throughout the generations, but during this emerging crisis, they were at last properly heard and embraced. They proved to be *the* difference in the functioning of marae, often under extreme circumstances.

The recent appointments of their wāhine counterparts,[†] plus the new leaders' lack of enthusiasm for the traditional kaupapa (agenda) of debate, meant that the last of the original kaumātua found themselves struggling

---

[*] The Crown did not have a formal policy or law that banned te reo in schools, but as Sir James Henare remarked, there was a very effective gentleman's policy.
[†] Wāhine literally means female, but in this context, it refers to the younger female members of the marae community (compared with the kuia or whaea).

to maintain the steadfastness of tikanga Māori and tikanga marae as they once knew it.

The 1970s and 1980s can be seen as a continued period of turmoil and struggle for tikanga marae. It also heralded the establishment of the taumata (representative speakers) system as we recognise it today in Ngāpuhi and in Te Tai Tokerau. The taumata arrangement has the kaumātua-appointed speakers of the marae sitting and conducting proceedings from their marked-out position in the meeting house. This is also now recognised as the top position for speakers within a marae. Female representative leaders like the kaikaranga might also sit close by. The taumata has the benefit of people being able to identify who the speakers might be, while the old system – in which speakers sat where they pleased within the whare – offered a form of protection and strategy. An enemy could take out all the leaders in one go if they were positioned together, but it would be difficult to do so if the leaders were scattered or hidden within a group, as in the traditional system. Political positioning of the speaker and his community was achieved from various corners or parts of a house. The taumata system took away this layer of strategy. Speaking was all about mana, but the field of play began to change when the taumata was introduced.

Additionally, the 1970s and 1980s saw the allowing of children into the wharenui during hui tangihanga, unlike the days of old where they were banned because of the importance of the kōrero flowing within. Children were seen as a distraction. A rite of passage was once in operation where junior members – including children – of a community first had to serve an apprenticeship to learn how the marae and rituals operated and how te reo was spoken. They began in the kāuta (cooking area) or wharekai (dining hall), and even as keri poka (grave diggers). Then when they had proven their worth, they could progress into the whare. In some cases, though, the apprenticeships were not happening and children instead came into the whare earlier on. Of course learning would take place within the whare, but the dynamics and forums of learning were beginning to change.

These changes, sanctioned by the kaumātua, indicated that the time had come to hand over the reins to a new leadership: a generally younger generation who were brought up with a different value system. The elders had no choice. Age, perhaps illness, counted them out in the eyes of the new generation. But, in the elders' view, the new systems were better than nothing at all and so they conceded. This transition of authority was a sensitive period as elders came to realise and accept, albeit reluctantly, that the reign of old had in effect come to an end. Many observed future proceedings in reflective submission.

Except perhaps for tangihanga, where te reo o te kaikaranga (the welcoming call of the female leader), the mihi whakatau (the welcome from the taumata and tapu-lifting speeches) and the response of the manuhiri are heard, an uncomfortable silence often descends and prevails within the wharenui. It is not uncommon for routine conversations between parties or individuals to be mostly conducted in English, including out in the kāuta and wharekai, which is often recognised as the 'whare wānanga' or place of learning of a marae.*

It was during the 1970s and 1980s also that another alarming threat arose. Crucial roles such as the kaikaranga and the taumata on marae throughout Ngāpuhi and Te Tai Tokerau were noticeably not being filled, resulting in many embarrassing, if not also hostile, confrontations between hosts and visitors.

The utilisation by host marae of young, inexperienced tāne and wāhine, including schoolgirls and schoolboys, was a stop-gap solution to an obvious problem, but was frowned upon by the manuhiri who from time to time voiced their displeasure categorically. The severity of their verbal attack was seen as an expression of their bitter disappointment and disbelief that the hosts could allow things to decline to such a point. It was strongly believed, for example, that a young girl performing the karanga could not in any way understand or capture the tapu (sacredness) or wairua (spiritual) content of the task, because of age, the lack of tuition and experience. A similar argument applied to the young tāne, no doubt coerced into the unenviable duty of speaking on the taumata. It was not uncommon for his effort to be targeted in various ways by different kaumātua. Some elders might have praised and complimented him, perhaps offering encouraging words, 'kia

---

* The meaningful exchange of kōrero during the preparation and cooking of food, and the many lessons learnt in the execution of duties, have led to these areas being referred to as the whare wānanga for many aspiring future leaders.

kaha' (be strong; keep trying), but others would have condemned the marae for trivialising such a pivotal position. The tūturu kaumātua (experienced elderly leaders), for instance, are of a generation who under no circumstances will allow the trampling of their mana or their dignity and will not respond to young male speakers. Instead, these elders bow their heads as in a pose of defiance, and remain silent.

Occasionally, the depth of a marae's problem has been tragically highlighted by the stepping forward of its hau kāinga kuia (elder female leaders of the resident community) in order to assume the role of the taumata. With a heavy heart, such a kuia apologises for the marae's predicament and the probable embarrassment to manuhiri, and asks permission to perform the tikanga process of mihi whakatau herself. Despite the obvious difficulty, her fulfilment of a tikanga obligation is generally received with the praise it deserves in acknowledgement of a growing concern, and of her courage.

During the 1980s and 1990s, the problem of limited, or no, male elders was still evidenced on most marae in Te Tai Tokerau, and the people searched and prayed for a miracle remedy. The establishment during this period of kōhanga reo, followed by kura kaupapa Māori and other Māori-language initiatives, offered only a spark of hope for the future. Unfortunately, they did not rectify the immediate crisis that many marae were experiencing. Marae plodded on regardless, tolerating the ongoing view of optimism that things would take a turn for the better.

To the New Millennium and Beyond

It is in the decade of the 1990s to the 2000s that I take my position on the taumata of my marae alongside my tuakana (older relative). There we operate in tandem, casting aside the tikanga regarding teina (younger relative)/tuakana speaking rights, because of the lack of tāne kaikōrero.

This period also realises the introduction and the advancement of a promising new initiative within the marae of South Hokianga, including our whanaunga (relative) marae of Te Roroa – Waipoua. In recognition of the ongoing problems of filling the taumata, the hau kāinga kaumātua (who is often on his own) extends to the manuhiri kaumātua an invitation to sit alongside him and share the responsibilities of attending to visitors and issues. This happens during hui tangihanga in particular, and the idea of support also extends to other positions, including the role of kaikaranga and of the ringa wera in the kitchen. It is my view that this kaupapa will gain momentum as its popularity grows and the obvious benefits are realised. It gives effect to the principle of reciprocity, and support may be offered elsewhere in exchange for the support given to the taumata.

Through the encouragement of a few inspiring individuals, the participation at marae functions including wānanga (intense learning), fundraising, hui a iwi (tribal meetings) and weddings will culminate in the rekindling of close relationships between the people of the marae; relationships that were long lost, and that our mātua and tūpuna have often reminisced about. Marae-based hui are also welcome chances to discuss and share problems encountered on our marae, not least those that are about the apparent softening attitude towards tikanga Māori and kawa marae (local protocols) in order to accommodate a younger participating generation.

In conjunction again with the elder hau kāinga iwi, we are also addressing a growing concern regarding our young nursing mothers and their newborn babies. Their presence is of course welcomed not only by their mātua and their tūpuna, but also the whānau whānui, ensuring continued close relationships, plus the chance of making new acquaintances. It is gratifying to note that many of the young mothers are aware of the tikanga surrounding tapu and the partaking of food during hui tangihanga. And so rather than cause affront or challenge tikanga, many try to cater for their babies as best they can by going out of the wharenui to their vehicles irrespective of weather conditions, or to the ablution blocks, irrespective of what environment these offer for nursing or attending to babies. The reality is though, neither of these options offers the best of situations for the mokopuna (grandchildren), who are our future prospects. It is common knowledge that most Tai Tokerau marae are ill-equipped to accommodate such a need. It was probably far from the minds of our mātua tupuna (ancestor) designers and builders. Today, though, there is mounting pressure from all sides, not least the women, to allow our young mothers to tend their babies within the comfort of the wharenui, even during hui tangihanga. Appropriate protocols in respect of nursing babies at marae are important, as is discussing all viewpoints in depth. The final decision on what should be done centres on two key arguments. Firstly there is the tikanga concerning tapu and the partaking of food, which is an antithesis of tapu. Secondly there is the issue of the appropriate care and wellbeing of our future generations such as our young mothers and our mokopuna. In complete contravention of tūturu tikanga Māori as imposed many years ago by our tūpuna, we today agree to the latter, whereby the mothers can tend their babies within the comfort of the wharenui. Nappy-changing, breast- or bottle-feeding can now be carried out without the fear of reprisal. The changing tikanga is seen by many as a welcome one, and aids in the further utilisation of a marae.

In the 2000s and 2010s, the first few years of the twenty-first century, it is noticeable that other marae have not yet embraced our concept regarding the young mothers and their babies. Reasons no doubt vary, but could include the desire of some to maintain the tikanga of tapu prevailing within the house. In other cases, it may be that they have adopted a 'wait and see' attitude.

Mo Āpōpō: For Tomorrow

> Auē – taukiri ē
> Kei hea wa tāua rangatira mo āpōpō?

An underlying message of the tangi mōteatea referred to earlier – where are the leaders for tomorrow? – continues to reverberate around the rohe, from the mountain tops to the valleys below, where the marae stand. In their constant vigil, the ahi kā roa kuia (female elders of the home communities) still hope, anticipate and expect that the message will reach the ears of the absent menfolk and others, and urge them to return home to their marae.

In the future when the accolades are handed out or spoken about, recognising the survival of a marae and everything it represents, the efforts and the contributions of the kuia and the wāhine hau kāinga will certainly be to the fore.

STEPHEN McTAGGART is one of eight children born to Scottish parents who migrated to Aotearoa in 1949. He grew up under the shadow of Maungarei–Mt Wellington in Tāmaki Makaurau–Auckland.

He has a background in both Māori and Pacific people's research, and is currently finishing his Ph.D. in Sociology at the University of Auckland. His thesis investigates the changes in marriage and cohabitation trends in New Zealand over a 25-year period. He also works as a social researcher at the University of Auckland. Many of his publications focus on the wellbeing of family and whānau in New Zealand. Stephen has taught sociology and research methods at the National University of Samoa, Auckland University of Technology and, most recently, the University of Auckland.

CHAPTER EIGHT

TE REO MĀORI AND THE TAMARIKI OF TE TAI TOKERAU: A TWENTY-FIRST-CENTURY DEMOGRAPHY

STEPHEN McTAGGART

Ko Te Reo te mauri o te mana Māori
Language is the cornerstone of what it is to be Māori
– Sir James Henare, 1985

To kōrero – to tell, say, speak, read, talk, address – is vital for the overall health of any culture. Speaking, reading, writing and listening in any language captures, infers and reproduces the nuances of that people's history. As Pierre Bourdieu suggests, language provides linguistic capital with which to negotiate various fields of opportunity (Harker, 1990). It helps to prepare a people for the future. The transmission of te reo Māori needs the cooperation of the people within and between generations in the teaching, reading, speaking, writing and listening aspects of the language. Multiple forums, networks and media exist for this purpose. The wellbeing of te reo is observable through its use by elders, parents and children. Numbers and statistics also tell a story about the health of te reo Māori. The aim of this chapter is to give an overall demographic picture of te reo use in

Northland–Te Tai Tokerau for the 1991 to 2006 period. More specifically, this chapter focuses upon the evolution of te reo Māori use by young Māori across Te Tai Tokerau.

To provide some historical context for understanding the health of te reo in Northland, the chapter begins with a very brief account of the decline and renaissance of the language in Te Tai Tokerau and Aotearoa New Zealand as a whole over roughly a century. It then summarises the formal and informal language strategies that have been developed and used in Aotearoa over the 15 years to 2006. To discuss the use of te reo by tamariki (children) and mokopuna (grandchildren) of Te Tai Tokerau, it is necessary to provide a picture of the larger demographic context in which this takes place. Therefore, we first examine te reo use at the national level, making observations on the percentage of all people in Aotearoa who can kōrero Māori. Second, we examine the linguistic practices of all Māori: which languages they speak and specifically what proportions of them kōrero in te reo. Third, we examine the use of te reo by Māori in Northland and compare this information with other regions in Aotearoa. We also compare and contrast te reo use in the Far North, Whangārei, and Kaipara districts.

These analyses provide a background for understanding the impact that gender, age, geographical location and iwi membership (over time) have on te reo use in Te Tai Tokerau. Therefore, the fourth section of this chapter compares and contrasts age, gender and te reo use at the geographical and community levels. Finally, the chapter examines te reo use by Northland iwi. As with the geographical analysis, we consider the influence of age and gender upon the health of te reo. A summary and discussion of the research findings follows.

Strengths and Limitations of the Study

The geographical- and iwi-based analyses within this chapter are useful for understanding the past and probable future health of te reo in the Northland region. They can shed light upon the performance of recent language education strategies, both formal and informal, that were refocused to the level of hapū (sub-tribal groups) and iwi in the late twentieth and early twenty-first centuries. The demographic findings of this chapter must be understood in both historical and methodological contexts. In essence, the measuring tools of te reo competency, such as the New Zealand Census of Population and Dwellings, used by Te Puni Kōkiri and Statistics New Zealand, are necessarily succinct. These tools do not necessarily reflect the range, depth and quality of the language used on a day-to-day basis. Nor do they qualitatively reflect the attitudes of the people of Aotearoa to te reo Māori or its present and future health (see Te Puni Kōkiri, 2001; 2006). The geographical and iwi-based results presented in this chapter are also unable to reflect the clustering of highest- and lowest-quality Māori language use among speakers of te reo in Aotearoa.

However, the results shown here provide numerical evidence of Māori making a statement about their language. The results indicate the frequencies of people who want to be counted as being able to converse about (a lot) of everyday things in their native tongue (hereafter, 'converse in te reo' is used). The results also tell us in which geographical areas and social groupings Māori are making this political and cultural statement. On a more pragmatic level, the results tell us which age groupings are gaining language skills and which are suffering language attrition. In addition, the results show us the influence of gender upon use of te reo Māori. Numerical comparisons of these geographical and social factors are possible because of seamless collection, presentation and publication of reports and data taken from Statistics New Zealand's Census of Population and Dwellings.* Additional information found in this chapter comes from publications by Te Puni Kōkiri and Te Taura Whiri i Te Reo Māori (the Māori Language Commission), among others.

The Decline and Renaissance of te Reo Māori

As with much of Māori society prior to World War II, Tai Tokerau Māori lived in predominantly rural settings. This relative geographical

---

* The Māori ethnic population is the count for people of the Māori ethnic group. It includes those people who stated Māori was either their sole ethnic group or one of several ethnic groups to which they belonged.

and social insulation allowed for the control and regeneration of culture and language by local Māori. Te reo was the default language used in Māori homes as it had been for generations past, but the language suffered an unfortunate decline in post-World War II Aotearoa, in both public and private life (Te Puni Kōkiri, 2009). The number of native speakers dropped dramatically in this period, influenced by a number of factors. First was the historical use of English in schools: as far back as the 1930s, English was the principal language in Tai Tokerau schools. This was supported by local communities and national leaders as a rational and strategic decision (Te Puni Kōkiri, 2009). Right through the 1950s and 1960s, many Māori parents, both rural and urban, thought that the learning of English by children in schools would help their future success in the fields of education and work. These decisions directly affected the future health of te reo.

A second influence upon the decline of te reo in the home was the significant rural to urban post-war migration of Māori seeking employment. Government accommodation strategies at that time engineered an ethnic integration scheme known as 'pepper potting', which placed Māori families within largely Pākehā communities. These strategies had two effects. First, they slowed or prevented the formation of urban Māori communities. Second, they stretched – and in some cases decimated – the social and cultural networks that had existed for families in rural communities. In a pre-internet world, geographical and indeed physical proximity was important for the normalisation, transmission and reproduction of language skills. More importantly the use of Māori language, which was perceived as 'usual, natural and commonsense' in the rural setting, was considered a little redundant in the urban social environment. This is not surprising, considering English was spoken almost exclusively in the workplace and was the medium of instruction in schools (Te Puni Kōkiri, 2008).

Pockets of practice and promotion of Māori language occurred in urban centres at this time. Religious organisations such as the Auckland Maori Catholic Society and Ngāti Poneke Young Māori Club in Wellington encouraged and used te reo Māori in many facets and practices of their organisations (Te Puni Kōkiri, 2008). These socio-structural factors were to have far-reaching effects on the transmission of te reo skills for whole generations of urban as well as rural Māori.

A renaissance of Māori identity and Māoritanga occurred in the late 1970s. Crucial to this renaissance were strategies for the revitalisation of the Māori language. The early 1980s saw coordinated marae-based initiatives such as Whakatupuranga Rua Mano (Generation 2000), a 25-year plan for the institution of marae wānanga reo – week-long immersion courses (Te Puni Kōkiri, 2008). This period also saw the institution of kōhanga reo for pre-school children and Te Ātaarangi language schools for adults. By the mid-1980s, kura kaupapa Māori immersion schools began to appear, with Māori-language (immersion) and bilingual units also evolving in non-immersion schools at this time (Te Puni Kōkiri, 2008). In the 1990s, Māori tertiary institutions or wānanga were established as another vehicle for promoting te reo and Māoritanga.

Yet the long-held perception (by Pākehā and Māori) that te reo was a dying language persisted, leading to the assumption that it had limited utility. In 1987 Te Taura Whiri i Te Reo Māori (The Māori Language Commission) responded by trying to 'promote the use of Māori as an ordinary medium of communication' at a society level (Te Puni Kōkiri, 2008, p. 5). Importantly, 1995 saw the Māori Language Commission, Māori academics and others refocus their te reo revitalisation efforts at community and iwi levels. This theoretically gave ownership of and responsibility for the revitalisation project back to local Māori. An example of this 'relocation of ownership and responsibility' is the 'Guide for Iwi and Hapū to the Preparation of Long-term Māori Language Development Plans' by Te Taura Whiri i Te Reo Māori (2000). More recent legislative initiatives aimed at language development at the levels of whānau, community, marae, iwi and hapū include the Community Based Language Initiative administered by the Ministry of Education and the Mā Te Reo fund administered by Te Taura Whiri i Te Reo (Te Puni Kōkiri, 2008, p. 5). In particular, the 'Guide' mentioned above is an important document for language strategies, as it provides a practical blueprint for the revitalisation of te reo at iwi and hapū levels.

Strategies for the Revitalisation of te Reo Māori in Te Tai Tokerau

As with most cultural practices, the growth of te reo for tamariki, mokopuna and adults of Northland depends on a number of factors. These include the stimulation of interest in the practice, to make it relevant and to promote the value of using it by emphasising its utility in multiple situations and cultural locations. Perhaps most importantly, there is the need for educational frameworks and strategies in which te reo is nurtured. The national efforts to promote te reo and Māori culture through Māori television, Māori radio and Māori-specific internet sites and other cultural initiatives are also present in Te Tai Tokerau. These include iwi-based radio and television programming, and other forms of informational and artistic expression (Te Puni Kōkiri, 2008).

Language initiatives in Te Tai Tokerau have been multiple. One formal strategy was the formation in 1999 of the charitable trust Te Reo o Te Tai Tokerau, a collective of iwi and hapū leaders and teaching professionals, whose mandate was to coordinate the multiple aspects and efforts of Māori-language education for the foreseeable future. In addition, in 2004, a 25-year te reo strategy for the Far North/Te Hiku o Te Ika was developed from a hui that the Far North Education Council coordinated (Te Puni Kōkiri, 2008). This strategy was comprehensive in its approach, focuses and goals. It encompassed schooling and early childhood; teachers and tutors of te reo Māori; marae; increasing the use of te reo Māori; and leadership and coordination. Projects like this have needed to involve the use of te reo at the levels of the whānau, the hapū and the iwi.

The Ethnic Distribution of Aotearoa, 1991–2006

New Zealand society can be understood as multicultural, bicultural or homogeneous, depending on one's point of view. In addition, the ways ethnic identity is subjectively and objectively understood and measured continue to shift in the twenty-first century (these arguments have been rehearsed elsewhere). In this research, the Māori population consists of people who stated that they were of Māori descent on census night in 1991, 1996, 2001 and 2006. Inclusion in a particular iwi within census information was determined by Māori stating their specific iwi and hapū (Statistics New Zealand, 2009a).

To discuss te reo use in Te Tai Tokerau, it is necessary to provide a larger demographic context. The population of Aotearoa increased over the study period. More interestingly, the ethnic proportions of the population shifted.

Table 8.1: Distribution of ethnicities in Aotearoa New Zealand for the census 'usually resident' population, 1991-2006

	1991		1996		2001		2006	
	Count	%	Count	%	Count	%	Count	%
European	2,783,028	79.7	2,879,085	83.1	2,871,432	80.1	2,997,051	77.6
Māori	434,847	12.5	523,374	15.1	526,281	14.7	565,329	14.6
Pacific peoples	167,070	4.8	202,233	5.8	231,798	6.5	265,974	6.9
Asian	99,759	2.9	173,502	5.0	238,176	6.6	354,549	9.2
Other	6597	0.2	15,804	0.5	24,885	0.7	36,237	0.9
Total with ethnicity specified	3,345,741		3,466,515		3,586,641		3,860,163	

Source: Ministry of Social Development, 2009
Note: Statistics New Zealand data are randomly rounded to protect confidentiality of the respondents. Individual figures may not add up to totals, and values for the same data may vary in different texts, tables and graphs.

Table 8.1 shows us a numerical and proportional snapshot of ethnicities within Aotearoa. While people within the largest proportion of the total population continue to define themselves as 'European', this declined over the 1991–2006 period. This is in part due to the increase in Pacific and Asian peoples now residing in Aotearoa. Table 8.1 also shows us that there was a growth spurt in Māori from 1991 to 1996 with a levelling off in the following ten years. The proportional growths within ethnicities are more telling. The number of people identifying as European increased by only 8 per cent in the 15 years between 1991 and 2006. Over the same period, the number who identified as Māori increased by 30 per cent; Pacific peoples increased by 59 per cent; and Asian peoples increased by 255 per cent. While people of all other ethnicities still made up less than 1 per cent of the population in 2006, over those 15 years they had grown in number faster than any of the major ethnic groups, by 440 per cent (Ministry of Social Development, 2009).

One can argue that critical mass or size of a population will influence the production and reproduction of culture within. In addition, this culture is defined in two ways: as a unifying practice and marker of the people within it and as indicators of difference to other groups. Reproduction of similarities and differences is also influenced by the subjective importance or relevance of elements of a culture that foster its nurture, adaptability and survival.

Te reo Māori is an integral element in the cultural survival of Māoritanga. Although the focus of this research is to map the success or failure of language initiatives (both formal and informal) in the Māori youth of Te Tai Tokerau, it behoves us to understand their te reo Māori competencies by viewing them both close up and in a wider context. Therefore, a comparative analysis is needed at the national level, the Northland level, and most importantly at the level of local iwi of Te Tai Tokerau.

Languages Used in Aotearoa

New Zealand is a place of multilingual communication. English is the most common language used, but a significant proportion of the population use it in combination with one or more other languages. Table 8.2 and Figure 8.1 give a broad demographic picture of the counts and proportions of languages used in Aotearoa.[*]

Overall, a proportional consistency exists among languages used over the period. English continued to be the most commonly used language with approximately 95 per cent of all people using it in the census. Te reo use remained constant over time – between 4.1 and 4.5 per cent of the population reported that they were competent in this language between 1996 and 2006.

---

[*] Language categories are not exclusive. People could state the use of more than one language in the census.

Table 8.2: Distribution of languages spoken in Aotearoa New Zealand for the census 'usually resident' population, 1996-2006

	1996		2001		2006	
	Count	%	Count	%	Count	%
English	3,290,451	95.3	3,425,304	96.1	3,673,623	95.9
Māori	153,666	4.5	160,527	4.5	157,113	4.1
Samoan	70,875	2.1	81,033	2.3	85,428	2.2
NZ Sign Language	26,589	0.8	27,285	0.8	24,087	0.6
Other	307,764	8.9	384,858	10.8	509,358	13.3
None	91,830	2.7	76,053	2.1	75,567	2.0
Total people specifying one or more languages	3,452,937		3,563,796		3,830,757	

Source: Statistics New Zealand, 2006a

Figure 8.1: Distribution of languages spoken in Aotearoa New Zealand for the census 'usually resident' population, 1996-2006 (logarithmic scale)

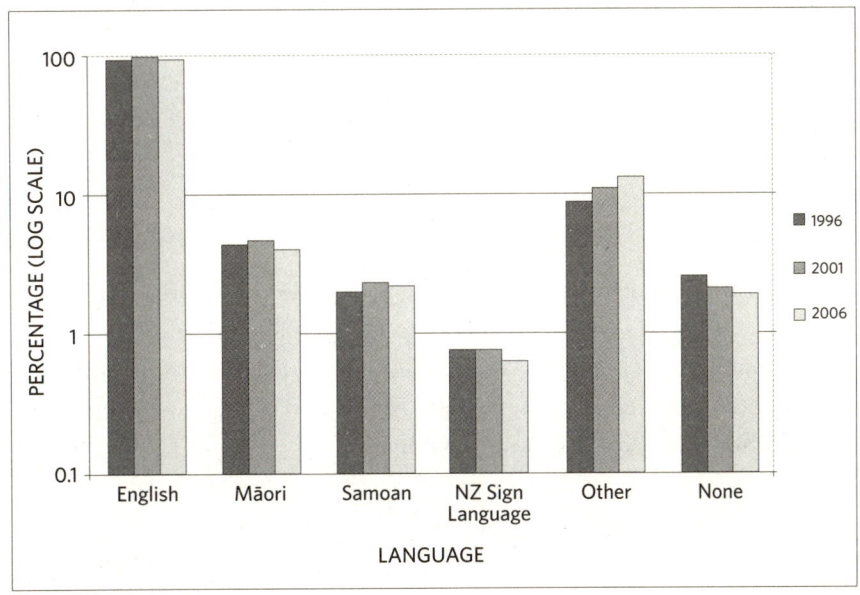

Source: Statistics New Zealand, 2006a

Māori Speaking te Reo Māori

The number of Māori who speak te reo continues to rise. Table 8.3 shows an increase of 2577 from 1996 to 2006. The proportion of Māori speaking te reo reached a peak historically in 2001 at just over 25 per cent before a slight drop to almost 24 per cent in 2006 – overall it remained fairly constant between 1996 and 2006 with not much more than 1 per cent fluctuation across the three census periods.

Table 8.3: Distribution of languages spoken by Māori in Aotearoa New Zealand for the census 'usually resident' population, 1996–2006

	1996		2001		2006	
	Count	%	Count	%	Count	%
English	481,488	93.2	494,679	95.4	530,892	95.8
Māori	129,033	25.0	130,482	25.2	131,610	23.7
Samoan	3765	0.7	4074	0.8	3693	0.7
NZ Sign Language	6264	1.2	6549	1.3	5538	1.0
Other	8733	1.7	9063	1.8	9264	1.7
None	23,151	4.5	17,376	3.4	15,576	2.8
Total People Specifying One or More Languages	516,744		518,730		554,355	

Source: Statistics New Zealand, 2006a

A significant proportion of Māori speak one or more languages. Bilingualism for Māori is most likely to be English and te reo. In 2006, approximately 24 per cent of Māori had this skill set. A very small number of Māori (204) stated that they spoke Māori and a language other than English (Statistics New Zealand, 2007).

Te Reo Māori by Geographical Region in Aotearoa

The proportions of the Māori population who can hold a conversation about everyday things in te reo varies by geographical region (Statistics New Zealand, 1996; 2001; 2006c).* Table 8.4 and Figure 8.2 (overleaf) show the ranked differences for the eight Te Puni Kōkiri-defined regions in Aotearoa.

Table 8.4 gives a clear indication that a larger population size is not necessarily reflected in a large proportion of te reo speakers. Te Waipounamu, for example, has a population of 62,300 Māori, of whom 16 per cent speak te reo. In contrast Te Tai Tokerau has a smaller Māori population (43,500) but 28 per cent speak te reo. In fact, Te Tai Tokerau has the smallest population size but ranks second, behind only Waiariki (30 per cent), in the percentage of Māori-language speakers.

Table 8.4: Speakers of te reo Māori in the Māori population, by regions defined by Te Puni Kōkiri, 2006

	Able to speak Māori	Total Māori population	Percentage of those in Māori population who speak Māori
Te Waipounamu	9900	62,300	16%
Tāmaki Makaurau	27,900	140,000	20%
Te Upoko o Te Ika/Te Tau Ihu	14,600	67,300	22%
Te Taihauāuru	11,300	48,500	23%
Waikato	16,400	65,400	25%
Te Tairāwhiti/Tākitimu	16,500	62,300	26%
Te Tai Tokerau	12,100	43,500	28%
Waiariki	22,900	76,000	30%

Source: Te Puni Kōkiri, 2009

---

* In the 1996, 2001, and 2006 census forms, individuals were asked, 'In which language(s) could you have a conversation about a lot of everyday things?' The form offered multiple choices, of which te reo Māori was one. This allowed for the recording of monolingual, bilingual and multilingual abilities. A space for recording other languages spoken but not listed on the form was also provided.

Figure 8.2: Speakers of te reo Māori in the population, by regions defined by Te Puni Kōkiri, 2006

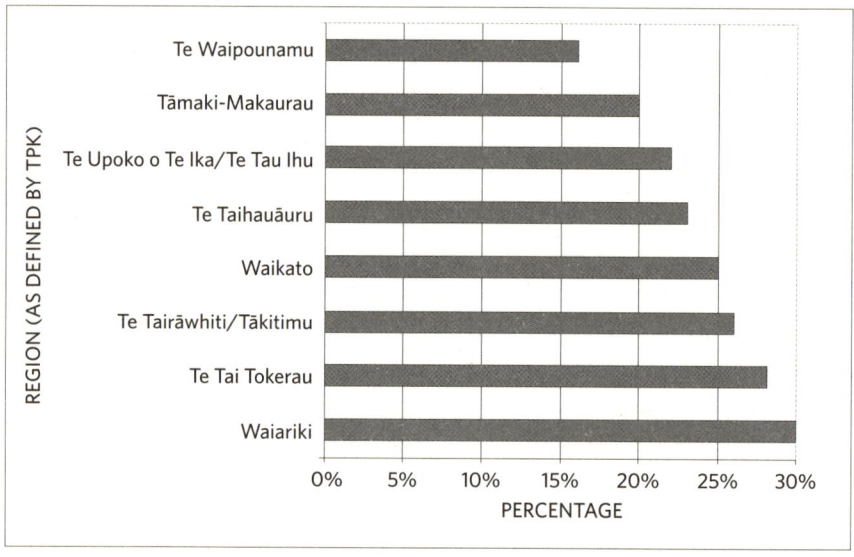

Source: Te Puni Kōkiri, 2009

Te Reo Māori in Northland

The aim of this section is to provide a demographic outline of te reo use in Te Tai Tokerau, the northern part of New Zealand. More specifically, it aims to show the impact that various factors, in aggregate, have upon te reo use within a particular geographical region, namely Northland (Te Tai Tokerau). These factors include age, gender and iwi. Iwi is an important concept that transcends, but does not fully exclude, geographical boundaries. The iwi population can be spread over a number of geo-locations, local and international. The reasons for population location and movement are well documented elsewhere, but include rural to urban drift for reasons of employment opportunities or pressures, and educational necessity. As was the case nationwide in 2006, English was the language most commonly spoken in Northland. Significantly, 10 per cent of the Northland population, compared to 4.1 per cent nationwide, could speak te reo. This is no doubt influenced by the larger proportion of Māori in the Northland population. While Pākehā remain the largest ethnic group there, making up 68 per cent, 31.7 per cent of the Northland population belong to the Māori ethnic group.* This is more than twice the national proportion of 14.6 per cent for Māori. Overall, 28.5 per cent of Māori in Northland in 2006 could speak te reo Māori – 4.8 per cent greater than the national average of 23.7 per cent (Statistics New Zealand, 2006d). In addition, Māori people in Northland were more likely to be bilingual or multilingual than Māori elsewhere in New Zealand; 29.9 per cent of Northland Māori spoke more than one language, where the national average for Māori was 26.6 per cent.

The Whangārei, Far North and Kaipara districts make up the Northland region. Whangārei has the largest population, with just over 68,000 people in 2006. The Far North had approximately 48,000 and Kaipara just over 16,000 people. The proportions of people speaking English and te reo in each of these areas differ – related to both the ethnic composition and the density of Māori-language centres, marae and networks of cultural dissemination in each area.

The Kaipara District

The proportions of the general population who speak te reo and English in the Northland sub-districts differ quite markedly.† Language use in Kaipara, the smallest of the three sub-districts, is summarised in Table 8.5 and Figure 8.3.

The proportion of the general population in the Kaipara district speaking te reo declined slightly in the study period, dropping from 6.4 per cent in 1996 to 5.6 per cent in 2006. The 2006 figure was still greater than the national average of 4.1 per cent, but less than the Northland average of 10 per cent. These figures, the author suggests, are related to the proportions of Māori and non-Māori living in this district.

---

* In 2006, the English-language version of the New Zealand census form offered 'New Zealand European' as an option to define one's ethnicity. The te reo Māori version of the form offered 'Pākehā' as an option. The author has chosen to use 'Pākehā' in this document.
† The general population is the 'usually resident' population at the time of information gathering.

Table 8.5: Distribution of languages spoken in the Kaipara district for the census 'usually resident' population, 1996-2006

	English		Māori		Samoan		NZ Sign Language		Other		None	
	Count	%	Count	%	Count	%	Count	%	Count	%	Count	%
1996	16,188	96.6	1074	6.4	33	0.2	117	0.7	549	3.3	432	2.6
2001	16,029	97.6	975	5.9	36	0.2	114	0.7	618	3.8	315	1.9
2006	16,707	97.8	960	5.6	30	0.2	93	0.5	747	4.4	279	1.6

Source: Statistics New Zealand, 2006a

Figure 8.3: Distribution of languages spoken in the Kaipara district for the census 'usually resident' population, 1996-2006

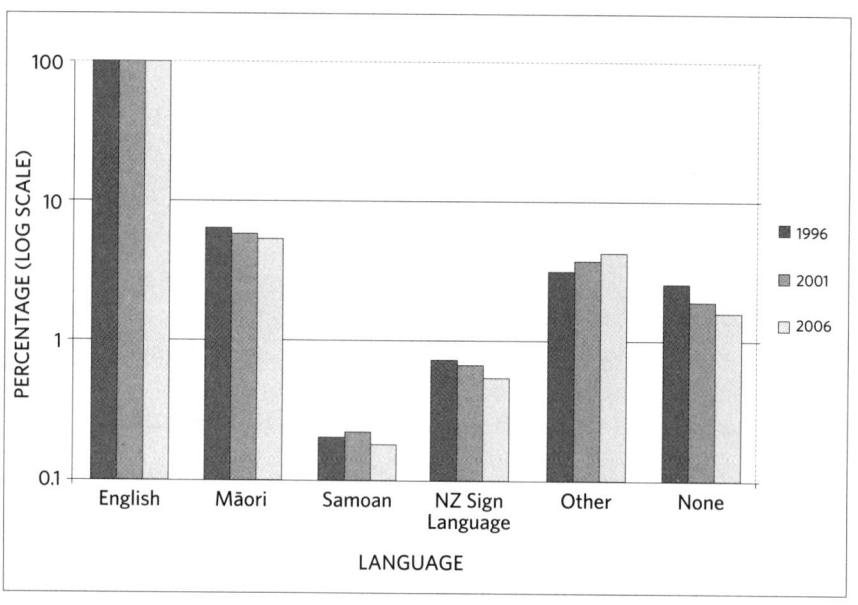

Source: Statistics New Zealand, 2006a

The Whangārei District

The Whangārei district contains the largest population within Northland, growing by approximately 10 per cent over the study period. Table 8.6 and Figure 8.4 summarise the languages spoken there.

Table 8.6: Distribution of languages spoken in the Whangārei district for the census 'usually resident' population, 1996-2006

	English		Māori		Samoan		NZ Sign Language		Other		None	
	Count	%	Count	%	Count	%	Count	%	Count	%	Count	%
1996	61,206	96.5	4329	6.8	165	0.3	561	0.9	2745	4.3	1647	2.6
2001	62,259	97.5	4356	6.8	198	0.3	564	0.9	3129	4.9	1203	1.9
2006	68,061	97.6	4578	6.6	186	0.3	531	0.8	3957	5.7	1263	1.8

Source: Statistics New Zealand, 2006a

Figure 8.4: Distribution of languages spoken in the Whangārei district for the census 'usually resident' population, 1996-2006

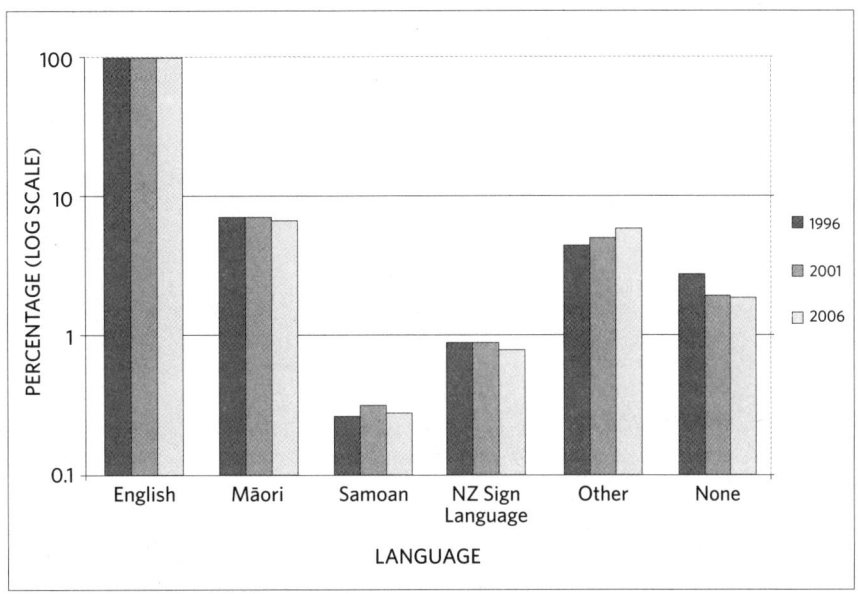

Source: Statistics New Zealand, 2006a

The proportion of people who could hold a conversation in te reo in Whangārei remained fairly constant (approximately 6.8 per cent) within the study period. As with the Kaipara district, this was greater than the 4.1 per cent national proportion but less than the 10 per cent recorded in Northland.

The Far North District

The greatest proportion of English–Māori bilingualism in the Northland region is found in the Far North. Table 8.7 and Figure 8.5 summarise its language distribution.

Table 8.7: Distribution of languages spoken in the Far North district for the census 'usually resident' population, 1996-2006

	English		Māori		Samoan		NZ Sign Language		Other		None	
	Count	%	Count	%	Count	%	Count	%	Count	%	Count	%
1996	45,741	95.2	7884	16.4	150	0.3	396	0.8	1977	4.1	1416	3.0
2001	46,830	97.1	7977	16.5	369	0.8	462	1.0	2295	4.8	870	1.8
2006	48,618	97.2	7914	15.8	192	0.4	357	0.7	2718	5.4	837	1.7

Source: Statistics New Zealand, 2006a

Figure 8.5: Distribution of languages spoken in the Far North district for the census 'usually resident' population, 1996-2006

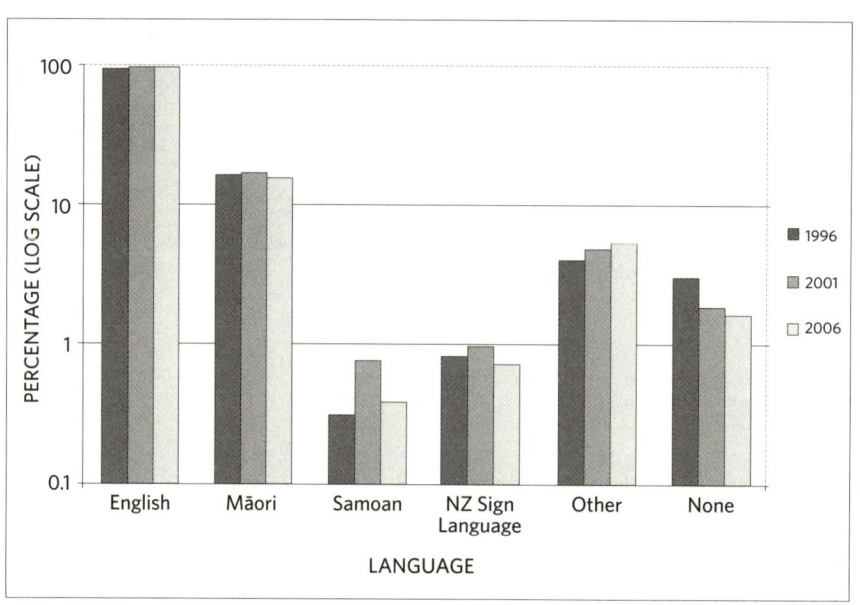

Source: Statistics New Zealand, 2006a

Whether influenced by the greater ratio of Māori to non-Māori people or other factors, a critical mass of te reo exists in Northland and in the Far North specifically. The proportion that can hold a conversation in te reo is much greater than the national average of 4.1 per cent. In 2006, 15.8 per cent of the total population of the Far North spoke Māori, slightly less than the 16.4 per cent who stated so in 1996.

Explaining the differences in the proportions of te reo speakers between the three sub-districts of Northland is problematic, given the data at hand. One possible explanation, however, is the critical mass of cultural activity that can occur due to increased population size and a concentration or close proximity of people within a particular geographical area. The density of a population, in terms of both geographic distance and social networks, appears to play a part in the uptake, use, teaching and promotion of te reo.

Speakers of Te Reo Māori among Different Age Groups in Northland

As stated, the transmission of te reo is achieved using multiple forms of communication. They include the stories told by kaumātua and kuia (male and female elders), books, films, TV shows, speeches and everyday conversations. The transmission can be formal or informal and may take place in any number of forums. Te reo can be, and is, maintained in multiple ways. By observing language abilities across age groups, we are in essence looking at the present, but also the past and the future. By looking to the mid-life to older populations, we can observe the effects of socialisation, and the decisions and practices of people's lives.

When we look at the language abilities of tamariki and mokopuna, we are observing the result of not only the personal initiative of these children but also the efforts – conscious and unconscious, structured and unstructured – of whānau, hapū, iwi and the general tāngata whenua (local people; people of the land) to educate and inculcate te reo Māori. These efforts can be as simple as overheard conversations in te reo at home, through to participating in Māori-medium learning, kōhanga reo and kura kaupapa Māori. It can be influenced by web resources or cool TV, which shows te reo as both serious and as fun.

Most importantly, the statistics we see within the under-15 and to a lesser degree 15–29 age groups are positive signs of the potential for improving the health of te reo (and Māoritanga). Tables 8.8 and 8.9 and Figures 8.6 and 8.7 look deeper into the use of te reo in Northland, by geographical area and age groups.

North Hokianga and South Hokianga had relatively high proportions of Māori speakers within all age groups, with 31 per cent and 27 per cent of all Māori respectively able to converse in te reo in 2006. For the under-15 age group, 27 per cent of Māori in North and 26 per cent in South Hokianga could converse in te reo. For the 65 and over age group, 50 per cent and 42 per cent of Māori in North and South Hokianga respectively could converse. The ability to kōrero in te reo was also strong in the 15–29 and 30–64 age groups in these areas.

Table 8.8: Te reo Māori speakers in Northland, by geographical area and age group, for 2006 (part I)

	Under 15		15-29		30-64		65 and over		Totals	
	Count	%	Count	%	Count	%	Count	%	Count	%
Kaitāia West	882	19	654	18	1158	17	558	13	3252	17
Kaitāia East	549	20	345	21	774	17	279	15	1950	18
Kaeo	126	14	75	24	216	14	75	16	495	16
Rāwene	108	22	48	25	207	19	75	28	438	21
Ōmāpere and Ōpononi	90	27	84	18	225	21	81	19	477	21
Hokianga North	528	27	321	29	867	28	246	50	1962	31
Hokianga South	720	26	372	25	1227	25	285	42	2607	27
Kaikohe	1329	21	762	24	1575	23	441	26	4113	23
Inlet-Hokianga Harbour	..c		..c		..c		..c		6	0

Source: Statistics New Zealand, 2006a
Note: ..c = numbers not available for reasons of confidentiality (Statistics New Zealand). This is invoked where counts are so small that the identity of citizens may be known if they are published.

Figure 8.6: Te reo Māori speakers in Northland, by geographical area and age group, for 2006 (part I)

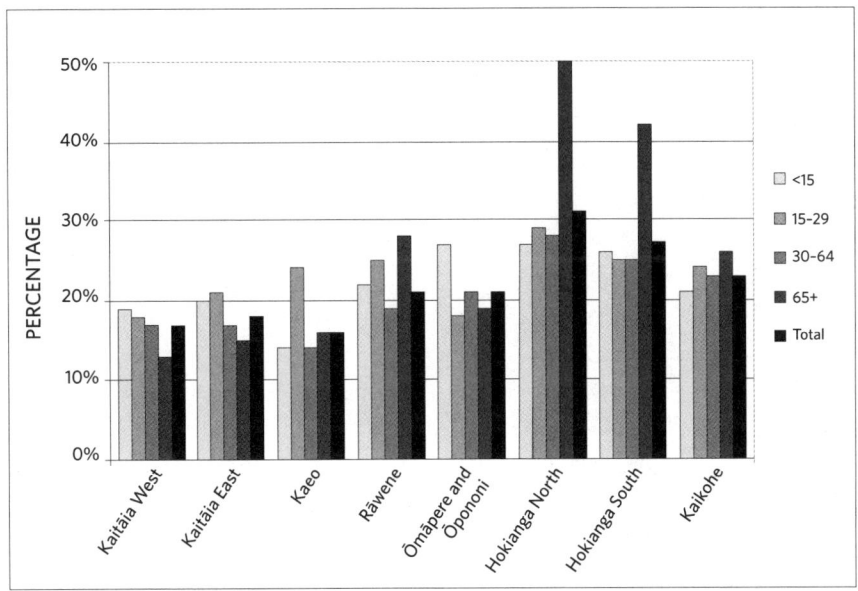

Source: Statistics New Zealand, 2006a

Table 8.9 and Figure 8.7 (overleaf) show that increased population size does not necessarily reflect the percentage of people within that population who can converse in Māori. Dargaville, for example, has a Māori population over twice the size of that of North Hokianga (1105 versus 528), but the proportion that speaks Māori is much smaller (7 per cent in Dargaville versus 31 per cent in North Hokianga).

Table 8.9: Te reo Māori speakers in Northland, by geographical area and age group, for 2006 (part II)

	Under 15		15-29		30-64		65 and over		Totals	
	Count	%	Count	%	Count	%	Count	%	Count	%
Marsden Point - Ruakaka	660	6	411	9	1329	5	516	2	2913	6
Ngunguru	243	5	144	8	729	4	309	3	1425	4
Te Kopuru	108	14	63	5	195	9	90	10	453	11
Kaipara Coastal	699	7	414	5	1506	6	363	6	2982	6
Dargaville	1005	8	711	10	1818	8	918	5	4455	7
Maungatūroto	213	6	186	2	327	5	108	0	837	4
Ruawai	90	0	54	11	192	14	90	7	426	9
Inlet-Kaipara Harbour North	..c		..c		..c		..c		..c	

Source: Statistics New Zealand, 2006a
Note: ..c = numbers not available for reasons of confidentiality

Figure 8.7: Te reo Māori speakers in Northland by geographical area and age group, for 2006 (part II)

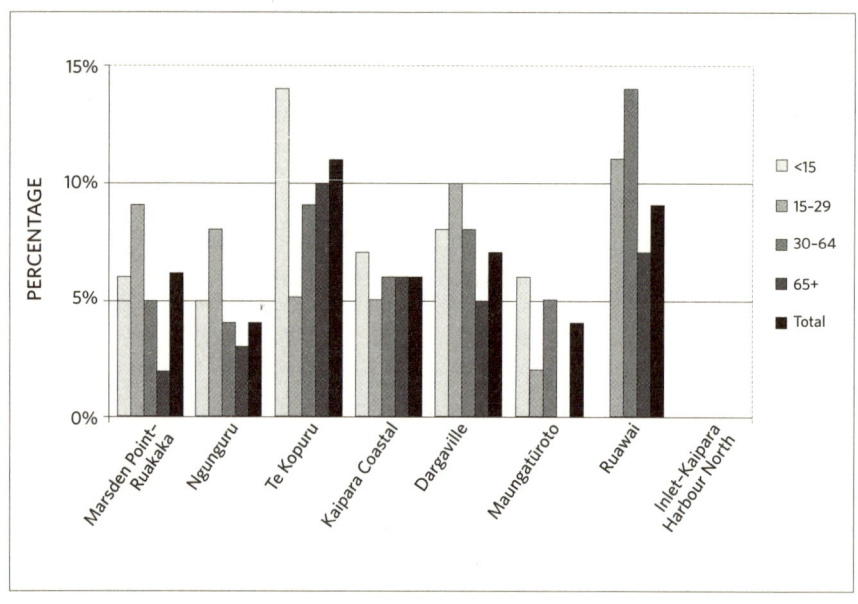

Source: Statistics New Zealand, 2006a

Te Reo Māori and Iwi

The analysis above is based upon the geographical location and grouping of Māori. It tells us much about the concentration, and the proliferation or decline, of te reo in Northland. This allows us to understand the impact that language and cultural initiatives such as the Māori-language revival and resulting kōhanga reo and kura kaupapa Māori have had upon te reo use by Māori youth. Adding another factor, iwi, to the investigation can further improve understanding. The levels of te reo use within and between iwi groups tell us some useful kōrero pono (true stories). Iwi are linked to geographical location but also transcend it, setting a context of inclusiveness or exclusiveness and of similarity and difference. They are identifiers of an individual's whakapapa (genealogy).*

It is important to examine use of te reo at the level of the iwi (and hapū). It is these social groupings to which organisations such as Te Puni Kōkiri and Te Taura Whiri i Te Reo Māori (among others) are offering language-planning advice, strategies and funding. By monitoring these iwi-based language competencies and comparing them with goals and strategies – not only those that government agencies have suggested and implemented but also those instigated by iwi and hapū over time – we can infer what progress has been made in revitalising the use of te reo.

Te Reo Māori for All Iwi of Aotearoa

In Table 8.10 and Figure 8.8 (overleaf), figures from the 2006 census show the relationship between the population who stated affiliation to one or more iwi,† and their use of te reo.

---

* Statistics New Zealand allows for the collection of multiple iwi affiliations for individuals in the 2006 census. It asks: '(a) Do you know the name(s) of your iwi (tribe or tribes)? (b) (If yes) mark your answer and print the name and home area, rohe or region of your iwi.'

† Within the New Zealand census, respondents are asked to record iwi affiliations and geographical locations. Iwi data therefore includes all of the people who stated each iwi, whether as their only iwi or as one of several iwi. Where a person reported more than one iwi, they have been counted in each applicable group. Therefore, there may be some cross-pollination of responses within iwi related tables and graphs (2006b).

Table 8.10: Use of te reo Māori and other languages for all 2006 census participants specifying iwi affiliation

Māori only		Māori and English only		Māori and other language		Total Māori spoken		Total all languages
Count	%	Count	%	Count	%	Count	%	
6453	1.0	112,767	17.5	8799	1.4	128,019	20.0	643,980

Source: Statistics New Zealand, 2006b

Figure 8.8: Use of te reo Māori and other languages for all 2006 census participants specifying iwi affiliation

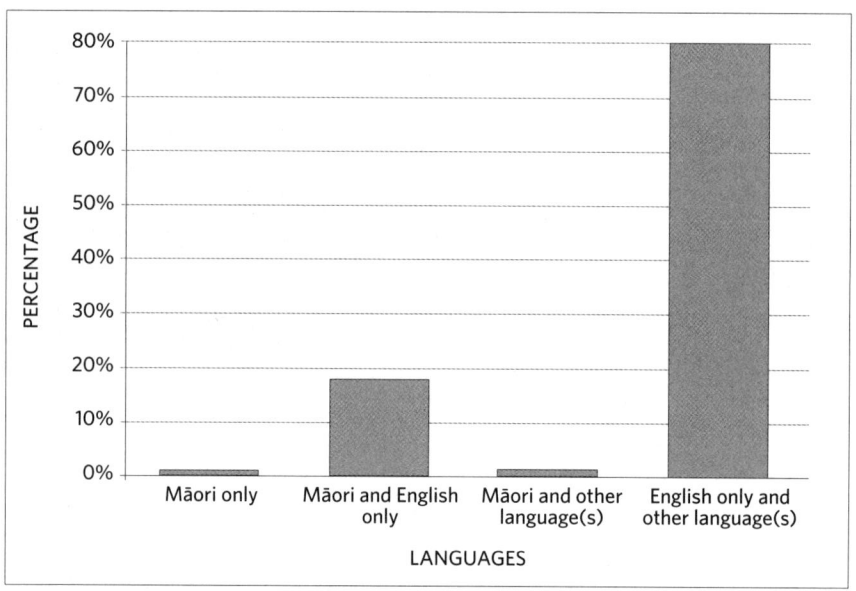

Source: Statistics New Zealand, 2006b

There is strong likelihood that a significant proportion of those who stated Māori as their ethnicity in the census, also stated allegiance to one or more iwi. However not all would have done so. Therefore, these figures must be interpreted as representative of a subgroup of the larger population of Māori who can converse in te reo. A very small but culturally significant proportion (1 per cent, numbering 6453) of our iwi subgroup conversed only in te reo, while 18 per cent were bilingual in English and te reo. A small proportion (1.4 per cent) could converse in te reo and at least one other non-English language. Overall, 20 per cent of Māori who stated an iwi could converse in te reo Māori; 80 per cent of this subgroup spoke only English and/or other languages (not including te reo).

Te Reo Māori for All Iwi Represented in Northland

Table 8.11 and Figure 8.9 (overleaf) show a comparison of use of te reo and other languages among the iwi of Northland in 2006.

Table 8.11: Te reo Māori and other language use for iwi represented in Northland in the 2006 census

	Māori only		Māori and English only		Combination of Māori and other		Total Māori spoken		Total pop.
	Count	%	Count	%	Count	%	Count	%	Count
Total Iwi Northland	639	1.4	10,614	22.4	621	1.3	11,874	25.1	47,295
Te Tai Tokerau*	15	1.9	267	33.3	18	2.2	300	37.5	801
Te Aupōuri	21	0.9	861	35.7	45	1.9	927	38.4	2415
Ngāti Kahu	39	1.5	840	32.0	48	1.8	927	35.3	2628
Ngāti Kurī	27	1.4	579	30.4	33	1.7	639	33.6	1902
Ngāpuhi	378	1.5	6672	26.8	363	1.5	7413	29.8	24,909
Ngāpuhi ki Whaingaroa**	9	1.5	195	31.7	3	0.5	207	33.7	615
Te Rarawa	63	1.4	1536	34.5	72	1.6	1671	37.5	4455
Ngāi Takoto	3	0.9	111	32.2	9	2.6	123	35.7	345
Ngāti Wai	18	1.0	513	28.0	48	2.6	579	31.6	1830
Ngāti Whātua	63	1.9	912	27.4	69	2.1	1044	31.4	3324
Te Kawerau	-	-	3	33.3	-	-	3	33.3	9
Te Uri-o-Hau	3	0.7	114	28.4	6	1.5	123	30.6	402
Te Roroa	6	1.2	153	30.4	6	1.2	165	32.7	504

Source: Statistics New Zealand, 2006b
Note: Because of random rounding of outputs to base three by Statistics New Zealand, row and column totals may not add up to 100%
* Te Tai Tokerau/Tāmaki Makaurau (Northland/Auckland) region, not further defined
** Ngāpuhi ki Whaingaroa–Ngāti Kahu ki Whaingaroa

Figure 8.9: Overall te reo Māori use for iwi represented in Northland at the 2006 census

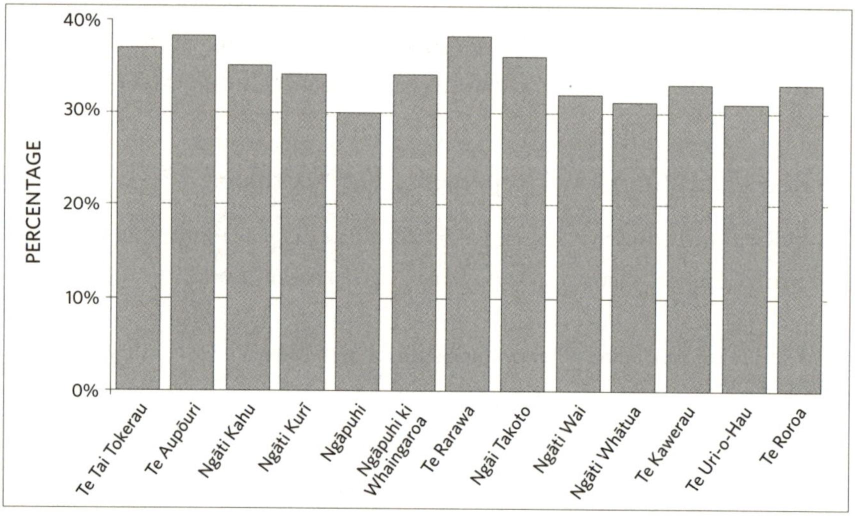

[Bar chart showing percentages by iwi: Te Tai Tokerau ~37%, Te Aupōuri ~38%, Ngāti Kahu ~35%, Ngāti Kuri ~34%, Ngāpuhi ~30%, Ngāpuhi ki Whaingaroa ~34%, Te Rarawa ~38%, Ngāi Takoto ~36%, Ngāti Wai ~32%, Ngāti Whātua ~31%, Te Kawerau ~33%, Te Uri-o-Hau ~31%, Te Roroa ~33%. Y-axis: PERCENTAGE, 0% to 40%.]

Source: Statistics New Zealand, 2006b

In all, 25.1 per cent of Māori in the iwi of Northland reported in the 2006 census, that they could hold a conversation in te reo. This was 5 per cent greater than the iwi total (20 per cent) for Aotearoa. The proportions of each Northland iwi who could speak te reo ranged between 30 and 38 per cent, figures significantly higher than the national iwi average of 20 per cent. The average proportion of te reo speakers for Northland iwi in 2006 was 31 per cent. In pure numbers, the largest iwi population in Northland was Ngāpuhi, with 24,909 people. Of these, 30 per cent (7413 people) could converse in te reo. The highest rate of te reo use, 38 per cent, was seen for both Te Rarawa and Te Aupōuri.

Te Reo Māori Use, Age and Gender in Iwi

Use of te reo varies by age group and gender within the Māori population. In 2006, just under half of Māori 65 years and over could converse in te reo Māori, compared to a quarter of those aged 15–64. Fewer young Māori (under 15 years), were able to converse in te reo than their older peers and elders. In this younger age group, one in six could converse in their native language. Males aged 65 and over were only slightly more likely to converse in te reo than females. Females were slightly more likely to use te reo Māori than males in the 15–64 and under 15 age groups (Statistics New Zealand, 2007).

Between 2001 and 2006, the proportion of speakers in the 55 or above age group has fallen 6 percentage points (from 57 to 51 per cent), reflecting the deaths of older native speakers and the entry, by aging, of a population group that has fewer speakers of Māori (Te Puni Kōkiri, 2009).

Table 8.12 summarises demographic distributions for Māori speakers in each of the Northland iwi, nationwide, for 2006. It also provides an overall comparison of te reo use between 2001 and 2006.

Table 8.12: Northland iwi members nationwide, by age, gender and use of te reo 2001-06

	Age groups			Gender		NZ iwi population count	Percentage Māori speakers	
	<15	15-64	65+	Male	Female		2001	2006
Te Aupōuri	24	67	9	45	55	9333	34	33
Ngāti Kahu	30	63	8	44	56	8313	32	30
Ngāti Kurī	25	66	9	45	55	5757	32	32
Ngāpuhi	29	64	7	46	54	122,214	25	23
Ngāpuhi ki Whaingaroa–Ngāti Kahu ki Whaingaroa	24	65	11	43	57	1746	35	34
Te Rarawa	26	65	8	44	56	14,892	34	32
Far North (Te Aupōuri, Ngāti Kurī or Ngāi Takoto)	25	66	9	45	55	14,193	33	31
Ngāti Wai	27	64	8	45	55	4866	30	28
Ngāti Whātua	30	64	7	44	56	14,724	27	28
Te Kawerau	..c	..c	..c	..c	..c	..c	..c	..c
Te Uri-o-Hau	21	73	7	42	57	1071	30	29
Te Roroa	24	63	12	43	57	1170	28	27

Sources: Statistics New Zealand, 2009a; 2009b; 2009c; 2009d; 2009e; 2009f; 2009g; 2009h; 2009i
Note: ..c = numbers not available for reasons of confidentiality

The drop in those speaking te reo Māori between 2001 and 2006 is reflected in the iwi-based data shown in Figure 8.10.

Figure 8.10: **Te reo Māori use for Northland iwi, 2001-06**

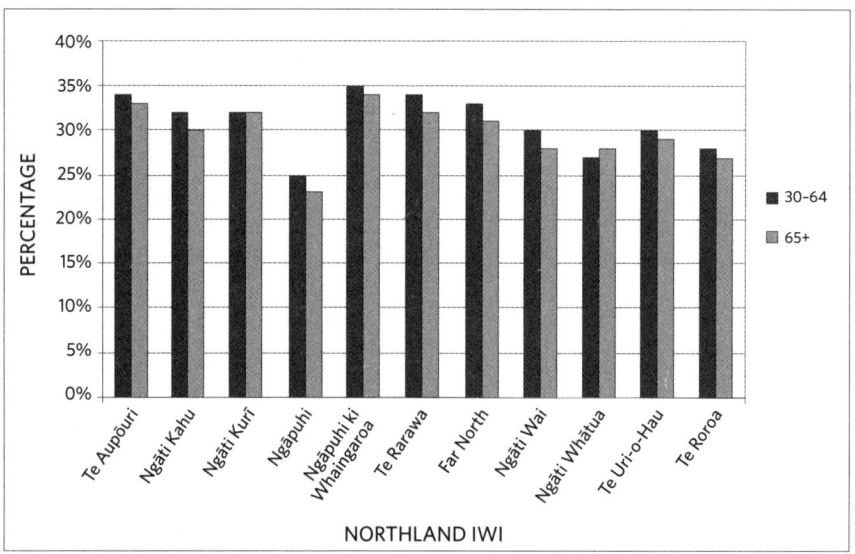

Sources: Statistics New Zealand, 2009a; 2009b; 2009c; 2009d; 2009e; 2009f; 2009g; 2009h; 2009i

The average proportion of te reo speakers in Northland iwi dropped from 30 per cent to 29 per cent between 2001 and 2006. All iwi, save Ngāti Whātua and Ngāti Kurī, experienced a 1–2 per cent drop in the proportions speaking te reo. Ngāti Whātua experienced a 1 per cent increase between 2001 and 2006, while Ngāti Kurī remained constant.

Age Groups, Iwi and te Reo Māori

As stated earlier, a correlation exists between age group and use of te reo. This is reflected in the age distribution for individual Northland iwi, as summarised in Figure 8.11.

On average, 26 per cent of all Northland iwi speakers of te reo were under 15 years old in 2006; 65 per cent of them were 15–64 years old, while those aged 65 years and older made up approximately 8 per cent.

Evidence also suggests that the age distribution of te reo users also differs between iwi. Te Aupōuri, for example, has the largest proportion (67 per cent) of those aged 15–64. In contrast, 30 per cent of the Ngāti Kahu population who could kōrero in te reo were under the age of 15. Most interestingly perhaps, 11 per cent of Ngāpuhi ki Whaingaroa–Ngāti Kahu ki Whaingaroa who could kōrero were 65 years and over.

Figure 8.11: **Age group distribution for Northland iwi speakers of Māori in 2006**

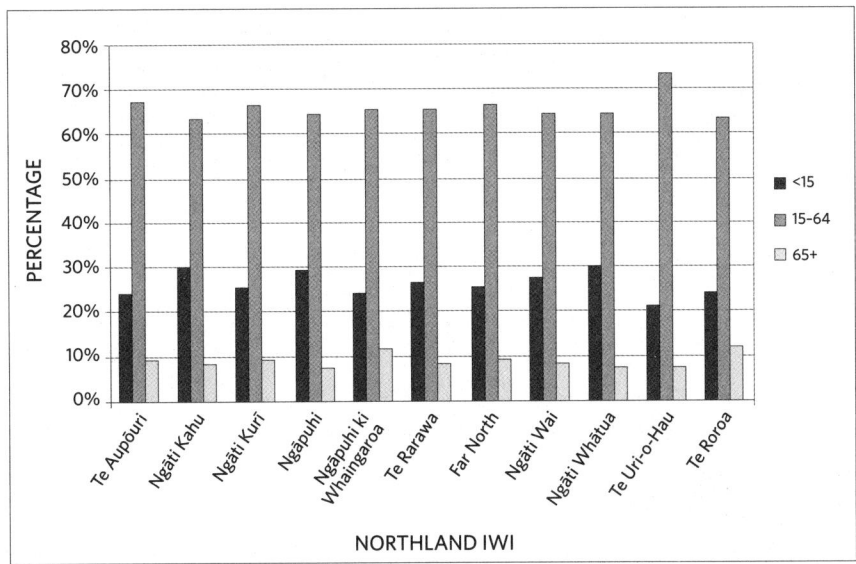

Sources: Statistics New Zealand, 2009a; 2009b; 2009c; 2009d; 2009e; 2009f; 2009g; 2009h; 2009i

Gender and te Reo Māori in Te Tai Tokerau

Females in all iwi around the country were more likely to kōrero Māori than males. In Te Tai Tokerau in 2006, females made up 54 per cent of all people in this region who could kōrero in Māori on a daily basis. This proportional distribution shifts little across age groups, something that the iwi-based data shown in Figure 8.12 (overleaf) also reflect, although the percentages of difference vary more than is shown in Te Puni Kōkiri surveys (Te Puni Kōkiri, 2009).

Figure 8.12: Gender distribution for Northland iwi Māori speakers in 2006

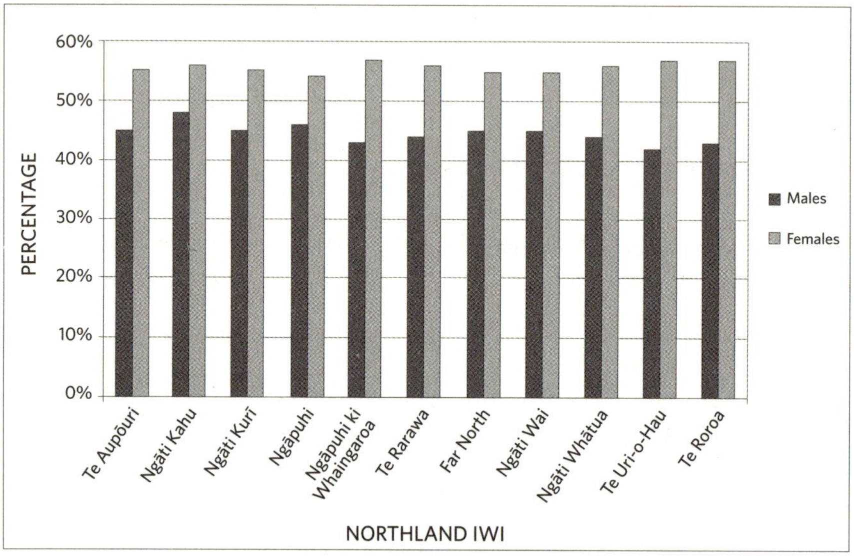

[Bar chart showing percentage of Males and Females for Northland iwi: Te Aupōuri, Ngāti Kahu, Ngāti Kuri, Ngāpuhi, Ngāpuhi ki Whaingaroa, Te Rarawa, Far North, Ngāti Wai, Ngāti Whātua, Te Uri-o-Hau, Te Roroa]

Sources: Statistics New Zealand, 2009a; 2009b; 2009c; 2009d; 2009e; 2009f; 2009g; 2009h; 2009i

For iwi around the country, the difference between males and females using te reo was 8 to 15 per cent, depending on the individual iwi. Across all iwi in Northland, the average difference between males and females using te reo was 11 per cent. Ngāpuhi, the largest iwi in the northern population, had the smallest proportional gender difference at 8 per cent. The proportions of males to females in all iwi who kōrero in te reo are very similar to the trends found within the geographical discussion.

Data Correlations and Discussions

This chapter was written to provide a resource for discussing, now and in the future, te reo Māori use by young people of Te Tai Tokerau. The author has also summarised the historical influences upon the decline and renaissance of te reo (for all Māori and the iwi of Te Tai Tokerau) in the twentieth and twenty-first centuries in Aotearoa. These included the employment-driven rural to urban drift of Māori in the early- to mid-twentieth century, which contributed to the stretching of social networks and family and cultural ties. The formerly culturally sustaining communities of Te Tai Tokerau and others were now atomised and diasporic in formation. Also influential was that English was (as it continues to be) the dominant, if not exclusive, language of public life, education and employment. This leaves the questions: in what contexts is te reo being used, and perceived as significant, in Te Tai Tokerau? These are addressed within the accompanying chapters of this book (see Hopeha, also Ngaha, this volume).

The author has also briefly highlighted the language strategies, whether positive or detrimental, designed and implemented by parents, elders, Māori leaders, religious groups, Māori organisations, iwi, and government agencies from the mid-twentieth century onward in Aotearoa. The utility of these strategies must be considered in their political, cultural and historical contexts. The cultural importance, promotion, cultivation and most importantly 'use value' of te reo have all been contested and consequently fluctuated over time. The frequencies and related competencies of te reo spoken by the tāngata whenua result from a combination of social, economic and cultural structures, tempered by the free will and agency of Māori and others to contest their place and power within those structures.

Self-reported competency in te reo has varied by geographical location, iwi, age, gender, and over time in Te Tai Tokerau and the whole of Aotearoa from 1991 to 2006. Greater proportions of Māori women spoke the Māori language than did men, both in the general population and in Te Tai Tokerau. The proportions of individuals who could converse in te reo were higher in Northland–Te Tai Tokerau than in most other geographical areas (save Waiariki) in Aotearoa. A significant proportion (28.5 per cent) of Māori in Northland in 2006 stated that they could converse in te reo, 4.8 per cent more than the 23.7 per cent national average (Statistics New Zealand, 2006d).

The proportion of the Māori population that could kōrero in te reo Māori varied between the three geographical districts that make up Northland. The Far North district had the highest proportion, followed by Whangārei and then the Kaipara district. There was a very slight decline in te reo use in all three areas, especially in the 2001–06 period.

As with the general population, this decline in proportions of te reo users in Te Tai Tokerau is linked to the passing away of members of the eldest cohort, and is compounded by the movement of the next youngest cohort, some of whom possess lesser Māori-language skills than their predecessors, into that older age cohort.

Interesting relationships between specific geographical location, age group and te reo competency are also evident in the data. North and South Hokianga both have relatively high proportions of Māori-language speakers within all age groups: 27 per cent of those under 15 years in North and 26 per cent in South Hokianga in 2006 could converse in te reo; for the 65 and over group, the figures were 50 per cent and 42 per cent respectively.

Also observed was an inverse proportional relationship between population size and ability to speak te reo in some parts of Te Tai Tokerau. Dargaville, for example, has a much larger Māori population than North Hokianga, but a much smaller proportion able to kōrero in te reo. Only 7 per cent of the Dargaville Māori population (1105) in 2006 could speak te reo while 31 per cent of the North Hokianga Māori population (528) felt they were competent in te reo.

A person's iwi, or indeed all of their iwi, can be linked to geographical locations but also transcends the firmament. It is also a marker of an individual's social networks, of their whānau and whakapapa, of cultural, social and economic capitals, of possibilities and predispositions for language success. The author suggests that the correlation between use of te reo and iwi membership or affiliation may reflect two things. First, it can infer the group/iwi habitus: the mindset and dispositions of that group towards language acquisition and education. Second, it can reflect real material conditions in which Māori construct strategies and attempt to implement them.

Of all Māori who stated allegiance to an iwi in the 2006 census, 20 per cent reported that they could converse in te reo. The remaining 80 per cent spoke English and other languages. A significant number and proportion of our iwi subgroup (6453, 1 per cent) stated that te reo was their principal language. Importantly, 18 per cent of all of the iwi subgroup were bilingual in te reo Māori and English.

As the geographical analysis of te reo reflected, a greater proportion of the people in the iwi of Northland (25 per cent) could converse in te reo Māori than the national proportion (20 per cent). Between 30 and 38 per cent of each individual Northland iwi could speak te reo in 2006. This proportion was also significantly higher than the national iwi average.

There was a slight drop in the proportions of Māori speakers for all Northland iwi from 2001 to 2006, from 30 per cent to 29 per cent. All individual iwi (save Ngāti Whātua and Ngāti Kurī who, respectively, had a slight rise and remained constant) experienced a 1–2 per cent drop between 2001 and 2006.

In 2006, the average proportional difference between males and females using te reo across all iwi in Northland was 11 per cent, with females consistently more likely to be Māori speakers than males. In addition, a correlation was shown to exist between age group and use of te reo within individual Northland iwi: in 2006, 26 per cent of all te reo speakers in Northland were under 15 years; 65 per cent were 15–64, and 8 per cent were aged 65 years or older.

Wider Cultural Context

We must consider the influence of social structures on te reo Māori competency in Northland and indeed Aotearoa. The author suggests that the importance of speaking te reo has shifted for Māori over time. In the twenty-first century, the struggle for identity, of which language is an important part, is a running battle for all New Zealanders. In immediate post-war New Zealand, individual identity was strongly linked to collective identity, social class, geographical location, occupation and ethnicity. In the 1960s, we saw beginnings of an individualisation of New Zealand society and the stretching of social networks. Among the factors that gave rise to this phenomenon were a furthering of immigration, the growth of capitalism, the internationalisation of labour and money, cultural and political revolutions and, most importantly, the globalisation of culture. In New Zealand's case, the 'cultural traffic' has been decidedly one-way. At risk is the possibility of homogenisation or 'McDonaldization' of Maori youth identity (Ritzer, 2013).

As stated, the health of te reo Māori for individuals was and is influenced by the Pākehā and Māori education systems and strategies. A less direct, more insidious influence is constraining the relevance and development of te reo in New Zealand. Globally diffused culture in all of its forms – including images, sounds, music, styles and language – must sit alongside local culture in the identities of all New Zealand people. These new forms of culture are present and available through multiple media such as movies, radio, television, print and the internet. Global culture is also manifest in the texts and objects used in everyday New Zealand life, which invariably share connections with, or refer to, cultures produced and lived in other countries. Clothing, music, food, motor vehicles, franchised retail stores and any number of other things are imbued with both international meaning and local interpretation of meaning. Competence in the language of global culture is necessary if the youth of Aotearoa are to have successful social interactions.

The influence of global culture upon te reo is not as institutionalised and obvious as the influences of government, hapū and iwi, but fights for space alongside colloquialisms and geographic linguistic idiosyncrasies in the dialects of the tamariki. Bauman (1998) suggests that living within global culture, and indeed within a consumerist society, has made the desire for instant gratification normal. This must influence the long-term, necessarily effort-intensive project that is te reo Māori promotion, acquisition and retention.

Hope and Strategies

Te reo Māori is a unique and living cultural entity. It is the cornerstone of what it is to be Māori. It is particularly alive in Te Tai Tokerau, compared to other regions. Recent dips in proportions of older people who can kōrero may be only short-term losses. They are the result of a particular generation (or two) that perhaps did not have the level of belief in te reo or the encouragement (and utility) of language strategies and resources that are available to present generations. Most importantly, a significant proportion of young Māori across Aotearoa (and specifically in the iwi of Te Tai Tokerau) now consider speaking in te reo Māori to be normative.

It is and will be second nature to kōrero in te reo. In several Northland kura kaupapa Māori that the author experienced first hand, children were living the language with pride and passion. These cohorts of young Māori (if nurtured) are likely to grow into adults who not only speak te reo but also use it in their homes, with their children.

Both Te Puni Kōkiri and Te Taura Whiri i Te Reo Māori (2000) have suggested that the path to an increase in the proportions and quality of te reo spoken by Māori is possible through an interconnectedness of language strategies locally, regionally and nationally. If present language strategies are monitored; improved in quality and consistency; accepted as relevant; and adopted and implemented at the levels of government agencies, hapū, iwi, whānau and individuals, Te Tai Tokerau can look forward to a continued revitalisation of te reo Māori.

It is worth quoting a second Māori proverb to restate the sentiment (and warning) concerning the future of te reo:

Ka ngaro Te Reo, ka ngaro taua, pera i te ngaro o te Moa
If the language be lost, man will be lost, as dead as the moa
(Department of Justice 1993, p. 7)

Bibliography

Bauman, Z., 1998. 'From Work Ethic to the Aesthetic of Consumption'. *Work, Consumerism, and the New Poor*. Buckingham: Open University Press: pp. 23–41.
Department of Justice, 1993. 'Report of The Waitangi Tribunal on The Te Reo Maori Claim'. Wellington: Brookers.
Harker, R., 1990. 'Education and Cultural Capital'. In: R. Harker, C. Mahar and C. Wilkes, eds. *An Introduction to the Work of Pierre Bourdieu: The Practice of Theory*. London: Macmillan.
Henare, J. (Sir), 1985. 'The Waitangi Tribunal: (Speech) Te Reo Maori Claim (Wai 11) 1985'.
Ministry of Social Development, 2009. 'The Social Report: 2009'. Wellington: The Ministry.
Ritzer, G., 2013. *The McDonaldization of Society*. Thousand Oaks: Sage.
Statistics New Zealand, 1996. 'Individual Form New Zealand Census of Population

and Dwellings: 1996 Census of Population and Dwellings'. From: http://www2.stats.govt.nz/domino/external/quest/sddquest.nsf/9f655b2a49f-64c256809000da4aa/17bd0e63a3bd0bfc4c25695a000adc4d/$FILE/individu.pdf

——, 2001. 'Individual Form New Zealand Census of Population and Dwellings: 2001 Census of Population and Dwellings'. From: http://www2.stats.govt.nz/domino/external/quest/sddquest.nsf/a0d89f655b2a49f64c256809000da4aa/136c4e6e24a41d10cc25698e007d3b0d/$FILE/Website%20IF.pdf

——, 2006a. 'Cultural Diversity – Tables and Reports'. From: http://www.stats.govt.nz/Census/2006CensusHomePage/Tables/Detailed/CulturalDiversity/3222.aspx

——, 2006b. 'StatsNZ, Iwi by Official Language Indicator, New Zealand, 2006'. From: http://www.stats.govt.nz/searchresults.aspx?q=official%20languages.

——, 2006c. 'Individual Form New Zealand Census of Population and Dwellings: 2006 Census of Population and Dwellings'. From: http://www2.stats.govt.nz/domino/external/quest/sddquest.nsf/a0d89f655b2a49f64c256809000da4aa/cac4ece534e3caafcc2571ce0016abbc/$FILE/English%20Individual%20Form.pdf

——, 2006d. 'QuickStats about Northland Region'. Statistics New Zealand. Wellington: Statistics NZ.

——, 2007. 'QuickStats about Maori'. Wellington: Statistics NZ.

——, 2009a. 'Iwi Profiles: Far North (2006)'. Wellington: Statistics NZ.

——, 2009b. 'Iwi Profiles: Ngapuhi (2006)'. Wellington: Statistics NZ.

——, 2009c. 'Iwi Profiles: Ngati Kahu (2006)'. Wellington: Statistics NZ.

——, 2009d. 'Iwi Profiles: Ngapuhi ki Whaingaroa–Ngati Kahu ki Whaingaroa (2006)'. Wellington: Statistics NZ.

——, 2009e. 'Iwi Profiles: Ngati Kuri (2006)'. Wellington: Statistics NZ.

——, 2009f. 'Iwi Profiles: Te Aupouri (2006)'. Wellington: Statistics NZ.

——, 2009g. 'Iwi Profiles: Ngapuhi (2006)'. Wellington: Statistics NZ.

——, 2009h. 'Iwi Profiles: Ngatiwai (2006)'. Wellington: Statistics NZ.

——, 2009i. 'Iwi Profiles: Te Uri-o-Hau (2006)'. Wellington: Statistics NZ.

Te Puni Kōkiri, 2001. 'Survey of Attitudes, Values and Beliefs towards the Māori Language'. Wellington: TPK.

——, 2006. 'Attitudes Towards the Māori Language'. Wellington: TPK.

——, 2008. 'Te Oranga o te Reo Māori 2006: The Health of the Māori Language in 2006'. Wellington: TPK.

——, 2009. 'Te Oranga o te Reo Māori i te Rohe o Te Taitokerau 2006: The Health of the Māori Language in Te Taitokerau 2006'. Wellington: TPK.

Te Taura Whiri i Te Reo Māori, 2000. 'A Guide for Iwi and Hapū to the Preparation of Long-term Māori Language Development Plans'. Māori Language Commission.

KIRI TOKI is of Ngāti Wai, Ngāpuhi and Ngāti Whātua descent. She holds a BA./LL.B. (Hons.) from the University of Auckland. At university, Kiri received the Ngārimu VC and 28th (Māori) Battalion memorial scholarship for undergraduates, the Auckland Women Lawyers' Association scholarship and the Simpson Grierson prize in law, as well as prizes in Māori and political studies. She also tutored various law and arts papers.

Kiri has a passion for all things Māori. Her interests include the growth of the Maori economy, the interrelationship between tikanga Māori and New Zealand's legal system, and the role international law can play in affirming indigenous rights generally. In 2010, she was a member of the Youth Caucus at the United Nations Permanent Forum on the Rights of Indigenous Peoples and at the Expert Mechanism on the Rights of Indigenous Peoples, and worked closely with other indigenous youth.

Kiri is currently a solicitor in the litigation team at Chapman Tripp. The views she expresses in this book are her own.

CHAPTER NINE

RENAISSANCE AND RE-ENGAGEMENT: A RANGATAHI PERSPECTIVE

KIRI TOKI

I was born in the 1980s, a period of cultural 'renaissance' for Māori, and was fortunate to hear and speak te reo Māori from a young age. But when many of my kaumātua (including my grandfather, the cornerstone of my Māoritanga) began to pass away, my whānau slowly stopped speaking Māori. Today, Māori is spoken only on our marae, and even here only on occasion. It seems that despite a renaissance in the 1980s, the state of te reo and tikanga Māori, for my whānau and hapū at least, remains precarious.

I see my situation as representative of the wider concerns facing Māori society. At face value Māori are seen to be successful. The Māori culture is revered, particularly by other indigenous peoples, as a culture that is alive and well. And through innovative investments and business leadership, iwi and other Māori groups have become successful commercial entities. But at a deeper level, we continue to face significant issues, such as the wellbeing of our people and the cultural survival of iwi practices. Here, from a rangatahi (youth) perspective, I will discuss two: the state of te reo Māori and the declining use of marae as a forum for dispute resolution. Although I believe that te reo and tikanga Māori continue to rest on a knife edge, I think we can continue the momentum of the Māori renaissance to secure the place of both.

The State of te Reo Māori

Te reo Māori is yet to become a language that all Māori speak, despite the fact that it is an official language of Aotearoa New Zealand and has been for more than 25 years. While there is no question that we must secure the place of te reo – it is after all a basic right of any indigenous person to learn their traditional language – *how* we do this remains to be seen. Whatever the answer looks like, I believe it must include increasing the number (and quality) of kōhanga reo and kura kaupapa Māori.

To me, teaching te reo to primary school children is the most efficient way to ensure that the language survives. Learning languages as an adult is tough at the best of times. A better option lies with increasing the number of speakers of te reo from an early age. This is certainly my experience. Living on my papakāinga, I did not attend a kura kaupapa Māori. My reo is shaky at the best of times, despite growing up with the language and taking te reo Māori courses at university.

Equally, I believe there is demand for kura. Most Māori would like their children to learn te reo. But whānau face constraints. For example, as it was for me as a child, it may be that there aren't any kura kaupapa in your local area. In Auckland, I know of only two kura kaupapa in the Auckland CDB, yet there are many, many more mainstream schools. Kura themselves sometimes struggle with demand. My younger brother's kura, for example, had to be very careful with the number of students they could take on, as they had only a certain number of teachers and resources for a certain number of students.

Clearly more needs to be done to cater for this demand. But what, and how, and by whom? The answer to these questions obviously involves whānau, iwi and the government; each has a role to play.

Although this is potentially an unattractive option in the current political climate, the government could increase the funding available to build more kura kaupapa and train more Māori teachers. This could be offered in conjunction with iwi. For more bang for its buck, the government could target areas with high Māori populations. Equally, for meaningful change to take place, control or mana of these schools should be given to Māori with appropriate support from the government.

But more schools, managed or overseen by Māori, alone will not produce fluent speakers of Māori, nor a vibrant or dynamic language that will continue to grow. Te reo Māori must be spoken in homes to survive. Whānau, hapū and iwi therefore have a complementary role to speak te reo and offer places for it to be spoken. This requires persistence and dedication, and is probably the true test te reo must face.

I believe that teaching our youth te reo Māori from the outset will have a flow-on effect. More speakers of Māori create more places where Māori is spoken, which in turn promotes the language as a normal feature of everyday life. This idea began in the 1980s; we can easily continue the momentum today. Flourishing societies start with pride and identity. Pride and identity are sourced from language.

The Declining Use of Marae as a Forum for Dispute Resolution

As a lawyer, I have a particular interest in the role that dispute resolution processes play in society. When I was younger, my kaumātua dealt with any dispute or problem, usually on my marae. Their decision was final. But as they slowly disappear, so too it seems that this wonderful and unique aspect of tikanga Māori is also disappearing. Today, I feel that my whānau prefer Pākehā institutions, like the police and the courts, to resolve disputes, rather than our own tikanga, even where our remaining kaumātua speak on a matter. Again, I do not think my experience is unique. Many iwi have also experienced this.

I am not suggesting that Māori set aside Pākehā ways of resolving disputes. These processes are useful and appropriate, especially in commercial contexts. I am highlighting that our traditional method of resolving disputes, held on marae, convened by kaumātua, are slowly disappearing. It is sad for me to see the loss of yet another unique function the marae played in traditional Māori society, and to sense that our people are having to abandon their own systems for others. One option to re-engage marae and people may be to empower marae committees, or kaumātua boards, so that they can legally enforce their decisions. However, the simpler option inevitably involves the revitalisation of our communities, whānau and hapū. The conversation needs to continue.

Re-engagement

I am proud of the steps Māori have made in recent years. Internationally, Māori culture is celebrated and is often a 'pin-up' for other indigenous peoples. More recently, iwi are becoming significant stakeholders in the national economy, perhaps heralding an 'economic' Māori renaissance. This economic power will probably create greater political power, if it hasn't already, and so is another small step to achieving tino rangatiratanga.

But this cultural awakening, as well as the more recent economic surge, has not solved the problems Māori continue to face, such as securing the place (and future) for te reo and tikanga Māori. Although change takes time, te reo remains uncomfortably close to disappearing forever, which should not be the case 30 years after a cultural 'renaissance'. We must find a way to re-engage people to use tikanga in their everyday lives. Clearly, more needs to be done.

Since graduating from the University of Oxford with a D.Phil. in Social Anthropology, **MERATA KAWHARU** (Tè Taoū, Ngaoho, Tè Uringutu o Ngāti Whātua; Ngāti Rahiri, Ngāti Kawa o Ngāpuhi) has been a full-time researcher, more or less. The 'breaks' from this lifestyle occurred when Piere (ten) and Freda (seven) were born. Another break was when she worked at the World Heritage Centre in Paris in 2008. She leads the James Henare Māori Research Centre and is an associate professor at the University of Otago. Merata has managed and coordinated many research teams and projects on Māori development, leadership, heritage, marae and te reo, and on te Tiriti o Waitangi subjects. She has written on her Ngāti Whātua community at Ōrākei in Auckland, but has also worked extensively throughout Aotearoa with many iwi, hapū and their leaders on Treaty claims and other issues.

Merata has worked on national and local boards, including the New Zealand Geographic Board where she is on a new learning curve, coming to terms with the complexities and politics behind the naming of places. She was greatly honoured to be named a Member of the New Zealand Order of Merit in 2012 for services to Māori education, but is even more honoured to be the daughter of the late Hugh and Freda Kawharu, who are her inspiration. Nō reira, e ōku mātua, takoto, takoto, takoto mai rā.

PARATENE TANE (Ngāti Rahiri and Ngāti Kawa) has completed a study on leadership concerning the geothermal hot springs and surrounding lands at Pārahirahi–Ngāwhā in Northland. For his efforts, he graduated (with Distinction) with an M.A. in Indigenous Development from the University of Otago. He has worked as a researcher for the Māori Maps project, the Te Wehi Nui project (both of which feature in this book), and most recently the Waka Wairua project, which investigates oral narratives within New Zealand, Tahiti and Rarotonga communities and archives relating to the entrepreneurial voyagers who first settled in Aotearoa.

Paratene has participated in international conferences and events including the World Heritage and the Pacific workshop in Maupiti, Tahiti (2008), the Negotiating Indigenous identity workshop in Osaka (2010), Information Technologies and Indigenous Communities conference in Canberra (2010) and as an observer at the United Nations Indigenous Peoples and Forestry expert working group session in New York (2011). He has also worked on the Te Ara: Māori pathways of leadership photographic exhibition and book project, which has taken him to the UK and Germany. At Hamburg, determined not to be overwhelmed at the enormity of the subject, he lectured on the challenges of Māori leadership into the future. Paratene is a doctoral candidate at the University of Otago. He is actively involved in his hapū.

CHAPTER TEN

CASTING A NEW NET: CONNECTING MARAE AND TE REO IN THE INFORMATION AGE

MERATA KAWHARU, WITH PARATENE TANE

I T COULD BE REASONABLY ASSUMED THAT 'BEING MĀORI' MEANS, FOR Māori, having some connection with marae and possibly also having some knowledge or competency in the Māori language. A growth since the 1980s in first-language speakers of te reo could also be reasonably expected, considering the pioneering efforts of Māori leaders such as Sir James Henare and Dame Iritana Tawhiwhirangi who helped to establish the kōhanga reo (Māori-language preschool) movement. As discussed in this volume and elsewhere, the kura kaupapa Māori (Māori-language primary schools) and other Māori-medium learning emerged in the wake of kōhanga. All these developments contributed significantly to revitalising the Māori language and promoting Māori values among the young. And in terms of a cultural revival in general, many tribal marae are being restored, built or rebuilt. The formal recognition of Māori as an official language, the establishment of Māori Television and the growth of Māori radio, the Māori-made mark, Māori cultural performance groups and national competitions, Māori tertiary providers and the settlement of Treaty of Waitangi claims, among other things, are all further positive developments and may be considered 'cultural successes'. One could surmise then that the indigenous culture and language of New Zealand is healthy and is growing.

Despite these significant efforts, however, marae and te reo, especially knowledge of regional forms of language such as sayings or idioms, may actually have little to do with the day-to-day lives of many Māori. The exodus to cities discussed by Tapsell and Robinson in this volume is still occurring. Marae communities are still depopulating and few members return regularly to 'keep the home fires burning' (ahi kā). Of course there are marae that continue to thrive and are strong both in the frequency of use and in the numbers of kin-group members using their marae. But elders commonly lament the difficulties of fulfilling marae roles when few competent speakers or elders are available. Marae – not necessarily all, but many – are facing crises.

We are left, therefore, with some dilemmas: for instance, how can marae operate and indeed compete with the employment 'clock'? Marae are people. But people cannot necessarily get time off work and this simultaneously removes the opportunity for their children to participate in marae functions. And how can marae remain vibrant and relevant to the next generation of Māori? Whatever the relative state of marae and language throughout the country, critical questions need to be asked and – more importantly – answers need to be found.

Taitamariki, or young Māori, are often seen as tomorrow's leaders. It seems obvious that engaging with them meaningfully through culture and language is important. This might not be so straightforward though given the variety of communities to which young Māori belong and activities in which they participate. These extend beyond marae and include school, sport and other extra-curricular contexts. They can be multi-regional if not international, as demonstrated through e-network sites such as Facebook, Twitter and other web 2.0 (interactive website) forums. A tribal marae may be just one of several communities of relevance to Māori, if marae play a part in their lives at all. But it may be that within their broadened, 'networked' and (ironically) 'connected' community environments are some ways to bring young Māori and marae and te reo closer.

We look at these dilemmas, beginning (in 'What Is the Problem?') by briefly outlining leadership challenges that confront marae communities concerning marae sustainability and language. We start from the premise that questions and answers cannot be found if there is no baseline data to inform them. In the first part of this section we explore themes and ideas that emerged from insights gained while visiting schools and marae communities between 2008 and 2010 in the North and South Hokianga, Patuharakeke and North Kaipara regions of Te Tai Tokerau. This was the 'community engagement' part of the Te Wehi Nui project and was based on kōrero (discussions) with community leaders and elders.[*] In this section we also explore the significant impact of Treaty claims on marae and leadership as well as the theme of te reo and leadership. These insights have also emerged from our own community engagements over the years. From this 'local' layer, we then explore how language and culture are viewed more generally, in a national study on Māori wellbeing.

These local and national contexts provide a backdrop and thinking space to consider more closely young people's thoughts about te reo and marae. In the second part of our essay ('Te Wehi Nui a Mamao Project: What Are Taitamariki Saying?') we explore some of these views that came out of questionnaires and focus-group discussions in the Te Wehi Nui project.

In part three, 'A "Connected" Solution? Tewehinui.com', we turn our focus to a way of addressing the problems. Of course, multiple problems call for multiple solutions. Increasingly, the internet is becoming a critical tool for hapū to connect dispersed community members and to share information and cultural knowledge. But with the internet come challenges as well, and we discuss some of these. Principal among them is to preserve marae values, knowledge and language in a contemporary e-learning environment. We consider the value of taonga (something treasured) in this context. We ask, what actually are taonga, and how can

---

[*] 'Kōrero' (rather than 'interview') as used here refers to the dialogue that, in almost all cases, included some kind of mihi (formal greetings) and then continued with traversing whakapapa (genealogy) and other connections. They were more than simply discussion on particular topics directed by an interviewer.

their integrity be maintained in an internet environment? How can such knowledge be protected using the checks and balances of the kinship system and in relevant ways today?

What Is the Problem?

What does it mean to 'be' Māori? What do young Māori say about that? What are they doing about it? We visited many schools throughout Northland and received glimpses into answers to these questions. Students welcomed us into their schools and into their marae. One school group, some 30 to 40 students, flanked by their teachers at the sides of the house, organised themselves and led a pōwhiri (welcome) for us. With only a little imagination, we could have been in a tribal marae setting being welcomed by kaumātua. At another school in rural Hokianga, the school children, aged from five to fifteen, also conducted formal rituals of encounter under the watchful gaze of the kaumātua and kuia of the community who had come in especially for the occasion. The five- and six-year-olds keenly sang the accompanying waiata (song) for the student representative who was around thirteen years old and who began the speeches of welcome. We were inspired. Marae-based knowledge and language were clearly being perpetuated, and confidently so, on both these occasions.

These welcomes, like pōwhiri given at other schools, showed what seemed to be all quite straightforward and routine. Certainly in some ways the students were being required to follow their teachers' instruction, but they undertook their roles with pride and enthusiasm. Young boys mustered the courage to stand before a crowd of strangers, while their supportive, but potentially critical peers, teachers and elders looked on. Tikanga (marae-based protocols) and te reo appeared to be vibrant and living. But are these realities the same within the hapū (kin group) context of marae? We may begin to answer that question by exploring more closely contemporary issues facing marae, and kaumātua views.

The View from Marae: A Contemporary Context
The Treaty claim process in one form or another has gripped most tribal communities over the past 30 or so years. It is a game-changer for

marae economic, political and cultural sustainability. The claim process has (re)produced knowledge on tribal history and traditions, and made this knowledge and related information – otherwise 'hidden' in public or private archives – accessible and published. This can be seen in the historical accounts of 'agreements in principle' (at, for example, the Office of Treaty Settlements website – http://www.ots.govt.nz), as well as the hundreds of research reports written for claimants and of course Waitangi Tribunal reports. These stores of knowledge may be a key contributor to broadening the cultural base in marae contexts, such as in helping to inform karanga (ritual calls of welcome) and whaikōrero (ritual formal speeches), if not also helping to inform regional forms of language (see also Tapsell, this volume, for broader discussion on Treaty settlements and marae). It might take a creative step to translate the formal Treaty reports or historical accounts into useful forms for marae and language development. The point, however, is that these are new stores of knowledge, as kaumātua have described to us in the Te Wehi Nui project and as claimants have said repeatedly in hearings and direct negotiation throughout Aotearoa. The information will be vital for marae community enhancement.

Another positive development in recent years in Te Tai Tokerau (if not also elsewhere) is the return home of families who have spent some years away from the tribal region. As another contributor to this volume, Te Rūnanga o Te Rarawa CEO Kevin Robinson, explained to us (pers. comm. 20 May 2011), this return has brought another layer of community capacity, particularly where individuals take on marae or trustee roles.

Equally important in these cases is that the cultural 'training ground' for young Māori is now their tribal marae – as opposed to when they lived outside their rohe or tribal territory, and the marae that they went to (if at all), belonged to other tribal groups or pan-tribal groups. The return of families to marae communities is perhaps the singular most effective way of rebuilding those communities.

For several rural schools in the north, particularly those in the Hokianga, Kaipara and the Far North, the marae plays a central or important part in their learning. The benefit is reciprocated for the marae, who receive the support of the schools in hui.

Wānanga, or cultural learning programmes, are also being held on marae, strengthening otherwise disparate communities and helping to revalidate the use and importance of customary marae-based knowledge and te reo. Marae-based wānanga such as those run by young Ngāti Whātua leader and kura teacher Anaru Martin in the Kaipara have been popular amongst 'next generation' Ngāti Whātua people. His and other wānanga initiatives take a special kind of leadership; one that recognises the problems and then results in the coordination (possibly new) of people and resources to effect change.

Certainly there is vibrancy in marae. The examples touched on (and there are others) indicate marae and language utility and relevance, if not also growth. But these kinds of vitality are not necessarily widespread, regular, or even evident, in marae. Many Treaty settlements remain outstanding in Northland: only a few have occurred, some as recently as Te Rarawa and Ngāi Takoto in October 2012. It will be some time, possibly years, before marae see *direct* benefits of Treaty settlements. In other areas that have had such settlements, the resulting legislation has not typically referred to marae specifically. Settlements are for their benefit, but usually the larger organisational structures receive settlement assets, develop and distribute them. As one tribal leader said, about a large tribal group who were among the first claimants to settle their Treaty grievances (and to receive many millions of dollars, land and other things), the place of marae in the settlement process is central, but much more work needs to be done so that they can directly benefit. The iwi has instead focused much of its attention on economic development of large assets and businesses. The key benefit arising out of these new enterprises is employment. However, several factors, including having the relevant skills and living locally, need to be in place before employment can materialise. Where marae do not directly receive a Treaty settlement, they may instead become a beneficiary of it – but with little, or no, autonomy to act in Treaty settlement terms, except perhaps as recipients of funds or resources that the Treaty settlement entity has allocated to them. It would be wrong to generalise or characterise the varied relationships between marae and Treaty settlement entities. But where those relationships are not clear, they could leave marae frustrated and unempowered;

the very opposite of what Treaty settlements are supposed to provide. It is not uncommon to hear of marae concerns about settlement and post-settlement processes.

Marae and Leadership

To widen the discussion: difficulties facing marae communities appear, in large part, to hinge on two major things – limited participation by young Māori, and limited leadership succession.

Customarily, kaumātua (more specifically, elders who represent a kin community on that community's behalf, particularly in marae contexts) usually fulfil marae leadership duties. Yet, today marae appear to have fewer and fewer kaumātua – generally through natural attrition – and limited, or no, replacement. Marae representatives within Ngāti Whātua, Ngāpuhi, Te Rarawa, Ngāti Kurī and other iwi have all too commonly lamented this predicament. Some communities have reported having no kaumātua. Kiri Toki (this volume) also speaks about this problem from the viewpoint of a young person. Out of necessity, younger community members are put into leadership positions. 'Kaumātua' of today are often considerably younger than the marae kaumātua of a generation ago. Training younger people to take on marae responsibilities has the obvious benefit of fulfilling manaakitanga (duties of care and hosting). However, there may be an assumption that kaumātua are present or able to provide guidance. This is not necessarily the case. Fraser Toi (also this volume) discusses the dilemmas arising from these situations in more detail.

Marae cope also by seeking support from kaumātua from other marae who might have more distant connections to the marae in question. A kaumātua well-known amongst northern iwi – and who regularly participates in marae hui throughout the north – illustrated the difficulties his marae faced, by describing the situation where the same small group of kaumātua is called upon to fulfil customary roles for more than one marae in a region. Of course, the help of kaumātua of other marae affirms and strengthens the whanaungatanga or familial relationships between marae. But when these elders are also the same individuals who take on an ever increasing range of tribal obligations, such as being involved in Treaty claim negotiations and/or broader tribal representation roles, the burden on these few is greater than ever before. In part, the heavy responsibilities often coincide with communities' recognition of certain individuals as leaders. Elders may be seen as being the most capable of representing their communities in multiple forums and contexts. This is not necessarily sustainable, though, over the longer term. If there is too heavy a reliance on a few and not enough attention on building leadership succession, there are risks for the community (such as not capitalising on new opportunities – perhaps new partnerships; not maintaining strategic political and economic relationships; limited understanding of marae tikanga and so on) when those leaders at the helm pass on.

Within marae, the burden is felt by a few: those who perform marae duties in receiving visitors, and those responsible for preparing and managing the logistics of a hui.* While circumstances differ between communities, marae are experiencing varying degrees of burden from one hui to the next. The toll can be great, especially for those elders who are expected to provide manaakitanga at tangi. Bringing visitors into marae, one group after another, can be fatiguing; more so if there is limited support such as for karanga or whaikōrero. Sometimes there are successive tangi. Yet the same elders fulfil the hosting duties, with little or no break in between the tangi. Unfortunately this is not an uncommon pattern across Te Tai Tokerau, as described to the project team in the Te Wehi Nui kōrero or in our (the team's) own communities.

Each community with whom we talked in Te Wehi Nui told similar stories of elders dying and not being succeeded. One of the elders lives three hours away from his marae, yet he is a key community leader and spokesperson on behalf of that marae. For those living locally, balancing day-to-day responsibilities (work, for example) with marae responsibilities is also not easy, but hui such as tangihanga do not conform with the workplace clock. Then there are the many whānau who live some distance away from marae (many in urban centres) and have less opportunity to participate than the resident hau kāinga people (those living within the

---

* For example, setting out a meeting house and organising catering.

marae communities). The effects of urban migration are often discussed in connection with the socio-cultural dislocation that Māori experienced in the 1950s and 1960s, when they moved to cities for employment reasons (see Tapsell, this volume). These are still very much realities decades later. If anything, the problems have only deepened or widened to include many more families and generations.

Negative net migration is a common concern for hau kāinga throughout Northland. Broadly speaking, local marae people worry about the cultural, economic and political sustainability of their communities because families have continued to flock to cities. Let's look at some demographic 'numbers', not least because at first glance, statistics and anecdotal evidence do not necessarily match up. That is, on one hand, communities – in the loose sense of the term – appear to see some growth (measured by, for instance, new businesses being created or even individuals having children at a relatively young age); on the other hand, marae community people also report that their communities are declining. Official statistics tell us that the Māori population in Northland slightly increased between 1996, 2001 and 2006 (the census years), though it had declined again by 2013. When we look more closely at what is meant by 'Māori population', even in 2013, we see that while there are increases amongst older people, there are decreases amongst younger Māori:

Table 10.1: Māori resident population in Northland, 1996, 2001, 2006, by age

	Age				
	0-14 years	15-39 years	40-64 years	65 years plus	Total
1996	17,900	17,600	8800	2100	46,400
2001	17,600	16,700	12,200	2500	47,100
2006	16,900	16,600	11,700	2900	48,000
2013	15,138	13,911	12,435	3447	44,931

Source: Statistics New Zealand, n.d.

While there appeared to be an overall population increase between the years 1996 and 2006, this did not translate into increased marae communities or increased marae involvement, according to many kaumātua in Northland.* In other words, even when the Māori population in Northland increased (though only slightly, according to the figures), it did not appear to have a significant effect at rural marae community level. There may be pockets of increases for some age groups. Further research would need to establish this,† but it may be that Māori population increases occur more in the towns and cities in Northland, rather than within marae communities. To take a contrasting view: when marae communities do in fact increase – purely on a population basis – this does not necessarily translate into sustainable leadership succession. This is not surprising when statistics tell us that the Māori population in Northland is aging. The Northland District Health Board adds to this point, stating:

> Northland's [general] population is 'ageing' because older age groups are increasing in both number and proportion, while those of children and youth are decreasing because of declining birth rates. Significant change in the age structure of Northland is projected between 2012 and 2026.

Motivated by the lack of local employment opportunities and the offer of jobs in cities (and in Australia), families inevitably move. Again this is not new. To take an example of the impact of depopulation in marae communities in northern Hokianga, from Mitimiti on the west coast to inland Mangamuka, the region once thrived with eleven kōhanga reo, with some 200 children attending. Today in northern Hokianga, only two kōhanga reo are still open (Far North REAP, 2012). One of the two local area schools has also suffered a significant decline in its roll. As a result it has become more difficult to attract and retain good teachers (see also Robinson, this volume, for further discussion on declining communities). Learning te reo at school has consequently suffered. And as described to us by kaumātua, marae support has been affected, especially where marae rely on the local school. Limited numbers at school have translated into limited support of the marae.

---

* These views have also been expressed by kaumātua to whom we have spoken over a number of years, outside the Te Wehi Nui project.
† Census data is very useful for many purposes but it cannot be broken down at marae level.

Leaders and te Reo

Perhaps ironically, while te reo learning environments aim to promote the language, some kaumātua in fact criticise 'the what' and 'the how' of language learning, and see the language being 'institutionalised'. Although supportive of the efforts of kōhanga reo and kura kaupapa, one tribal leader felt that it was not the job of schools to teach te reo from prescribed texts that are written for a general readership and not a particular area. (The Waitangi Tribunal also acknowledged that te reo has become standardised in learning texts [Waitangi Tribunal, 2011], meaning that local idioms or ways of writing te reo may not be reflected in them.) Rather, it was the role of whānau, parents and grandparents to provide the primary environment for children to learn Māori language and culture/tikanga associated with local marae. He further argued that the whānau can (or should) provide a more accurate interpretation of language and values relevant and applicable to the region. The level of interpretation and contextualisation of knowledge may not be obvious or offered in books.

A whānau learning environment also encourages a two-way dialogue and opportunity for discussion and debate. The kaumātua was not dismissive of the role of schools in learning – he came from a school teaching background himself – but he was clear about the role they should have in promoting the learning of te reo and tikanga. Schools, he explained, should be a secondary level of learning. Others have echoed these sentiments. And so while he saw the decline in kōhanga reo as a major loss, others did not see it as such a problem. But while the family (or marae) context may be the ideal environment for te reo and tikanga learning, often families are now ill-equipped to provide the learning in these terms. As explained to us by a northern leader who moved back to North Hokianga after several years away in Auckland, neither he nor his wife are fluent in te reo. Kōhanga reo provided the opportunity not only for their son to learn the language and values, but also for themselves to learn. This example is not isolated. It may be that Māori-medium schooling provides some basics, and fine-tuning occurs within the marae community.

With the decline in kōhanga reo; the lack of total immersion or bilingual language-learning systems of schooling; limited whānau environments where Māori is the first or dominant language in the household; and fewer elder role models, it is no surprise that the opportunities to maintain continual regional language and customary values transmission are becoming scarce. These circumstances present a very real crisis of marae-based cultural sustainability. With limited knowledge transfer, marae are inevitably struggling.

The developments outlined so far demonstrate a complex set of circumstances that directly affect hapū and marae identity and wellbeing. While the specifics differ from one iwi region to the next, the underlying crisis precipitated by ongoing negative migration appears to be recurring throughout Te Tai Tokerau, if not also more widely.

An important response to the cultural crises that marae face is the creation of vibrant economies; economies that may entice people to return home, even to relatively remote regions like Hokianga or the Far North. Economic development is a major focus for iwi, as northern iwi leaders explained to our research team, including scoping out new business and entrepreneurship opportunities.* Promoting new business in depressed or isolated regions is no small feat for anyone. The settlement of Treaty claims is crucial for this, as it can bring opportunities to create new ventures and to involve marae in settlement. But people's lives cannot necessarily wait for Treaty settlement, and such settlement does not necessarily involve marae directly, as discussed by Paul Tapsell in this volume. Whatever form it takes, enhanced economic development will potentially affect marae significantly by bringing greater whānau (re-)involvement, thus strengthening their cultural fabric. This point is well emphasised by Kevin Robinson (see his chapter, this volume).

A further reality though is that many families will not return to live permanently within their marae communities. If marae are about people (as Paul Tapsell discusses in his chapter) and the people are scattered, new

---

* One example is the mānuka honey project led by Te Rarawa. The tribal authority is hoping to support the development of mānuka bee business in the Far North where there is a high level of Unique Manuka Factor (UMF), a critical ingredient in certified mānuka honey. Higher levels of UMF enable the honey to be medical-grade quality. Another example is the broadband project: building broadband access in the Far North to connect rural areas, including the most remote.

ways of connecting marae communities will be important, in addition to focusing on local economic development. 'Connectedness' is a major issue and is discussed later in this chapter.

Questions of wellbeing, identity and connectedness are not new. One of the most comprehensive studies on these topics took place in the 1990s. To further contextualise the perspectives just given by northern leaders, we take a brief look at this study.

National Context: Te Hoe Nuku Roa

Te Hoe Nuku Roa was a longitudinal research programme conducted in the late 1990s by researchers at Massey University and led by renowned Māori studies scholar Mason (later Sir Mason) Durie. This study gives a broader context for considering cultural identity and marae.

The study was conducted among 655 households from Manawatū–Whanganui, Gisborne, Wellington and Auckland regional council areas. 1574 individuals were interviewed, 618 of them under 15 years old (Te Hoe Nuku Roa Research Team, 1999). It is this group of young Māori that provides some points of reflection in comparison to our project. Of particular note is the frequency of visits by tamariki (children) to their marae, and the frequency of visits each made to a marae for tangihanga or hui, as indicated in the following tables:

Table 10.2: Percentage of respondents who visited their own marae over the past 12 months

Not at all	40%
Once	17.6%
A few times	27.9%
Several times	12.3%
More than once a month	2.1%

Source: Te Hoe Nuku Roa Research Team, 1999, p. 125

Table 10.3: Percentage of respondents who visited a marae to attend a tangi or hui over the past 12 months

	Tangi	Hui
Not at all	53.8%	62.1%
Once	18.5%	15.0%
A few times	16.5%	14.4%
Several times	9.0%	6.0%
More than once a month	2.2%	2.5%

Source: Te Hoe Nuku Roa Research Team, 1999, p. 125

As Table 10.2 indicates, although 60 per cent visited their marae once or more over the preceding twelve-month period, the remaining 40 per cent had not visited their marae at all in the same period. The latter figure seems to suggest that of those surveyed, a large group of young Māori are disconnected from their marae. Those who went several times or more than once a month and, therefore, appear to have an active involvement in their marae, were comparatively few (14.4 per cent). Although many of those represented in the surveys were very young (under ten years) and possibly too young to have created an association with their marae, the surveys do indicate frequency of visits and possible limited direct engagement. Durie (1999, p. 352) does add, however, that other family members in a wider network may be more regularly involved. This involvement may mean that the young members who do not go to their marae often are not necessarily completely separated from marae life; even so, direct involvement appears to be by few.

Table 10.3 similarly illustrates limited engagement with marae. The question was framed more broadly than the first as it enabled the participant (or representative) to talk about any marae, not necessarily their own. More than half had not been to a tangihanga or hui (53.8 per cent and 62.1 per cent respectively) in the previous twelve months. Overall, the statistics do not present a particularly bright picture in respect of regular participation and marae sustainability.

Te Wehi Nui a Mamao Project: What Are Taitamariki Saying?

The views of kaumātua and other leaders, along with findings of the national study Te Hoe Nuku Roa, gave us a fairly stark illustration of the state of marae and te reo. Our research team wanted to see what young Māori had to say and how their views compared with this picture. So we now consider the views put to us by young Māori aged between 12 and 23 years old. These arise from 502 surveys and focus group discussions that we carried out in schools in Te Tai Tokerau, and which involved some University of Auckland students.[*] At the heart of the research was our intention to find out the extent of connection or disconnection between young Māori and marae. Are te reo and marae important and, if so, how? We began to answer these questions by asking in the survey:

- the types of schooling they had (whether it was Māori-language medium or mainstream, and how many years they had at these schools);
- whether and how Māori language was spoken in the home and with whom;
- other forums where Māori language was heard and whether they engaged in te reo;
- whether their tribal marae are important and why;
- whether and how often they visited their tribal marae;
- why marae were visited;
- what they knew about their marae; and
- the extent of youth participation in tribal/sub-tribal (iwi/hapū) marae affairs compared to other youth priorities.

The Importance of Marae
Defining 'distinct tribal identity' varied greatly from individual to individual, depending on any number of general factors including upbringing, schooling and degree of connection to home marae and

---

[*] Schools included were Broadwood Area School, Panguru Area School (Te Kura Taumata o Panguru), Te Kura Kaupapa Māori o te Tonga o Hokianga (at Whirinaki; sadly, now closed since mid-2013), Opononi Area School, Te Kura Kaupapa Māori o Kaikohe, Northland College, Bream Bay College and Otamatea College. Six university students participated in the survey.

community. These basic findings arose out of the key question, 'Are hapū marae important?' The students' responses to this question provided a window into understanding what 'tribal' identity might mean. Just over three-quarters of total respondents said marae are important to them. The finding was about the same for the 12–16 age group and the 16–23 age group. Females valued marae slightly more than males: 83 per cent compared to 73 per cent.

Table 10.4: Respondents' key reasons for going to a marae

Key reason	Number of responses	Percentage of all responses
Whānau	123	42.2
Kotahitanga	50	22
Identity, tikanga, history	179	73.99
Brought up on marae	13	5.78
Whakapapa	34	4.6
Learn language	4	1.2
Meeting place	1	0.06
No reason given	8	4.6
Other	17	1.2
Total	420 reasons; 255 responses	

Source: Te Wehi Nui a Mamao survey, 2009

Having established from a simple yes/no answer that marae are a part of life, and possibly a crucial part of life, it was necessary to establish why. It may have seemed obvious to the participants to state that marae are important, but explaining how they are important gives a good indication of connectedness, or lack of it. Basic questions that interested us included: What makes marae critical in the lives of young Māori? How does this measure against other things that they do? And what are the prominent marae values that stand out for them? Although asking students why marae are important was relatively straightforward, obtaining an answer was not necessarily so simple. It required students to be reflective and to think beyond the practical reasons of going to marae because, for instance, parents or caregivers take the family there, or, it is just what you do. Explaining why was difficult, as the number of responses indicated. Of the 502 questionnaires, only half (255) students answered the question. However, of those who did answer, the key reasons can be grouped into six main areas: (1) whānau, (2) kotahitanga (unity), (3) identity, tikanga, history, (4) brought up on marae, and (5) whakapapa. Table 10.4 indicates the relative weighting given to each.

As explained in the examples below, a number of reasons could be given. Not surprisingly, students from both mainstream and Māori-medium schools spoke overwhelmingly (70 per cent) about marae as a source of identity, as a place that gives them a cultural grounding in life and as a place that is integral to their wellbeing. Marae also acts as a place that defines who they were in relation to their tūpuna (ancestors), to their landscape and to each other. A sixteen-year-old from Hokianga more or less summed up these sentiments:

> Because though it is only a house, it is . . . full of spirits of our ancestors, also their histories and their life lies within that secret house. It is significant to me and priceless, without knowing where I am from I would be lost. Pērā i te moa ngaro noa.

'Pērā i te moa ngaro noa' (like the moa that has gone forever) is an apt reminder not only of the centrality of marae to the respondent's world – in 'positioning' or orienting her to what is important in culture and identity – but also of the fragility of marae. The connection that she speaks of also implies that if the marae is important, it calls for involvement in its community and, therefore, some degree of accountability to it. But this might be easier said than done, especially if the road between home and marae drives a geographic wedge between them. 'Keeping the home fires burning' is not so easy. For those who live away, maybe some distance, the moa analogy might act as a reminder of the risk of distance, possible disconnection and cultural loss. Losing connection with marae could also mean losing the context for whakapapa and understanding how people, place and values are interwoven. For those close by and who can engage in marae functions, marae are a vital source of 'community', as one 17-year-old simply stated, 'Because it is where I belong and it's home.'

Although few commented specifically on whakapapa, several reflections about marae inferred it. Marae bridge an ancestral past with the living:

> Because it's where we gather with all of our family and it's who I am and where I am from. Nā te mea tēnā te wāhi o tōku tūpuna.* (13 years old)

> Because I have been there since I was a baby and all of my ancestors have been there before me. (13 years old)

Notably, while several of the participants knew that the marae 'rules' or codes of behaviour (tikanga) are important, these were not really critically discussed. Tikanga was beyond the survey questions and focus group discussions, but it may also have been considered inconsequential – as 'just the way you should do things' – or possibly hard to define. Kaumātua such as Fraser Toi (this volume), Merimeri Penfold (also this volume), Renata Tane and others are concerned that marae rules or practices are not necessarily clear-cut or well understood by the dispersed marae community members. It is particularly a problem if there are few or no knowledgeable kaumātua to provide the guidance. Nevertheless, amongst the participants in the survey, there was a spirit of wanting to 'do the right thing' and give due respect to tūpuna and marae:

> Because we are the generations who have to carry on what our kuia and kaumātua have taught us so that our Māori tikanga wont [sic] be lost like the moa. (16 years old)

> Kia au nei, he tikanga kē te take he wāhi tino nui te marae ki au. He wāhi maumaharatanga ā ō tātou nei mātua tūpuna.† (16 years old)

> It's a place where we can learn our whakapapa and where we're from. (15 years old)

---

* Meaning, 'Because that's the place of my ancestor[s].'
† Meaning, 'To me, the marae is actually the embodiment of custom[;] it is a very important place. It is a place of remembrance of our ancestors.'

> Ko ngā maharatanga ō ōku tūpuna ngā pikitia ō ōku tipuna. Te wairua ki roto. Nō te mea he pai ana ahau ki te noho ki te marae.* (12 years old)

The last comment was by one of the youngest students who nevertheless had already formed strong views about the importance of marae: most likely s/he had been brought up close to it. Marae gave a sense of belonging, identity, and connection to tūpuna, who were remembered in the photographs that hung on the meeting house walls. (Also of note was that the student wrote both 'tipuna' and 'tūpuna', which are different dialectal ways of referring to ancestors.)

Further statements (almost half of those surveyed) give similar pictures of the values expressed so far and emphasise the centrality of marae in bringing together extended family and in affirming kotahitanga (22 per cent). The importance that the students gave to these values varied little between schools:

> My marae is very important in my life, because all my family get together and help the whānau pani [bereaved family]. And when we spend our happy and sad times together. Tino nui tōku marae ki roto i tōku ao, ka haere ahau ki tōku marae i ngā wā katoa kia tautoko ai tōku whānau, ki roto i ngā wā aroha, me ngā wā harikoa. (14 years old)

> Because it's where I learn about tikanga Māori. And it's where all the whānau come together. Ka hono ai te whānau ka whakatinanahia ngā mahi o ngā tūpuna. Ka ako i ngā tikanga Māori.† (14 years old)

> Marae are important to me because we have many family gatherings and we all meet different whānau members each time. (14 years old)

> Because it's the meeting house for the family and we have tangi there. (12 years old)

---

* 'The memories of my ancestors are [represented in] the pictures. The spirit [of the house]. I like to stay at the marae.'
† 'The family joins together and gives substance to the work of the ancestors. [We] learn about Māori customs/laws.'

The marae to me means just another house to me because I practically live up there. I love it up there. It is used a lot for different things, tangi, birthdays, meetings, hakari [feasts]. (12 years old)

Because that's where we have family reunion and get togethers. Ko tērā te tino wāhi mō te whakawhanaungatanga me te kōrero ngā tikanga o te ao Māori.* (14 years old)

Because it is a place where myself and whānau gather for both sad and happy events. A place I can always come home to. Very important to me in many ways. (16 years old)

Because that's where my family is from and I just know that our marae is important to me because my papa told me all about it and he use[d] to take me to visit the marae. (13 years old)

Several accounts demonstrate ease in conveying Māori values in te reo, as expected of those learning in Māori-medium schooling. Schools, especially Māori-medium ones, clearly have an important role not only in promoting te reo, but also in nurturing children in the cultural values that the language embodies. This is a significant reason to promote Māori language in schools. It applies even more to those whose opportunities for learning basic tikanga in marae contexts are limited.

A wider, but related, context for looking at the student responses is to see how many survey participants gave their answers wholly or partly in Māori, and to see what kinds of schools the participants attended (mainstream where English is the teaching medium; bilingual where Māori and English are both used for teaching; or kura where learning is through total immersion Māori).† It might be expected that those at bilingual schools would respond bilingually. Of the participating schools, there were two kura. At one of the kura all students responded in English and te reo. At the

---

* Meaning, 'That is the very place for family unification and discussion of the Māori world.'
† Only those who wrote a sentence or more in Māori were counted. Those who incorporated Māori words into their answers were not counted.

other kura, nine out of 26 gave answers that incorporated te reo. Of those nine, eight answered exclusively in te reo. Although as a percentage fewer students at the second kura answered in Māori or a combination of te reo and English; more answered in Māori only than at the first school. These were the only responses out of the 502 that were in te reo. This tally says something also about the overall low number of students who chose Māori as the preferred language of written communication (and who were responding to the questionnaire written in te reo), and correspondingly, the likely low proficiency in te reo among this group (although some of those who did not answer in te reo may have been able to).

Commitment to fulfilling obligations at marae was also explained by several young Māori:

> Because if someone in your family is there you must go and support your family. Ngā tangihanga mena kua mate tētahi mai i tōu whānau me haere koe ki te tautoko te kaupapa.*

> To me, marae are important . . . because when someone in your family has gone you have the privilege to take your whānau to the marae so the rest of the people can bring their respect and aroha to the tūpāpaku [deceased] and to the whānau pani.

> Because maraes are and [will] always be there waiting if you need to set up a hui or for a tangi.

> Cause marae are like a family gathering place, not only for the spirit or the lost but for the living also. It also feels good working on a marae. (14 years old)

Although the responses shown so far are a small sample, they are fairly representative of views that were expressed by many, if not most, who answered the question. They recognised the inherent duties of belonging to marae: to give, to receive and to repay.

---

* Meaning, 'Funerals, if someone in your family has died you should go to support [the family]'.

By far the main purpose in returning to marae was to attend tangi, with 81 per cent of taitamariki in the Te Wehi Nui project giving this as their primary reason. There was a big jump down to the next statistics: birthday (53 per cent); iwi/hapū meetings (43 per cent); wedding (40 per cent); marae committee meetings (37 per cent); and other reasons (23 per cent). Forty-one per cent said they went not for specific reasons but simply because their parents or caregivers were going and they were expected to go as well. That young people visit marae mainly because of tangi is possibly not a startling revelation. It does indicate, however, not only the continued importance of tangi, but also that marae are not necessarily central in a day-to-day sense and may be peripheral to people's lives. Is this an exaggeration? Are people actually participating in marae relatively frequently? We can consider these questions by looking at numbers again, namely the frequency of visits by the Te Wehi Nui participants:

Table 10.5: Percentage of respondents who visited a marae, by frequency

	Percentage
Weekly	13.9
Once or twice a month	28.3
Every six months	20.5
Once a year	17.5
Never	3.4
No response	16.5
Total	100

Source: Te Wehi Nui a Mamao survey, 2009

The results indicate several things. First, it could be said that a fairly high proportion of taitamariki, just over 42 per cent, attend their marae on a regular basis, i.e., weekly or once or twice a month. Second, if youth who go to their marae every six months or more are also included, then this total proportion increases to just over 62 per cent. This reality is perhaps not so surprising given that the schools have close proximity to marae. Urban-based statistics might give a different picture if Māori youth interviewed were affiliated to marae located out of urban centres.

Compared with the national survey by Te Hoe Nuku Roa in 1999, participants in our project may in fact be more engaged in marae – if we measure this by frequency of visits. However, a third observation is that a relatively high number, 17.5 per cent, said they rarely go to their marae and 3.4 per cent never go. In combination, this represents just over 20 per cent who are moderately to totally disconnected from their marae. (The number could be higher, as just over 16 per cent did not answer this question and some within this group may have limited participation in their marae.) This again has implications for schools and their role in local communities, not least how they might support cultural learning by fostering community relationships. It also has implications for marae and hapū, and for wider iwi authorities that are also seeking to connect to descendant communities. The need to transmit and enliven marae knowledge amongst taitamariki – the next generation of marae trustees – is critical.

New ways of engaging taitamariki with marae-based knowledge and local forms of te reo may be precursors or enticers to participation in marae. In our final section we explore what these new ways could be.

A 'Connected' Solution? Tewehinui.com

Without doubt marae and language are threatened, yet they remain important. The narratives and views expressed by kaumātua and taitamariki participating in Te Wehi Nui, along with statistical analysis, show why we must shape a pathway that has relevance for young Māori. We now live in a digitally 'connected' world and taitamariki perhaps more than any other generation are the most connected – in an internet sense. It is their world. Recognising this and the problems facing many marae communities, our project team began developing the web 2.0 site Tewehinui.com.* It contains kōrero or narratives about regional histories and ancestral landscapes as short film clips, written narratives

---

*   Tewehinui.com is administered by Michael Hennessy (see his chapter, this volume) and Merata Kawharu with the support of the James Henare Māori Research Centre and the Pro Vice-Chancellor (Māori), University of Auckland.

and historical and contemporary images. It promotes discussion on the site's material and plugs a gap in resources of its type (see also Hennessy, this volume, for further discussion of Tewehinui.com).

Creating the website is only one step, though, towards making regional traditional knowledge and language more accessible for taitamariki and others. In the process, there are several issues to address, principally relating to the ethics of managing cultural material on the internet. As explained below, while cultural knowledge may be launched into a new environment – for example, the internet – internet sites (containing cultural knowledge) may not be governed or regulated by cultural controls. In hui we attended, people raised the question of what control communities could have once kōrero is uploaded.* The questions essentially turned on the meaning and value of taonga in a contemporary digital environment.

To put these ideas into further perspective, it is useful to look at what principles of taonga need to be taken into account for Te Wehi Nui, which contains traditional knowledge, to be developed and appropriately maintained on the web.

As widely appreciated, interpretations of taonga are vast.† In principle, taonga may be conceived as any item, object or thing that represents the ancestral identity of a kin group (whānau, hapū, iwi) in relation to particular lands and resources (Tapsell, 2000, p. 13; 2006, p. 17). Taonga feature in numerous ways and include prized, tangible material items (for example, carved waka [canoes], cloaks, greenstone, bone, stone, weapons, pendants and jewellery). Through successive Treaty claims (for example, Motunui, Te Reo and Kaituna), taonga have come to include

---

* See Hennessy chapter for further discussion on the management and intellectual property issues associated with Tewehinui.com.

† In the wake of museum-held taonga being released of their 'curios' interpretation (McCarthy, 2007), a more appropriate appreciation of taonga has developed as a result of two dynamic movements. First, as Mead affirms, the revitalisation of taonga in New Zealand museums was heightened following the Te Māori Exhibition (1992, p. 164). Increasingly the articulation of taonga was reasserted to engage with a developing 'bi-cultural' New Zealand (Museum of New Zealand, 2004). Second, taonga were re-established and redefined in the wider New Zealand conscience through the endeavours of claimants presenting their grievances against the Crown to the Waitangi Tribunal (see, for example, the Kaituna Report, Te Reo Māori Claim, the Flora and Fauna [Wai 262] Inquiry and the Manukau Harbour Report).

ancestral lands (for example, marae, pā, mountains, rivers, lakes) and seascapes. Taonga can also be fundamentally intangible, such as those aspects of mātauranga (knowledge) performed in Māori and civic contexts and embodied in, for example, whakataukī (proverbs), waiata and kōrero (where kōrero include stories, orally transmitted knowledge and narratives associated with ancestors). Taonga may be further considered as spiritual personifications of ancestors (Tapsell, 2000, p. 13; 2006, p. 17). Because of the association of taonga with ancestors and succeeding generations, taonga also represent genealogical layers of mana as well as tapu.

One final concept that has relevance to our discussion of taonga is tuku – the release, allowance, use or giving of an item, land, knowledge or rights to another individual or kin group. These exchanges were commonly signified by the phrase 'taonga tuku iho'. A quality of most taonga was, and continues to be, that they are handed down like heirlooms from one generation to the next (Mead, 1992, p. 164). This is the primary association of taonga with ancestors: 'taonga tuku iho' – literally, 'taonga brought down'.

Taonga, Tewehinui.com: How Do We Deal with Customary Knowledge on the Internet?
If the 1980s and 1990s saw major initiatives like the Te Māori exhibition and Treaty claims entering into the national consciousness as assertions of both Māori identity and the significance of taonga, in the 2000s the growth of digital and internet technology extends taonga further into the wider world. Websites like Tewehinui.com and others like Māori Maps (see Tapsell, this volume), created in this new era, are new mechanisms for reconnecting the diaspora of hapū/marae communities, and in turn reconnecting hapū/marae-based knowledge with these communities.

Tewehinui.com exemplifies the values inherent in taonga. The kōrero contained within this technological kete (basket) that kaumātua and community leaders have provided are in some way concerned with ancestral-based identity, whakapapa, mana and tapu. Tewehinui.com may play a key role in transmitting these kōrero to descendants, like a metaphorical handing down, or tuku, of knowledge. The online discussions may also function according to tuku, or a releasing of ideas and interpretations, thereby building further layers or whakapapa, of interpretations.

Very real challenges face us now, though, because the site disperses mātauranga to a non-local, virtual, community. Knowledge transfer (such as between kaumātua and others) is controlled or closed within whānau or hapū, but this is not generally so in an internet context, where access to information is relatively 'open'. Kaumātua have given their consent for their kōrero to appear on the website; nevertheless they and in some respects their hapū and marae are exposed in an internet environment. Anyone can comment on their kōrero, and this is encouraged through the interactive (web 2.0) nature of the site. Debate or questioning of kaumātua perspectives by young people may not occur when this dialogue is presented on a marae. (Debate certainly occurs on marae on any range of topics, but there are rules or tikanga about how this occurs and who participates.) As a non-customary mechanism for disseminating traditional knowledge to communities, the website does not have the same systems of knowledge control and protection as marae provide. In other words, kaumātua do not have the same role as kaitiaki (guardians) of knowledge that they would otherwise have or perform in contexts such as marae, where mātauranga is customarily activated. Appropriate site and knowledge management processes are, therefore, essential.

A related concern is that mātauranga on the internet may only be partially understood if the broader context out of which it originated is unknown. That, unfortunately, is already the case for customary narratives now finding wide public exposure after being confined or hidden in archives for perhaps many decades. And if kōrero or mātauranga is separated from its original context, any associated mana and tapu may also be lost (Tapsell, 1998, p. 17). Archival material such as karakia (incantations), waiata, haka and pepeha (tribal sayings) may have already lost much of their customary cloak of context before re-entering the public space. Words or names that were spoken and written about long ago – decades or more than a century – may have lost their original significance but be meaningful in other respects now. However, with the challenges of managing information come new opportunities. Customary knowledge, once dormant, may now find new life. By becoming publicly accessible, narratives and knowledge may even become reunited with the source communities. Those communities may then once more take an active custodial role for that knowledge (as well as for knowledge given today) and, therefore, reignite some degree of authority or mana.

Source communities, possibly kaumātua, tribal authorities or other representatives should in principle have a role where information relates to them (see also Michael Hennessy chapter). Kōrero can be protected by controlling access to the site with logins and passwords and by monitoring newly added content. But while these mechanisms aim to protect the integrity of knowledge and associated groups, the site is not risk-free. New information 'upload' and discussion or comment on the site have only periodic monitoring compared to a marae, where control of discussion is immediate and depends on the participants. Although exploitation may be rare, it is still important to have processes that address potential problems, much as for any website, but also since Tewehinui.com concerns tribal identity and mana.

Concluding Comments, or New Beginnings?
Marae are at the crossroads of cultural sustainability. Schools are, to some extent, concerned with supporting local marae through their programmes, engaging with kaumātua and kuia in school initiatives and in marae-based functions. Of course some schools, especially Māori-medium ones, are more active than others. Schools may not be the primary 'agent' responsible for the learning of te mita (local or regional variations and pronunciation) of te reo or cultural knowledge about local ancestral landscapes, but they can make important contributions. Opinions of community elders and results of studies such as Te Hoe Nuku Roa and our Te Wehi Nui project all point to a common concern: widening gaps in cultural and language knowledge. Critical questions are, then: How can marae be relevant in the diverse lives of young Māori, and how can schools help to bridge these gaps? It is these issues that underlie the rationale for developing Tewehinui.com. This and other similar websites may become important cultural and language learning tools within schools and within marae communities.

However, Tewehinui.com – like any website that contains tribally based traditional knowledge – cannot replace marae. Marae function within a community context, which involves the activation of tikanga or protocols by their leaders, especially kaumātua. Like marae rituals of encounter, Tewehinui.com is also about two-way engagement. But the site is not, and cannot be, about preserving the mana of groups in the customary sense. In general, marae performances engage senior representatives of groups, while the website Tewehinui.com can engage all ages, not least the young. Tewehinui.com can, however, contribute to developing an understanding of tikanga, traditional knowledge and language as they relate to marae, and help taitamariki connect digitally with their communities. It can also assist by providing a basic layer of knowledge that will ultimately be important for leadership succession and the performance of marae and hapū representative roles.

There are challenges as well as opportunities in the digital world within which we live. Poia Rewi in his book *Whaikōrero* (2010, pp. 163–182) notes the risks as well as the opportunities of communication through media (like online social media) for maintaining the art of whaikōrero, especially as the greater Māori population lives in cities and may not have the ability to link closely with their marae. And so with the development of Tewehinui.com: it comes at a time when many marae are no longer able to generate culturally sustainable levels of knowledge transfer between their elder and younger generations. However, the enthusiasm and confidence shown by the young Māori in ritually welcoming our team to their schools provides a vital key for marae communities if they are to be vibrant in the lives of their descendants. Tewehinui.com may help to further ignite that enthusiasm. And being connected in the digital sense may lead to being better connected in the tribal sense. Time will tell.

Bibliography

Durie, M., 1999. 'Marae and Implications for a Modern Māori Psychology'. *Journal of the Polynesian Society*, vol. 108, no. 4, pp. 351–366.

Far North REAP (Rural Education Activities Programme), n.d. From: http://www.farnorthreap.org.nz/newsletter%20&%20publications/TRMS%20-%20report%20and%20recommendations.pdf.

McCarthy, C., 2007. *Exhibiting Māori: A History of Colonial Cultures of Display*. Oxford: Berg Publishers.

Mead, H. M., 1992. 'The Nature of Taonga'. *Taonga Māori Conference Proceedings, New Zealand, 17–27 November 1990*, pp. 164–169. Wellington: Department of Internal Affairs.

Museum of New Zealand, 2004. *Icons Ngā Taonga: From the Collections of the Museum of New Zealand Te Papa Tongarewa*. Wellington: Te Papa Press.

Northland District Health Board, n.d. 'People and Population'. From: http://www.northlanddhb.org.nz/Careers/LivinginNorthland/PeoplePopulation.aspx

Rewi, P., 2010. *Whaikōrero: The World of Māori Oratory*. Auckland: Auckland University Press.

Tapsell, P., ed., 2006. *Ko Tawa: Māori Treasures of New Zealand*. Auckland: David Bateman.

——, 2000. *Pukaki: A Comet Returns*. Auckland: Reed Publishing.

Te Hoe Nuku Roa Research Team, 1999. 'Te Hoe Nuku Roa Source Document: Baseline History'. Maori Profiles Research Project, Palmerston North: School of Māori Studies, Massey University.

Te Wehi Nui, n.d. From: http://www.tewehinui.com

Waitangi Tribunal, 2011. 'Ko Aotearoa Tēnei: A Report into Claims Concerning New Zealand Law and Policy Affecting Māori Culture and Identity'. Te taumata tuarua, vol. 2. Wellington: Legislation Direct.

Mauri ora rā ki a koutou ngā ngākau whiwhita, ko **POUNAMU JADE AIKMAN-DODD** tōku ingoa. Although I've lived throughout New Zealand, within both rural and urban landscapes, I consider the Esk Valley in the mighty South Canterbury my home. My whakapapa is just as colourful, with links to Ngāti Maniapoto, Tainui, Ngāi Te Rangi, Ngāti Awa, Ngāpuhi and the great Ngāti Kōtirana in the UK. I study, work and reside in Dunedin, and am completing my M.A. in Social Anthropology at the University of Otago, having completed my B.A. (Hons.) in Māori Studies in 2012.

Māori Studies, which I found to be both engaging and challenging, explored cultural history, language, and indigenous experiences, taking my pursuit of knowledge into the stratosphere of critical thinking. Thus, I am deeply passionate about my focus (anthropology), and enjoy involvement in the academic arena. My master's thesis explores the importance of marae to their descendant and home communities today. Of particular interest to me are the stories of the many people who live far from their marae and tribal homelands, and how their perspectives fit into the phenomenon that is marae. In pursuing my passion of anthropology, I hope to reciprocate the many privileges I have received by continuing to relay the stories of grassroots communities, and by giving volume to the voices of our people and of our society.

CHAPTER ELEVEN

MADE OF MANY THREADS: IDENTITY AS A VIBRANT TAPESTRY

POUNAMU JADE AIKMAN-DODD

To find meaning in life it is necessary to explore, and explore widely. The poet T. S. Eliot, in famous lines from his poem 'Little Gidding', writes of exploration as a ceaseless process in life, and a circular one, in which reaching 'the end' means arriving in the place where we started, but with knowledge that we previously lacked. The idea of exploring can encompass the stereotype of the eager anthropologist far from home 'exploring' an exotic tribal culture or it can describe simply breaking the bonds of routine. My parents have taught me that gaining experience and perspective through exploration is the most important underlying and informing philosophy in life; that it broadens the mind and removes any residue of ignorance or non-understanding. This is what I strive towards. In the exploration here, this brief narrative of my life, I reflect on the desire to continually expand my horizon of understanding and perspective, with a focus on family values and cultural connectedness.

When asked the question 'Nō hea koe?' (Where do you call home?), I find it difficult to provide a coherent answer. Having lived in numerous places as a child, I struggle to identify one specific landscape of particular significance. My genealogy is embedded in the north of both the United Kingdom and New Zealand, descendant of tribes from Scotland, the Waikato Tainui region, and the Bay of Plenty, and so for me this is the best starting point in answering where I hail from and what I identify with. From there, well, it is a long story indeed.

Mum has always reminded me and instilled in me the idea that I 'must learn to walk in both worlds, Māori and Pākehā. In fact, you may need to walk in five worlds, but you know what I mean'. Perhaps it is only now, on completing my undergraduate studies, that I really understand. In growing up in New Zealand, embracing and occasionally rejecting elements of identity has been my experience. Due to the ebb and flow of familial obligations, whānau (family) health, and employment, much of my early childhood was spent travelling. After arriving back in New Zealand from Australia, Mum took me to live with her parents in South Canterbury. From that place and time I will always remember the aged colours of autumn that so matched the wisdom and serenity of my grandparents: the light afternoon breeze would stir the autumn leaves into a dance encircling Grandma and Grandad's house. After I learned to walk on my own, Grandma would take me on expeditions to the central park gardens, or Grandad and I would search for pinecones amongst the discarded foliage of the season.

From the South Island, we moved north to Poverty Bay, before shifting to various suburbs in the expansive metropolis of the Auckland region. Living from Manukau to Ponsonby, I experienced vastly distinct lifestyles and communities where, for example, my company included a retired High Court judge or a television personality – or I'd be with my numerous cousins, all of us bunked down in Nan and Pop's small cork-floored house in the suburbs. After Mum's dad died in the mid-1990s, I spent a lot of time in South Canterbury again, close to Grandma and our other whānau. My sister and I completed our secondary schooling there and then, like many of my form, I left to become (supposedly) enlightened at university.

Mum always explained that travelling around so much would prove invaluable, in learning to adapt to new and unfamiliar environments. I greatly appreciate the truth of her words as I reflect upon the last two decades of my life.

One of my earliest memories is of crawling around the retirement home Mum had recently helped to establish, in Gisborne. While in Poverty Bay, I attended kōhanga reo ('language nest' or Māori-language preschool) from about 1991 to 1995, and became very proficient in speaking Māori. Neither of my parents spoke te reo, and the language of the home was English. Mum was very keen to have me learn Māori and attend the kōhanga. She saw it as important because her generation was largely isolated from Māoridom – especially her family, who grew up in the Queenstown district. When not at kōhanga, I was at the rest home visiting the numerous koro and kuia (elderly folk) in their respective rooms. While, naturally, I of course was motivated by the potential reward of a chocolate or lolly that inevitably lay in the bedside cabinet of these many nannies and poppas, my early years of life were genuinely characterised by the adage that it takes a village to raise a child.

When I was in about J2, Grandma taught me my eleven times-table, and I fondly recall her sitting on the ground with me, exhibiting an incredible and unparalleled patience in describing the intricacies of 11 multiplied by whatever. Grandma is of Tainui and Maniapoto descent. On occasion, if I am fortunate enough, she will recount a few stories of her early youth, in which her grandfather (who was an adviser to the Tainui king) and grandmother raised her in what she describes as 'the old ways of life'. If ever she was sick, Great-great-grandfather would carry her to the water, whereupon he would recite complex karakia (prayers and ritual incantations) and bathe her in the river to heal her illness.

Other memories and stories from my childhood do not evoke such nostalgia. I often felt that some of my paternal family had a tendency to 'other' Pākehā people, almost suggesting a gulf existed between 'them Pākehā' and 'us Māori'. This always made me feel uncomfortable, especially because my maternal grandfather was of Scottish–Canadian descent, something I have always been very proud of. For me, this did nothing more than dichotomise stereotypes of what it meant to be *either* Māori *or* Pākehā, reinforcing a social construct that was divisive in nature. For what does it mean to be either 'Māori' or 'Pākehā' when one's ancestry is embedded in both worlds (something shared by many people today)? Must the choice of identity be presented as two simple categorical opposites?

More importantly: *why can one not be both*? The valuable lesson that all of this has taught me is that whānau and whanaungatanga (familial connectedness) are diverse and multifaceted.

In retrospect, I see that upon moving down to live in the South Island with my grandmother, I rejected (both consciously and unconsciously) many elements of my Māori cultural heritage and identity. This was a partial result of my environment and context. I was one of very few Māori children at my primary school, and I resented the fact that my skin was a different colour than that of my peers. During this time, I modelled my pronunciation of Māori words on teachers and classmates who spoke in a typical New Zealand accent, despite my knowing how to say them correctly. If I linguistically distanced myself from being Māori, perhaps I would turn white! To use more formal language: I consciously diverted my ethnic and cultural identity away from Māoritanga (the essence of what it is to be Māori), and towards the dominant culture expressed by the people in the area I was living.

I did not yet know what 'living in two worlds' really meant. In a similar vein, I did not enjoy going to marae or partaking in marae-based rituals, such as tangi (funeral rituals). Again, it was a representation of Māori identity that I wanted to distance myself from. This was exacerbated as I regarded the marae as a space of death, primarily as a result of my paternal grandfather's tangi in Whakatāne at the turn of the new millennium, when I was ten. Even in secondary school, I was more than content to contribute to negative stereotypes of Māori by propagating racial slurs and jokes that are, I now recognise, deeply offensive. Ironically, during my schooling it was assumed that as I was Māori, I had unqualified authority on things Māori within the school curriculum and cultural activities. This occasionally meant that I was called out of class to direct classroom activity regarding Māori culture, history, or rituals. While I did perhaps possess a slightly wider appreciation of Māori ideas and rituals, more often than not I saw this as a convenient way to dodge a history lesson or astonishingly boring statistics class.

The beginning of my university career heralded a significant change in attitude and mindset. In my first few years of tertiary education, learning the Māori language and culture in an institutionalised setting greatly increased my understanding of Māoritanga. The tipping point for me was the first class of a second-year paper, where my lecturer first uttered the words which put me on the path to pursuing a degree in Māori studies: 'What is whakapapa?', he asked, before explaining that 'whakapapa is, if anything, a philosophy of the universe and all that exists within it'. Almost instantaneously, learning about Māori culture, philosophy, and epistemology became my passion. For the first time, I began to celebrate my Māori identity, finding camaraderie among other Māori students at university. However, after a parenthesis (genuine Māori cultural connectedness had been rare from the end of my time at kōhanga until university), I subconsciously over-compensated in solidifying links to my Māori identity, sacrificing to a degree other elements that had come to define me. I became staunch in my beliefs, to the extent where, for example, I began correcting others for mispronunciation of Māori words. Such behaviour was so blind in its execution that I tended to forget how rude and arrogant I appeared, and Mum had to remind me of this on a few occasions. (Thanks, Mum: you were wise, as always, and I, typically unwilling to listen.) Yet it was during my tertiary studies that I began to appreciate central concepts of Māori culture – specifically, the cultural institution of the marae. I became more interested in philosophies and underpinning values, such as reciprocity, whakapapa and generosity, which were embodied in the rituals and world view surrounding the marae space.

Expanding my mind in an attempt to remove the vestiges of ignorance and arrogance allowed me to appreciate the genius of my ancestors and the culture and values they have come to represent. In most of the latter part of my undergraduate study, I felt I did not need to display Māori cultural connectedness in a staunch or overt way (as I had done previously) because, for me, being an entity of numerous identities did not require me to grasp one identity at the expense of another. Rather, I arrived at the realisation that I am a reflection of my ancestors, from both the northern and southern hemispheres. In this way, I am able to celebrate all that has come to define them, and by extension, to define me. Everything is not black and white, but a kaleidoscope of colour. The anthropology and philosophy of marae fascinate me, and although geospatial distance from my ancestral homelands makes frequenting them difficult, it has not stopped me 'being

Māori'. By the same token, it has not prohibited me from engaging in other elements of my identity. Even now, my connection to Māoridom is not characterised by extensive engagement with tribal identity, but a more pan-tribal ethnic Māori identity. My hapū (subtribal affiliations), marae, and iwi (tribal affiliations) are all-important to me, and despite the tyranny of distance, in the future I hope to be engaged with them and to contribute to their wellbeing. My immediate maternal whānau is the most important thing to me, and beyond that, the other facets of my identity radiate out in correlation to their importance in my life.

For my mother, wairua and aroha (spirit and love) characterised her connection to Māoridom. 'Being Māori' meant spirituality, compassion and love, and she has instilled these in me from the outset. Just as her Māori identity was specific and relative to her, my engagement with Māori identity continues to be an idiosyncratic exercise that is uniquely relevant to me. Although I learnt Māori as a toddler, transitioning into English-medium schools effectively removed it from my mind. Relearning Māori at a tertiary level for the past five years has been challenging, but I now converse with my friends, colleagues, koro, kuia and kaumātua (elders) in te reo.

The common threads throughout my life narrative are the core values espoused by my mother. Mum has always taught me respect, empathy, moderation and justice: to listen before speaking, and to think before replying. I strive to live according to these principles; doing so allows me to walk in the many worlds in which we live, and to celebrate the many nuances of culture. Indeed, my diverse array of ancestors do share similar basic values. Thus, constructing a personal identity does not require a choice between 'either this way or that way', but rather a conscious selection of various modes of identity, relaying their relative importance to oneself as an individual at a particular point in time and space. My tapestry of identity reflects such beliefs that I hold, and is ever changing through life, its crises, and its achievements.

In the words of one of my koro, 'Kua rahi o tēnā: that's enough for now.'

MICHAEL HENNESSY is a producer, director and oral historian. He has worked in the broadcast and media industries for twenty years, producing digital media projects, videos, exhibitions and websites as well as directing television commercials, a TV series, a music album and documentaries.

In the past decade Mike has worked with kaumātua and kuia from around the country, filming and documenting their iwi/hapū oral traditions and histories. Mike lives with his partner and two children in Auckland, where he runs his oral history and digital media consultancy – Ab Ovo. He has a Bachelor of Science (Zoology) and a Master of Creative and Performing Arts (Documentary), and is currently embarking on his doctorate.

CHAPTER TWELVE

NGĀ TAONGA KŌRERO AND THE MODERN WORLD

MICHAEL HENNESSY

Everything is held together with stories. That is all that is holding us together, stories and compassion. – Barry Lopez, 1994

IN HIS BOOK ABOUT THE INDIGENOUS IDENTITY OF AMERICAN INDIANS and New Zealand Māori, Chadwick Allen concludes that indigenous writers and activists of the past century have 'created an interdependent and essentially inseparable triad out of "blood," "land," and "memory,"' and that 'this triad has come to define minority indigeneity, its celebrated past, its contested present, and its imagined futures' (Allen, 2002, p. 220).

It is this triad that encircles the work of oral history recording and oral tradition telling – and it is this same triad that continues to drive the modern multimedia projects and websites that contain traditional knowledge into the future.

Storytelling through oral history and oral tradition dates back to the beginnings of human existence and the development of language. Tales told around the campfire informed the gathered members of a community and schooled them in their family history, their genealogy, their belief systems, their landmarks and their burial sites. This telling of their own stories reinforced individual, family and tribal identity.

Whilst western communities have largely replaced the traditions of oral transferral of knowledge with the written word, many indigenous peoples worldwide still nurture their oral traditions as a touchstone of their identity. And for those tribal communities faced by ever-increasing diasporas and movement into urban areas, the oral tradition remnants that remain – primarily amongst the older community members – have provided the flashpoints of their cultural 'renaissance'.

For Māori communities, various forms of cultural, economic and political renaissance have occurred, particularly in recent years. For example, new economic and cultural initiatives have followed Treaty of Waitangi claim settlements; Māori-language-learning preschools and primary schools; Māori cultural performance; Māori sports and so on. Historically, there was the revival of traditional arts and carving in the 1920s through Sir Apirana Ngata's programmes. Oral tradition, oral history and te reo have been vitally important elements in these cultural renaissance efforts, but the simple fact is that these traditional story-telling methods are struggling to survive in today's society. Quite simply, the haukāinga (local people of the marae) are under pressure to preserve what remains of their traditional knowledge and transfer it to their descendants.

One possible salvation for these tribal communities appears to lie in communicating their cultural traditions to descendants by utilising ever-improving access to the internet and technology in general. Arguably, the opportunities to reconnect with traditional tribal knowledge through these forms of new media are often stronger for urban-based tribe members, than for those living in largely rural papakāinga and on their ancestral landscapes. However, whether they are urban or rural, for younger iwi and hapū (tribe and sub-tribe) members who seek to reawaken or preserve their interest in traditional knowledge and storytelling, this media environment offers a great deal of potential. It can frame this knowledge in a way which prompts them to reconnect with their whakapapa (genealogical narratives) and traditional knowledge. Engagement is useful and meaningful when it ties them back to their land and enables them to recognise their kin-group relationships and ties.

This chapter argues that a key tool for achieving and inspiring re-engagement and re-connection is oral tradition and oral history, presented in new ways for a new generation that is more upwardly mobile and technologically savvy.

An insight into this future can be gained by exploring the research-based journey of the team that I was a part of, the web resource – Tewehinui.com – that we have built to hold and share the narratives that we recorded, and the stories and images that we collected (and continue to collect and upload).

This chapter has several parts. It first discusses oral tradition as a context for addressing intellectual property, ethical and identity issues that are explored throughout the rest of the chapter. It then provides an overview of the filming project that took us to marae and homes of kaumātua (male and female elders) and community leaders. Third, it details differences between oral history and oral tradition to set the scene for considering the material on our website. Fourth, with traditional knowledge as its focus, it discusses the changing dynamics of knowledge transfer.

It is this contemporary reality to which our website responds, by acting as a bridge between home marae and the dispersed descendant communities. In providing traditional knowledge in an online environment, we as creators of the website are conscious of the ethical issues now in front of us. In the fifth part of this chapter, I explore property rights, then in part six discuss Māori intellectual property and the public domain. This leads into part seven where I discuss intangible culture and new media. The chapter ends with some reflections on Tewehinui.com.

New Zealand and other countries with indigenous peoples are at a major crossroads where the digital highway intersects with customary knowledge. We face opportunities but constraints. too, as Kawharu and Tane also outline in this volume. Our web resource offers hope for the future preservation of oral tradition and oral history, at a time when more traditional methods are too often being undermined or compromised by modern lifestyles.

Oral Tradition

In te ao Māori (the Māori world), oral tradition could be considered amongst the most powerful taonga (treasures) that a hapū or iwi can care for. These spoken traditions originate from the time of the first migrations to Aotearoa, and then move forward over a thousand years of settlement – encapsulating the cherished identity of a hapū, their tūpuna (ancestors), the lands that they have lived upon, died on and been buried within.

Today though, only a decreasing number of select elders or community leaders can recite these oral traditions. Where they were once passed down through the members of the community that lived close to the home marae, this population is now scattered. Descendants are no longer exposed to these stories in the same ways they once were. Sadly many of the nuances these oral traditions previously held are passing into the spirit realm with the death of each kuia (female elder) and kaumātua. Stories that are vital to tribal identity are often now confined to written records and/or audio recordings – still valuable and still taonga, but bereft of the subtleties that would otherwise be present in a face-to-face context, perhaps sitting at the feet of the elders and learning them in a 'traditional' manner. It is not that this learning process should necessarily be the same today; that would be a romantic and unrealistic ideal as culture is dynamic and fluid. Rather, the challenge is to maintain the validity and relevance of cultural knowledge amongst a kin-group community that has changed demographically.

Over two years the research team of which I was a member travelled throughout Te Tai Tokerau capturing and documenting the oral traditions of the region's marae communities, and the oral histories of their members, in a project called Te Wehi Nui a Mamao. But rather than creating an historical record for academic study and consigning these testimonies to an archive in Auckland, our goal instead was to re-package our recordings of these treasured histories into a new and more modern environment: an online archive. By recording, protecting and then re-presenting these stories via a website we hoped that youth, in particular, could better engage with them. However we first needed to address concerns over the protection and guardianship of the knowledge and history being filmed. These are addressed later in this chapter.

The Filming Project

Whilst one part of the team conducted surveys and focus groups with young Māori, my role was slightly different. It involved photographing landscapes and documenting on film the stories that surround them. Along with sometimes one or two other researchers on any one trip, I recorded the life experiences and stories of kaumātua and kuia belonging to districts within Te Tai Tokerau – North Hokianga, South Hokianga, Takahiwai (south Whangārei), North Kaipara, Matauri Bay and the Bay of Islands – through filmed oral interview. We conducted these interviews on their marae as well as at family homes at each of these locations, and also in Auckland and Wellington.

Our initial questions for these elders included: What do they remember of marae life from their childhood and upbringing? How much te reo Māori was spoken in those times and where was it spoken? What were (and are) the dialectal differences in their language that set their hapū apart from others? What tribal kōrero (stories) relating to the landscape did they know? How did mātauranga Māori (traditional Māori knowledge) survive? Or indeed has it survived? What have been the challenges of sustaining the marae and tribal knowledge over their lifetimes? Have these challenges changed in recent times?

Soon, however, for many of our participants these interviews became an opportunity to talk to us at a deeper level. Rather than simply providing an oral history of their lives, experiences and perspectives, many desired also to talk to us about marae practice, belief systems and the tribal memory that they held. These were sessions more focused on oral tradition than oral history (to be discussed in the next section), but many participants considered that one could not happen without the other.

This deeper connection did not happen immediately. We spent a significant amount of time contacting, talking to, and sitting with these elders before bringing a camera into the room, let alone turning it on. But as is often the case with oral history practice, once a level of trust or familiarity was reached, we were privileged to be able to listen to and record many hours of tribal memory, which few will have heard. As a result of this evolution, we started moving into new areas of questioning and knowledge gathering. We asked them to tell us about the kōrero that surrounded their landscapes and their marae, the origins of the names for these places, important tūpuna they could remember and what part they played in the history of the tribe, battles and conflicts fought, traditional waiata (song) and karakia (incantations, prayers) that they could remember and the meanings that they held.

The reasons why we were provided with this level of access to tribal memory were not always clear. However, several kaumātua talked about the importance of imparting this knowledge on tape and so ensuring that a record of their knowledge and memories would outlive them. Despite initial reservations some held about losing control of such traditions and knowledge when kōrero was taped, the desire for preservation largely outweighed anything negative.

When recording oral histories, implicit responsibilities are assumed, but also need to be explained. To begin with, the generosity shown by our participants in sharing their kōrero was acknowledged, respected and understood. We then acknowledged that although the recordings would travel with us away from the communities involved, and time would pass before we could make use of them within the context of the project, the stories would remain theirs. By receiving and recording this knowledge, we accepted that we were taking on a kaitiakitanga or guardianship role.

A primary goal of the project was to re-present the filmed interviews to home communities via the website Tewehinui.com. As previously mentioned, by doing so we were seeking to reconnect the young people (and indeed their parents and wider families) with individual memories and tribal heritage, using a medium that they might find engaging – the internet. However, before looking more closely at the website, we should consider in more detail the concepts of oral tradition and oral history as a background to understanding the context for the site.

Oral Tradition versus Oral History

In essence, oral tradition within the Māori world involves transferring both simple and complex messages of tribal knowledge and identity from one generation to the next.

Through whaikōrero and kōrero (formal and informal speech), waiata and karakia, iwi and hapū have maintained their knowledge and unique tribal identity over many generations. It is out of this culturally rich environment that Māori oral tradition has grown. Centre points of Māori oral tradition include stories and explanations of the 'behaviour' of the natural environment and the necessities of daily life; the places to gather food; when to plant; the passing of the seasons; events, battles, marriages and other life celebrations; the reasons why certain places hold certain names and are tapu (restricted; set apart) or are significant and so on.

Although often confused with oral tradition, oral history is significantly different. Whilst oral tradition may be considered to hold deeper meaning and value, oral history is more focused on the recording of the life and times of the speaker, as well as their personal opinions and perspectives of the events that they have lived through. Although oral history is more often than not an eyewitness account of events and a perspective about one's life and experiences, it can also include the family stories, songs and traditions that have been passed down, perhaps through a number of generations.

To further explain, my own maternal family line (Johnstone) has a rich experience of oral history storytelling from its English heritage, and this was centred on my grandfather, who recently died at the age of 90. He was the consummate storyteller, who for the first 35 years of my life I am sure rarely told me the same story twice, unless I asked him to. His stories focused on his own immediate family, his father, mother, brothers, sisters and friends and his World War II experiences. These stories provided a rich tapestry of humour and personal experience, and whenever I visited him he demonstrated to me the art of 'a story told well'.

Conversely my family on my paternal side experienced a dramatic loss of 'story' or oral history, with the death of my other grandfather in the same war. In an instant his own personal stories were largely lost, and whilst the memories of the wider Hennessy family are still retained, they are snapshots and 'grabs' of second-hand oral history from which my own father has fashioned a smaller and primarily genealogical, whakapapa version that now sits within our own small family unit.

This scenario is no doubt familiar to many families across New Zealand, where a rich collection of stories about one's own family exists (or does not). This kōrero is not oral tradition: rather it is oral history.

Indeed, it could be argued that there are very few, if any, oral traditions left within the Pākehā world in New Zealand. The population of primarily Celtic and European peoples living in Aotearoa for perhaps three, four or more generations, and who originate from other lands and peoples, have stories that most often only start when their ancestors first set foot in the country. Links with their original homeland were cut off and largely lost within a few generations. Perhaps the most that exists within Pākehā society is a long series of oral history perspectives and stories that date from their first landfall in this country, but with very little that extends further back than that. Within Pākehā society there are of course exceptions to this generalisation, and I have in my career interviewed some of these families. But they are in the minority.

This historical loss of oral tradition in western society is in part related to the advent of the written word, when the preservation of knowledge and stories was moved from the spoken word to paper. Science, organised religion, the legal system and fundamental economics may also have played a part, creating a world view of ownership and exploitable resources that did not have time for what western society considered the more esoteric aspects of oral tradition. In the New Zealand context though, this loss amongst the Pākehā community is also undoubtedly related to a physical dislocation from original birthplaces, and a desire to forge a life for their families in a new place.

Oral tradition loss has also happened in Māori society. The problems of urbanisation and dislocation from home communities and marae that Tapsell outlines (this volume) are contributing factors. And as communities affected by land loss and poverty sought to improve wellbeing through, for example, Christian-based movements, often oral traditions lost their vibrancy and could not compete with the new value system.

To return to the dichotomy between oral tradition and oral histories: the relationships between these two styles of 'storytelling' are complex and involved. Can an oral history eventually become an oral tradition? And if so, when does this happen?

There are many perspectives on this. Some might emphasise that the stories being told must be held in common by a group of people over many generations – and it is this which distinguishes oral tradition from 'testimony' or oral history. It is of course much more multifaceted than this and it could be said that what was once an oral history can transform into an oral tradition when it is still being told many generations later.

Oral tradition might also be considered to be more about the underlying message and meanings rather than simply the words or description of events themselves. The cultural material that an oral tradition contains is often shared by more than the nuclear family unit and becomes part of the template of a community's identity over many generations. This is unlikely to occur much today where our lives are often urbanised and disengaged from each other; however, in the case of some communities (iwi, hapū and whānau for instance), these 'once were oral histories', dating perhaps from many hundreds of years ago, have now become taonga and are the oral traditions that shape their tribal identity. Similarly, some stories told about tribal leaders and events of today, may become oral traditions to their descendants in times to come.

Although oral traditions do contain the personal stories of tūpuna, they are also redefined and reworked to relate to larger issues such as community ethics, codes of behaviour, identity, political status, tribal landscape and tribal history.

Our project, Te Wehi Nui a Mamao, began with a goal of collecting the oral histories of tribal members and their own personal perspectives on tribal identity, language and cultural survival. However, the project soon evolved into an opportunity to create an 'ark' of hapū and whānau cultural tradition and belief systems which could be preserved for future generations.

Whereas normally oral history interviews are conducted primarily in audio, we filmed our sessions to ensure that we could expand our project beyond the usual verbal forms of communication and into the realm of gesture. Visual actions help to communicate and enhance particular messages, stories and emotions, in parallel with the spoken word.

This use of gesture is particularly apparent in the recording of interviews with kaumātua or kuia, where the kōrero might for instance, include facial expressions or motioning towards 'this mountain' or 'that river'.

Through the documenting of these non-verbal gestures on film, the kōrero itself comes alive and enhances the spoken word, creating nuance and a depth of understanding that may otherwise not exist.

Technology has created opportunity. But it has also delivered challenges that we have had to address. For instance, why were we taking these oral histories and traditions outside of their realms of protection and exclusivity, and into a world where anyone could access them? To understand this dilemma more fully, it is important to consider traditional knowledge and its place in the context of the discussions so far.

Traditional Knowledge and the Changing Dynamics of Transfer

Author Barry Lopez writes of 'the vast and particular knowledge of the Eskimo, garnered from hundreds of years of their patient interrogation of the landscape' (Lopez, 1986). This is one way to describe traditional knowledge, which is possessed and passed on by peoples who are still connected to their roots and their environment. To understand how the passing of knowledge from one generation to the next is changing, we first need to understand what traditional or 'cultural' knowledge is within an iwi and hapū context, and why it is so important. Traditional knowledge typically distinguishes one community from another.

The term 'traditional' preceding 'knowledge' is not to infer that knowledge is static. Like the term 'culture', it is dynamic and is integral to shaping identity. It may also have a deeply personal and spiritual meaning. It intimately connects ancestors with descendants.

Hapū have depended on this knowledge for their economic, social and political survival for generations. As previously stated, it was this traditional knowledge that once encapsulated the norms expected of community members. Traditional knowledge has also provided many kin groups with the impetus to rejuvenate their identity and status. It is this knowledge upon which iwi and hapū increasingly depend for their cultural revival. Moreover, traditional knowledge is undoubtedly having a growing impact on New Zealand society in general in, for example, cultural tourism, education/school curriculum, resource management and planning.

Devon Peña writes of 'traditional environmental knowledge' which, he claims, refers to a 'particular form of place-based knowledge of the diversity and interactions among plant and animal species, landforms, watercourses, and other qualities of the biophysical environment in a given place' (Peña, 2005, p. 29). In New Zealand, iwi and hapū are playing important roles in deciding how land and resources should be used, accessed and managed. Their guardianship is being acknowledged, and they are increasingly exercising such kaitiakitanga through their traditionally based knowledge (Kawharu, 2002). This is a result of the growing involvement of Māori in discussions, policy and decision-making particularly at regional levels, primarily as a result of the Treaty of Waitangi settlement process, and new laws recognising Treaty principles and kaitiakitanga.

This transformation has the potential to take wider societal understandings of the traditional value systems of Māori away from tokenism and into a space where these values and their knowledge may influence everyday life. Such influence is already seen in, for example, district plans that govern how water is used and managed (a topic that was particularly relevant in late 2012, and remains so), how social services are accessed, how our coastline is managed and developed and how we manage our fisheries.

Some observers may point to international academic studies which postulate that traditional knowledge is actually more a reflection of so-called power struggles. Indeed there may be individuals who use traditional knowledge out of context and on occasion exploit 'their' version to enhance the role their iwi or hapū may have played in a particular event. By and large though, traditional knowledge within te ao Māori can be confirmed in marae forums and elsewhere in written form such as the Māori Land Court Minute books and Waitangi Tribunal reports.

Māori, like indigenous communities more generally, value traditional knowledge because of its holistic nature and because of its link with lands and resources. When the Canadian government first informed the Gitksan people in British Columbia that – in its opinion – the government owned their land, the Gitksan replied by asking: 'If this is your land, where are your stories?' (Chamberlin, 2010).

I wonder whether this response could have been made to the New Zealand government by Māori when considering the 2012 discussions on 'ownership' of water. They might have asked the government, 'If this is your water, then where are the stories that demonstrate your rights?'

'Ownership' as a concept when discussing oral traditions or traditional knowledge is fraught with difficulties and needs to be reconsidered in light of tikanga. At the simplest level of understanding, Māori do not have a tradition of 'ownership' over knowledge that resembles western forms of private ownership. Instead there are clear traditions of custodianship over knowledge. Historically, customary law guided who could use different kinds of knowledge at particular times, contexts and places. There are also obligations that accompany the use of this knowledge. In one of our presentations to the home communities towards the end of our project, these challenges became glaringly apparent when we were reminded that the medium we were choosing to re-present their stories back to their communities was not the traditional method of communication by which traditional knowledge was imparted. The same rules and controls (of the marae, see Kawharu and Tane chapter) in relation to traditional knowledge did not apply in the internet site that we were creating. From their perspective, misappropriation and misuse of the knowledge that was freely given by the elders could be offensive.

We were always aware of these sensitivities from the start of our project. Indeed it was part of our kaupapa to be respectful of these views and to respond to them appropriately. Many of our team members also came from these communities, but it was right to be reminded of our obligations and to be told that this knowledge was not ours to use as we wanted. This was not said to us in such direct terms, but the message about protecting the 'intellectual property' or traditional knowledge was made clear. Now, of course, practitioners in this field generally acknowledge that if 'others' are to record and use the traditional knowledge of indigenous and local communities, respect and sensitivity are warranted. These are fairly basic principles to adhere to, but film-makers, academics and others have not always been this responsible. It is not difficult to find community experiences where 'outsiders' have gone into communities, recorded knowledge and left without any sense of accountability.

Critics of traditional knowledge may maintain that such demands for 'respect' are really an attempt to prevent unsubstantiated beliefs from being subjected to the same scrutiny as other knowledge (Muyingi, n.d.). This has particular significance for the management of land where some argue that traditional knowledge is used wrongly to justify any activity, or indeed to try to stop any activity.

A recent example of this might be the efforts in Ngunguru on the east coast of Northland where the local hapū Te Waiariki, Ngāti Korora and Ngāti Taka, as well as other residents, attempted to stop a development that Landco proposed for wāhi tapu – lands set apart or 'sacred' – beneath the mountain Whakairiora (Piper, 2011). The Ngunguru sandspit had long been considered an area of significant archaeological value by the community (both Māori and Pākehā), with pā, terraces, middens, and urupā or burial grounds. As is often the case, however, no comprehensive archaeological survey had been undertaken, with the result that no sites or wāhi tapu had been assessed for registration under the Historic Places Act. To add to the issue, the area was largely in private ownership. Landco and Todd Property Group's proposal prompted objections from not just the local hapū, but also the local community and environmentalists. Over the course of the imbroglio, those in favour of the development disputed whether the traditional knowledge and memories of the local hapū had any significance. However, the combined efforts of the objectors eventually resulted in the protection of the sandspit in 2011 (Piper, 2011). The irony of the whole process, however, was that in four separate assessments from 1982 to 2004, the Ngunguru sandspit was ranked as nationally significant.

As discussed so far, traditional knowledge is important to communities for cultural, economic and political reasons. As creators of an internet site that contains traditional knowledge, we were reminded by participants in our project of the importance of this knowledge, and that we must carefully manage when it is made available in a different environment than that in which it was traditionally passed on (i.e. the marae). These points lead me to discuss intellectual property.

Intellectual Property Rights: An Overview of Issues in New Zealand and International Instruments

Intellectual property concerns have arisen when, for example, traditional knowledge is used out of context. Publicly prominent cases relating to the 'ownership' and protection of Māori traditional knowledge include the haka *Ka Mate*, the rapidly expanding prevalence and adoption of tā moko (tattooing), and the use of traditional design on inappropriate media (such as watches and cigarette packets). Māori have largely resisted or have been wary of the misuse of traditional knowledge and designs used in things like logos, fashion and advertising. They have also been unhappy at the patenting of traditional uses of medicinal plants by companies or others who have not consulted or obtained consent from local communities. Similarly, Māori have strongly argued against the copyrighting of their tribal stories and narratives without their consent. These examples are all in some way concerned with the protection of traditional knowledge.

Māori have also wanted greater protection and control over traditional knowledge and resources, as argued in, for example, the Treaty of Waitangi claim commonly known as 'Wai 262' (Milne, 2011; Waitangi Tribunal, 2011).* Where control has proven difficult, tribal groups have sought to ensure that their traditional knowledge is used fairly and within the boundaries and restrictions defined by them.

Intellectual property laws and instruments have been emerging in recent times to preserve, protect and promote traditional knowledge, so it is useful to briefly survey some of these.

The international Rio Declaration on Environment and Development (1992) broadly recognises indigenous and local communities as distinct groups with special concerns that should be acknowledged and addressed (United Nations, 1992). The Convention on Biological Diversity (CBD, also 1992) recognised in particular the close relationship many indigenous and local communities have to their resources, and the importance of traditional knowledge in the use of these resources.

---

* This informal name for the claim relating to culture, identity, flora and fauna comes from the Waitangi Tribunal claim number.

As a result of these and many other initiatives, the collective human rights of indigenous and local communities were increasingly recognised over subsequent years, culminating in the Declaration on the Rights of Indigenous Peoples (United Nations, 2007). In New Zealand, after a lack of support from the previous Labour Government, the new National Government with the support of the Māori Party eventually ratified the declaration in 2008.

This is broadly the landscape into which our project entered, and while our engagement with community members was open and honest – with our intentions and kaupapa clearly expressed – there was, by some initially, a cautiousness about fully engaging with us or perhaps seeing the value of our work. In the early days, at a hui in the southern Hokianga, some iwi members expressed reservations about us recording their tribal knowledge. This was despite some of our team coming from those tribal groups. Their concern was that this knowledge should remain exclusively within the tribe, and control and mana would be forever lost if it was recorded and taken away from these home communities.

The inherent difficulty with the process we were involved in comes back to the issues outlined at the start of this chapter: the marrying of Māori and western value systems. The intellectual property 'system' uses ideas and terms that are incompatible with traditional Māori concepts; for example, it favours the commercialisation and 'ownership' of such traditions and knowledge. Concepts of ownership were naturally resisted by the iwi and hapū with whom we spent time and they were instead concerned to ensure that their knowledge would be protected according to a system of trusteeship or kaitiakitanga.

Te Wehi Nui website and similar sites which disseminate essentially traditional knowledge are governed by western law. However, in order to be truly successful, western laws and indigenous lores need to work together in projects such as these, so that kōrero is properly protected.

Māori Intellectual Property and the Public Domain: A Broader Context

Despite the contrasting approaches that western law and Māori guardianship have towards protecting knowledge, Māori recognise the usefulness of the western systems and are keen to work with them to ensure that the uniqueness of their identity is retained and not wrongly commercialised or lost. Control and protection are particularly important in the digital age where the online delivery of content is becoming more ubiquitous, and historical audio and video collections are finding a pathway out of the archives and towards a modern audience.

In the public realm, the traditional television and radio channels have been, by default, the collectors of oral histories and tribal knowledge for many years. Interviews conducted as part of programmes produced since the 1970s now hold the hidden treasures of a generation of kaumātua. *Waka Huia*, first broadcast in 1987, has since delivered more than 500 hours of programming, with many more hours of interviews in the archives. Originally devised as an archival series to document te reo and mātauranga of the elders, this collection has now become a taonga of considerable value. Other repositories of mātauranga include the collections of Radio New Zealand, Archives New Zealand, the National Library of New Zealand, the Archive of Māori and Pacific Music at the University of Auckland, as well as institutions such as Te Papa Tongarewa and the Auckland War Memorial Museum. Michael King's and Barry Barclay's landmark six-part series *Tangata Whenua*, first broadcast in 1974, and the archives of Radio New Zealand, museums, libraries and production companies together hold thousands of hours of interviews. These are in varying states – some languish on problematic formats with many others held in unsuitable conditions and therefore, subjected to ongoing degradation – but they are nevertheless taonga for the knowledge they contain and the connection they provide to individuals and to ancestors. Many of the recordings that do have physical protection do not necessarily have a tikanga-based layer of protection where elders or community representatives have a role in their preservation and use. Tribal communities often do not have knowledge of where repositories are, let alone any say over how their contents are 'used' by institutions, not least because it is the institutions that *legally* own the archives.

Recorded Traditional Knowledge and Re-presentation on the Internet: Issues for Te Wehi Nui

It is important to ask: how can the physical and the metaphysical essence of these resources and recorded taonga be properly protected, and by whom? We considered these questions before production of Te Wehi Nui began. We approached the interviews with the attitude that we were merely the means by which these oral taonga could be recorded and preserved. Our role was to gather kōrero (once permission was granted) for the benefit of present and future generations, and to manage the information appropriately, whilst it is slowly disseminated.

The following opinion, from a First Nations people in the United States, provides a guide to institutions who are in possession of traditional knowledge such as theirs:

> No matter how old it is, or whether the interviewees have long since passed on, these resources will always belong to the people and tribes from which they have sprung. The Tulalip Tribes of Washington State have said that . . . open sharing does not automatically confer a right to use the knowledge (of indigenous people). . . traditional cultural expressions are not in the public domain because indigenous peoples have failed to take the steps necessary to protect the knowledge in the Western intellectual property system, but from a failure of governments and citizens to recognise and respect the customary laws regulating their use. (Graber and Nenova, 2008, p. 174)

Related to these issues of protection, and directly informing our work in this project as discussed above, are questions concerning the use of these recordings within a purely digital environment: should they be on the internet for all to see?

A primary benefit of the internet for disparate Māori communities is the ability to access knowledge and information on their traditional tribal communities that would otherwise be hard to retrieve. For example, reports from the Waitangi Tribunal are available online and are valuable resources for research into whānau, hapū and iwi history. This ease of access contrasts with the levels of effort required when accessing physical copies of manuscripts and Native Land Court minute books, which are often old and at times hard to find and to read. Online Māori dictionary and language sites generally act as a guide for people searching for the meaning of Māori words and help with the maintenance of basic Māori-language greetings. Tribal websites provide basic information and knowledge specific to a kin group. Websites administered by the Ministry of Culture and Heritage, such as *Te Ara Encyclopedia of New Zealand* and 'New Zealand History Online' (http://www.teara.govt.nz and http://www.nzhistory.net.nz.), contain historical knowledge and also deliver general information on tribes. There are, however, no websites providing detailed traditional knowledge that would inform a descendant on the nuances of their own tribal heritage.

Te Wehi Nui attempts to address this internet-based knowledge gap. It does not aim to replace local, community-based sources, nor does it contain detail such as genealogy or ancestral land sites or other knowledge that is more appropriately locally held and possibly closed. The site aims to be an information tool used by schools, communities and kin groups; one that complements traditional forms of marae-based discussion and communication. It is not a replacement for the traditional means of knowledge transfer, but in the absence of close connections with home marae communities, the website provides an opportunity for learning; in a sense, an ark of rediscovery.

The site provides a pathway or bridge of discovery particularly to youth or urban-based descendants who, as the progeny of the diaspora to the cities or overseas, have grown up away from their tribal homelands and marae. It opens a door and provides a safe environment within which they can in some way reconnect with their tribal communities, learn something about their ancestral landscapes and listen to some of the elders and leaders who work and live in their tribal homelands today. The site is a bridge between cultural knowledge and those who may be 'entering' tribal communities for the first time, or those who may be re-engaging after an absence.

Although Tewehinui.com and other Māori sites, like those mentioned above, aim to educate, revitalise and recognise traditional knowledge, there are sceptics about the advantages of the internet. Alastair Smith (1997), for instance, believes that the way digitised objects (such as videos, images and manuscripts) are treated on the internet produces more harm than good because there are 'few controls' on how they are used. Although we believe that this is not the case with Tewehinui.com, we agree that it is necessary to consider concerns about intellectual property rights, loss of control of information, accuracy and authority, as well as access to the internet.

For example, when the Auckland Art Gallery first placed the digitised portraits of rangatira (tribal leaders) painted by Gottfried Lindauer on its website in 1996, this concerned some Māori who felt that there should have been consultation with descendants beforehand (Smith, 1997). In another (offshore) example illustrated by Smith, a US tattoo site displayed an image of preserved moko mōkai (preserved Māori heads) hung on meathooks (Smith, 1997). Indeed even now, an online search for 'mokomokai' reveals many images that Māori would find upsetting and offensive.

Smith, however, accepts that the internet provides 'an attractive method for communication by indigenous peoples', and that Māori are 'making increasing use of this capability' (Smith, 1997). The main priorities are to somehow ensure active and positive input from Māori communities and perhaps most importantly, to ensure that they simply have access to the web so that they can contribute to the wider discussions on the proper use and care of their customary knowledge on the internet. And indeed it should be noted that the Auckland Art Gallery has since launched an award-winning website devoted to Lindauer's portraits, which involved considerable consultation with descendants.

A key challenge for our team was how to effectively reach the target audiences. Many Māori have limited access to the internet, particularly if they are rurally located and do not have broadband or cannot afford it. However, schools and community facilities are fast becoming more 'connected', particularly as the government, telecommunications companies and indeed rūnanga (tribal councils) themselves continue to roll out broadband cabling to enable all children and their parents to learn via the internet.*

The new media environment offers considerably more opportunities to preserve, protect and communicate elements of traditional knowledge and intangible culture than ever before. Further, these opportunities outweigh the negative possibilities, if sites are carefully built and managed.

Intangible Culture and New Media

Intangible culture is that part of a culture that is not physical but which involves thought, memory and action such as song, music or performance and – in the context of our project – traditionally held knowledge. To provide an example from a Māori perspective: while tangible culture might be a carving, or the physical taonga itself, intangible culture is the traditionally held knowledge that informs the carver, which he brings to the creation of the taonga and subsequently passes on to his descendants.

Online indigenous mapping resources and websites such as Te Wehi Nui provide a means by which some of this knowledge can be stored, preserved and passed on. As the World Intellectual Property Organization puts it, new technologies 'offer enhanced means to safeguard and restore intangible cultural heritage, especially elements in danger of erosion and disappearance. They can also facilitate educational and scholarly opportunities, as well as enhanced cultural exchange' (World Intellectual Property Organization, 2010, p. 16).

These new web-based tools and technologies build upon and can sometimes even replace traditional tools used by earlier ethnographers and anthropologists; who through the written word, camera and sound recorder documented the intangible culture of indigenous peoples, creating a cultural record that now resides in the collections of institutions around the world.

---

* For information regarding the government's broadband policy in rural areas, see http://tvnz.co.nz/politics-news/govt-signs-off-rural-broadband-proposals-3418256.

The foundation stones of the Māori cultural renaissance that many consider to have been underway for the past 30 or so years are shaped by intangible culture. It is this culture that has informed and supported the Te Wehi Nui a Mamao project and the resulting website Tewehinui.com, which contains regional language (te reo), proverbs (pepeha), waiata, karakia and oral history.

Returning to the question posed at the start of this chapter: who gave us the right to record and preserve this intangible culture in the way we have, and to present it back to the world via this new website? The simple answer is that the communities did. Marae communities recognised an opportunity that they could control – by agreeing to the filming and transference of their kōrero onto the website – and thereby create a resource that they could make use of.

While our New Zealand experiences guide us in matters such as those discussed above, international examples provide further perspective.

Intangible culture in recent years has been classed a 'human treasure' by the United Nations (Kurin, 2004). As early as 1950, Japan established a law protecting intangible culture (Agency for Cultural Affairs of Japan, 2009). Although this was possibly more a national response to US occupation and intended to preserve Japanese culture as a whole, rather than to protect the cultural identities of their indigenous populations such as the Ainu, it still places Japan apart from most other countries.

In 2003, UNESCO adopted the Convention for the Safeguarding of Intangible Cultural Heritage and in 2006 the convention came into effect for those countries that had adopted it. Primary amongst other intangible culture programmes is the Proclamation of Masterpieces of the Oral and Intangible Heritage of Humanity. This list, which began in 2001 with nineteen items, now numbers more than 150 (Agency for Cultural Affairs of Japan, 2009). As yet, there is nothing from New Zealand.

The World Intellectual Property Organization (WIPO, mentioned above) has devoted considerable effort to securing the 'effective protection of traditional knowledge (TK), traditional cultural expressions (TCEs) and genetic resources (GRs)' in international law (WIPO, n.d.). Specifically, it provides 'assistance to communities and cultural institutions wishing to record, digitise and disseminate their traditional music, performances, art, designs and other creative expressions of traditional cultures for safeguarding, promotional and commercial purposes' (WIPO, n.d.[b]).

In the context of the discussions so far, our project is riding the crest of a technology-driven wave where the institutionalised paradigms of ownership and control are being re-imagined. The essential and spiritual elements of the kōrero have not been diminished by our recording of these histories, and we are working towards ensuring that the participating communities can assist in overseeing the resource that they have created with us. We aim to establish a management committee and a trust entity. By doing so, we hope to make certain that misappropriation and misuse of the resource does not happen, and that the conventions governing access and usage include rules derived from customary laws and practices.

Although the technologies we are using with Te Wehi Nui a Mamao are providing the participating communities with a fresh opportunity to document and to digitise expressions of their intangible culture and traditional knowledge, we are acutely aware that this process can leave their cultural heritage vulnerable.

As this project progresses, it documents the oral traditions that are at the heart of these communities as well as the history that is happening now. The strong desire that they feel – to preserve, promote and pass on their cultural heritage to succeeding generations – matches our own. Intellectual property issues infuse all aspects of our daily life working in this world, whether we are recording, collecting, cataloguing or disseminating.

Another international example gives us a further perspective to reflect on the value of our work, and look to its future use.

A New Oral History: A Case Study
The First Nations of North America have a long tradition of preserving history and culture through oral storytelling, such as the tale of Crazy Horse, a war leader of the Oglala Lakota during the late nineteenth century (NASA, n.d.).

Where Words Touch the Earth is a video documentary series of 15-minute episodes sponsored by the US space agency, NASA, in which students from First Nations communities documented the environmental changes observed by their elders over the years. NASA scientist David Adamec came up with the idea for the project when he visited the Crazy Horse monument in South Dakota and wondered, 'Why not take advantage of the information contained in oral history and combine it with the climate resources we have at NASA?' He wanted the students 'to tell their stories – that's the only way you're going to get a jewel' (NASA, n.d.).

The students controlled the production of each episode and its content. They were responsible for every single aspect of the documentary, from researching and writing, to directing, camera work and editing. In 2008, students from Haskell Indian Nations University in Lawrence, Kansas filmed a segment. The result was an episode that explored dramatic changes observed in the plains ecosystem. In another location students from the Northwest Indian College in Bellingham, Washington portrayed how climate change has affected the salmon populations of their coastal lands. And elsewhere, tribal colleges in New Mexico, North Dakota and Wisconsin are beginning to film desert, prairie and woodland environments respectively. These student films are reaching and educating students across the United States.

At the same time, a production house started working with the Bureau of Indian Education providing digital content for students and teachers, involving themselves at the 'intersection between traditional tribal communities and science education' (NASA, n.d.). Eventually an online collection was launched that 'disseminates re-purposed versions of the documentaries' (NASA, n.d.) for integration into the school curriculum, allowing teachers to download short clips, essays and other content. The exchange goes both ways. 'We might have assumed a disconnect between the traditional tribal community and hard science, but there's not,' one contributor said. 'Being connected to tradition doesn't mean you can't be a scientist' (NASA, n.d.).

Today the interaction continues between the tribal communities and NASA, and they are creating a new oral history. This may indeed contribute to the sum total of knowledge of the tribes and may itself in time start to inform the oral traditions of the tribe that are remembered generations from now.

Te Wehi Nui a Mamao: Some Reflections

Ultimately, our hope is that iwi, schools and communities will take over a degree of 'ownership' of Tewehinui.com. By allowing for this transfer of guardianship over the site, the kaitiaki of the knowledge contained in this digital environment – who are actually the descendants of these oral histories – are able to be directly responsible for the kōrero and be responsive to current knowledge needs.

In time we hope for such levels of engagement that the participating communities start to produce content supporting, or adding another layer in the interpretation of, the knowledge we have uploaded. Of course, as this process continues, discussions may move in directions that we cannot conceive of now.

At the launch of the initial beta website in 2010, I sat with a member of one of the communities, who could immediately see the potential of the site to contain information on gardening, seasonal planting and food gathering. He imagined his students listening to the stories told by their elders and then uploading their own responses and experiences to add to the sum total of knowledge available. It is responses such as this which inspire us to continue working towards a site that provides a true online representation of some of the history and traditions of the marae communities.

Too often over the years, traditional oral history projects, interviews and productions have collected stories only for them to be boxed and, in some cases, lost. Libraries, museums, archives and backrooms are filled to overflowing with reel-to-reels, audio cassettes, camcorder tapes, VHS and Beta tapes, DV tapes, mini-DVs, DVDs, and CD-ROMs. The list seems endless and many of these interviews, particularly with indigenous communities, are degrading with every year that passes. Instead of drawing on 'grabs' of this content for a documentary, or transferring excerpts from an abstract or transcript into a book, we need to rework these treasures and bring them back to life again, as well as to film and record our own stories from the history that is happening now. If we do not change our approach to these treasures, then we end up with bite-sized pieces of a culture that is devoid of nuance and increasingly homogenised. Rather than losing the oral nature of these interviews at an early stage, practitioners within this field (ourselves included) need to support the descendants to rediscover the heritage contained within these recordings and to move confidently towards an identity that they can recognise and be comfortable in.

Cultural, economic and political renaissance within the Māori world has undoubtedly occurred in recent years. Yet our ongoing research indicates that tribal descendants throughout Aotearoa continue to experience a cultural crisis that cannot be ignored. There continue to be considerable difficulties retaining te reo and native speakers. Individuals who have knowledge of tribal histories, genealogies and narratives and who are also fluent speakers of te reo, are dying. In the home communities, marae are increasingly bereft of people, resources and knowledge, with their relevance in a modern world being challenged with every year that passes. Marae communities want to reconnect with their descendants, but they may not have the resources to do so. Fewer and fewer hapū members have sufficient time or opportunity to listen to oral traditions in a marae context. It is these circumstances to which Te Wehi Nui a Mamao responds, providing a modern-day strategy that goes with the change of paradigm.

At the start of this chapter, I alluded to the fact that it is waiata, karakia and kōrero that wrap around tribal history and geneology, and have provided iwi and hapū with the foundation stones of their cultural identity. Despite the intent of our project, however, we fundamentally accept that the transfer of deeper traditional knowledge must still happen face-to-face, in a secure and controlled environment.

A bigger question still remains: how do tribal communities and practitioners such as ourselves open the door to those younger members of the tribe who are increasingly dislocated and physically distant from their marae, and assist them to step across the threshold on a journey towards cultural reaffirmation? Te Wehi Nui a Mamao creates a new framework within which te ao tawhito, the old Māori world, is talking once more to its descendants; through a digital environment.

It is not everything, and it is not the whole solution. But it is a start.

Bibliography

Agency for Cultural Affairs of Japan, ed., 2009. 'Protection System of Intangible Cultural Heritage in Japan'. Japan: Asia/Pacific Cultural Centre for UNESCO.

Allen, C., 2002. *Blood Narrative: Indigenous Identity in American Indian and Māori Literary and Activist Texts.* Durham: Duke University Press.

Chamberlin, J. E., 2010. *If This Is Your Land, Where Are Your Stories? Finding Common Ground.* Canada: Vintage Canada.

Graber, C. B., and Nenova, M. B., 2008. *Intellectual Property and Traditional Cultural Expressions in a Digital Environment.* Gloucester: Edward Elgar Publishing.

Intercultural Institute of Montreal, 1992. 'Living with the Earth: Conference Proceedings'. Montreal, Quebec: Intercultural Institute of Montreal.

Kawharu, M., 2002. *Whenua: Managing Our Resources.* Auckland: Reed Publishing.

Kurin, R., 2004. 'Safeguarding Intangible Cultural Heritage in the 2003 UNESCO Convention: A Critical Appraisal'. *Museum International*, issue 56, pp. 66–77.

Lopez, B., 1986. *Arctic Dreams: Imagination and Desire in a Northern Landscape.* New York: Vintage Books.

——, 1994. In: A. Evans, 'Leaning into the Light: An Interview with Barry Lopez'. *Poets and Writers.* March/April 1994, vol. 22, issue 2.

Milne, J., 2011. 'Wai 262 and Maori Ownership Rights'. *New Zealand Listener.* October 1–7 2011, issue 3725. From: http://www.listener.co.nz/commentary/wai-262-treaty-claim-and-maori-ownership-rights/

Muyingi, Hippolyte, N., n.d. 'IPR for IK and the Survival of IK in the Emerging Global Village'. From: http://www.ir.polytechnic.edu.na/bitstream/10628/292/1/Muyingi.%20IPR%20for%20IK....pdf

NASA, n.d. 'A New Oral History: Where Words Touch the Earth'. From: http://www.nasa.gov/topics/earth/features/climate-oral-history.html

Peña, D., 2005. *Mexican Americans and the Environment: Tierra Y Vida.* Arizona: University of Arizona Press.

Piper, D., 2011. 'Ngunguru Sandspit Celebration'. *Whangarei Leader.* From: http://www.stuff.co.nz/auckland/local-news/northland/whangarei-leader/5525657/Ngunguru-Sandspit-celebration

Smith, A., 1997. 'Fishing with New Nets: Maori Internet Information Resources and Implications of the Internet for Indigenous Peoples'. Paper presented at INET'97, Kuala Lumpur, 24–27 June 1997.

Te Wehi Nui, n.d. From: http://www.tewehinui.com

United Nations, 1992. General Assembly. 'Report of the United Nations Conference on Environment and Development'. Rio de Janiero. Principle 22. From: http://www.un.org/documents/ga/conf151/aconf15126-1annex1.htm

——, 2007. United Nations Permanent Forum on Indigenous Issues. ECOSOC. DESA. From: http://social.un.org/index/IndigenousPeoples/DeclarationontheRightsofIndigenousPeoples.aspx

Waitangi Tribunal, 2011. 'Ko Aotearoa Tēnei: A Report into Claims Concerning New Zealand Law and Policy Affecting Māori Culture and Identity'. Te taumata tuatahi. [Commonly known as 'Wai 262'] Wellington: Legislation Direct.

World Intellectual Property Organization, n.d. Intergovernmental Committee, summary of mandate. From: http://www.wipo.int/tk/en/igc/

——, n.d.[b]. 'Intellectual Property and the Safeguarding of Traditional Cultures: Legal Issues and Practical Options for Museums, Libraries and Archives'. Written for WIPO by Molly Torsen and Jane Anderson, 2010. From: http://www.wipo.int/export/sites/www/freepublications/en/tk/1023/wipo_pub_1023.pdf

——, 2010. 'International Symposium on Intellectual Property and Traditional Knowledge, Traditional Cultural Expressions and Genetic Resources: Towards Sustainable Development for Indigenous Communities'. Draft concept note prepared by the International Bureau, WIPO, 20 October 2010.

ACKNOWLEDGEMENTS

Tuatahi, ko ngā mihi ki a rātou kua waihotia ngā tapuwae i te mata o te whenua. Nā rātou i tuku te tōmairangi o te māramatanga, nā rātou i tuku te wero ki a mātou kia mau te tikanga o te marae, kia mau tonu te reo. Tuarua, ka hoki ōku mahara ki ōku mātua, ki a Freda rāua ko Hugh. Kua māturuturu iho ā kōrua nei hua me ngā ritenga o te ao Māori ki ahau. Moe mai kōrua. Tae noa ki tēnei wā, ko ngā mihi tuatoru ki ngā kaumātua, ki ngā kaituhi me ngā ihu oneone kua whakatinanahia te pukapuka nei. He mihi nui, he mihi maioha ki a koutou, ā, tēnā koutou katoa.

Maranga Mai! has been a journey and an emergence of a team of some special people over the past five years. It has been more than just editing a book. There are many I would like to acknowledge, not least those kaumātua and other leaders who welcomed our research team and me into their worlds when we travelled throughout Tai Tokerau between 2008 and 2013 to undertake much of the research that underpins these pages. Ko ngā mihi nui ki a Merimeri Penfold (contributing a chapter), Joe Cooper, Bobby Newson, Kevin Robinson (also contributing a chapter); John Klaricich, Ben Morunga, Helen Edwards, Hirini Wikaira, Patu Hohepa and South Hokianga people, and Fraser Toi (also an author in *Maranga Mai!*); Anaru Martin; Mere Kepa, Luana Pirihi and Patuharakeke, Deborah Harding, Te Tuhi Robust, Renata Tane and Nau Epiha. I'd also like to acknowledge schools throughout Tai Tokerau including Broadwood Area School, Te Kura Taumata o Panguru, Te Kura Kaupapa Māori o te Tonga o Hokianga, Te Kura Kaupapa Māori o Kaikohe, Northland College, Bream Bay College and Otamatea High School, all of whom welcomed us. They were central to the Te Wehi Nui research project discussed throughout this book.

Special thanks also to Jim Peters, Pro Vice-Chancellor (Māori) at the University of Auckland, who has supported *Maranga Mai!* over these years, along with Kori Netana. Raaniera Te Whata, Mereana Te Whata and Jane McRae gave excellent translation expertise. Claire Gummer and Anna Hodge provided editing finesse and guided the book into the publishing world. Katrina Duncan lent her brilliant design skills to the project and Krzysztof Pfeiffer's photographs provide beautiful windows into Tai Tokerau. And Sam Elworthy, thank you for encouraging me to persist with 'getting it right'. I would also like to thank the Royal Society of New Zealand for their financial support to publish. Finally, Paul Tapsell and Hirini Tane, both of whom have also contributed material to the book, have been the patient and wise 'thinkers' who have come up with great ideas when I come to full-stops. Kia ora rawa atu koutou katoa.

INDEX

Page numbers in *italics* refer to text in te reo Māori.

agriculture 47, 48, 49–50
ahi kā (keeping the home fires burning) 182, 197, *see also* haukāinga (home people of the marae)
āhu (coral slab wall of Pacific marae) 40, 41, 42
   in Aotearoa 43, 44
ātea (basalt plaza of Pacific marae) 40, 41
   evolution into semi-ritualised public leadership space 42, 44
atua (gods, great ancestral beings) 43
Auckland Art Gallery, digitisation of Lindauer portraits 237
Auckland Maori Catholic Society 142
awa (rivers) 74, 88, 89, 120, 122

babies in wharenui, changing tikanga 136–137
Bay of Islands (Pēwhairangi) 47, 114, 223
Bay of Plenty 48
bee school, Kaitāia 100, 192
Benton, Richard, *The Māori Language* (NZCER survey) 2, 75, 76, 78, 80, 115
bilingualism 148, 149, 151, 154, 160–161, 168
   education 110, 111, 116, 117, 119, 121, 143, 191, 200
Bledisloe, Lord 50

census data 4, 5, 72, 76, 141, 146, 149, 151, 159, 190
children, *see* tamariki (children)
church and religious activities, te reo usage 80–81, 142
Church Missionary Society 114
cities, relocation to, and city life 36, 51–52, 57, 59, 65, 67, 75, 98, 99, 132, 142–143, 166–167, 182, 188–189, 190, 192, 202, 208, 220, 226, 236

colonisation, impacts 46–49, 50, 51, 58, 103, 104
Community Based Language Initiative 143
Convention on Biological Diversity 232
Cook, James 43, 46
cross-cultural encounters, Māori and early Europeans 46
culture
   global culture 169–170
   intangible culture, and new media 238–241
   language key to perpetuation of culture and knowledge systems 103, 108
   Pacific based 37, 38, 40, 41, 42, 50, 58
   role of schooling in regeneration 108–113
culture, Māori 175, 178, 181–182, 220, *see also* mātauranga Māori (Māori knowledge, world view); tikanga Māori (custom, correct procedure); wānanga (tribal knowledge)
   marae-based 15, 26, 129–137
   and native schools system 115
   teaching in Maori-medium schools 110, 112, 116–117, 119

Department of Education, *see* Education Department/Ministry
diglossia 106
dispute resolution, declining use of marae as a forum 177–178
Durie, Sir Mason 193

education, *see also* Māori-medium education; schools
   bilingual 110, 111, 116, 117, 119, 121, 143, 191, 200
   compulsory 109–110, 115
   early childhood 109, 110, 117
   Te Tai Tokerau: historical context 113–117

Te Tai Tokerau: today 117–118
Education Act 1877 115
Education Act 1989 116
Education Department/Ministry 3, 109, 112–113, 116, 132, 143
   Ngā Haeata Mātauranga – Annual Report on Maori Education 110
Education Ordinance 1847 114
elders, *see* kaumātua (male elders); kuia (female elders); leadership (rangatiratanga)
English language, New Zealand
   code mixing 84, 85, 86
   imposition on Māori 108, 142
   most commonly used language 146, 147, 150, 167
   spoken by Māori 148, 150, 154
   use of Māori words 85
essentialism 72–73
ethnic population distribution, Aotearoa 144–146, 151
ethnolinguistic vitality theory 73

Far North (Te Hiku o Te Ika) 11, 12, 14, 22, 25, 100, 117, 144, 185
   languages spoken 154–155
   te reo use 11, 22, 163, 164, 165, 166, 167
First Nations of North America 235
Where Words Touch the Earth, collaboration with NASA 240–241

generations, differences in te reo spoken at home 81–82
global culture 169–170
grandparents, role in revival of language and culture 5, 80, 81, 82, 116, 191, *see also* kaumātua (elders)
greetings, *see* harirū (greetings); hongi (pressing of noses); mihimihi (formal greetings)

hā (breath) 85, 86
haka 45, 206
   Ka Mate 232
hākari (celebratory feast) 45, 85, 200
hapū (communities) 4, 6, 22, 43–44, 47, 48
   guardianship and transmission of cultural knowledge and values 74, 103–104, 121, 192, 228–229, 231, 233
   impact of colonisation 48–50, 58
   kin support necessary for survival 58–60
   and Maori incorporations 49–50
   realignment as iwi 46–47
   and taitamariki/rangatahi (young Māori) 74, 88, 89, 90, 120, 121, 122, 203
   te reo revitalisation 140–141, 143, 144, 155, 159, 177
   and Treaty settlements 54–55, 59
harirū (greetings) 131
haukāinga (home people of the marae) 56, 59, 188–189, 220, *see also* ahi kā (keeping the home fires burning)
Heke, Hone 48
Henare, Sir James 2, 66, 68, 132, 181
Hokianga 47, 97, 98–99, 135, 156, 157, 168, 184, 185, 190, 223, 233, *see also* Motutī Road, Hokianga
hongi (ritual greeting) 45
Hongi Hika 47, 113–114
hui (meetings) 89, 107, 120, 122, 136, 185, 188, 201, *see also* tangihanga

identity, bicultural 211–216
identity, Māori
   cultural markers 88–90
   and marae 2, 5, 36, 42, 55, 57, 58, 59, 98, 196, 197, 199, 215
   and mātauranga Māori (Maori knowledge, world view) 225, 227, 228, 234, 243
   pan-tribal 216
   taitamariki/rangatahi (Māori youth) 73, 87–88, 169, 184, 195–196
   and te reo 2, 5, 66, 68, 71–94, 169, 177
indigenous languages, *see also* te reo Māori
   and academic success 108
   as a basic right 103, 176
   diglossic existence 106–107
   Graded International Disruption Scale for Threatened Languages 106

indigenous languages *(cont.)*
   intergenerational
      transmission 105–106
   key to perpetuation of culture and
      knowledge systems 103, 108
   regeneration 104, 105–108
   role of schooling in loss and
      regeneration 104, 108–113
indigenous traditional knowledge 228, 229, 235, 238–240
integration policy, government 142
intellectual property rights 232–233
   Māori intellectual property and the public domain 234–235, 237
intergenerational transmission of language 105–106
   te reo Māori 80, 81–82, 116, 139
internet
   connection opportunities 57, 59, 100, 106, 182, 203, 205
   and intangible culture 238–240
   and te reo ability 155
   Te Wehi Nui website 72, 74, 91, 123, 203–208, 221, 224, 233, 236–237, 238, 239, 240, 242–243
   transmission of mātauranga Māori: risks, benefits and protection 206–208, 221, 228–231, 233, 235–238, 239, 240, 243
   websites containing information for and about Māori 144, 235–236, 237
iwi (people, extended kinship group)
   dialects *13*, 24
   economic development 175, 178, 186, 192
   guardianship and transmission of cultural knowledge and values 66, 68, 103–104, 112–113, 121, 175, 228–229, 233
   hapū realignment as iwi 46–47
   partnership with Ministry of Education 112–113
   percentage of Māori population who do not know their iwi 5
   Recognised Iwi Organisations (RIOs) 54–55
   and taitamariki/rangatahi (young Māori) 88, 89, 90, 120, 121, 203
   te reo revitalisation 140–141, 143, 144, 155, 159, 176, 177
   te reo use within and between iwi groups 159–166, 168–169
   world views 66, 68

James Henare Māori Research Centre, University of Auckland 6, 68
Japan, law protecting intangible culture 239

Ka Mate haka 232
kaikaranga (female leader who performs customary calls) *21*, 31, 99–100, 130, 133, 134, 136
   utilisation of young, inexperienced wāhine 134
kaikōrero (speaker) *18*, 28–29, 65–66, 67–68, 130–131, 135, *see also* taumata (representative speakers)
kāinga (home marae communities) 36, 43, 51, *see also* papakāinga
   Tiriti o Waitangi concept 52
Kaipara district 104, 117, 151–152, 167, 185, 186, 223
kaitiakitanga (guardianship, stewardship) 224, 229, 230, 233, 234, 242
kapa haka (cultural group) performances and activities 6, 79, 87–88, 90, 91, 121
karakia (incantations, prayers) 107, 206, 213, 224, 225, 239, 243
karanga (formal ritual calls) 6, *15*, *21* 26, 31, 99, 107, 134, 185, 188
kaumātua (elders) 3, *11*, *12*, *16*, *18*, *21*, 26, 28–29, 32, 44, 45, 65, 67, 74, 80, 91, 98–99, 106, 129, 130, 131, 132–135, 155, 177, 184, 208, 234
   declining numbers 132, 133–134, 135, 137, 182, 187–190, 192, 198, 222, 243
   manuhiri kaumātua 135–136, 187
   Te Wehi Nui a Mamao project 223–224
   transfer of knowledge via internet 206
   tūturu kaumātua 135
   views on te reo learning 191–193
kāuta (cooking area) 133, 134
Kawharu, Sir Hugh 52

Kawiti 48
keri poka (grave diggers) 133
kete kōrero (kits of knowledge held privately) 130
kete mātauranga (kits of worldly knowledge) 130
knowledge, *see* indigenous traditional knowledge; mātauranga Māori (Māori knowledge, world view); wānanga (tribal knowledge)
kōhanga reo (Māori-language preschools) 109
   children entering English-medium primary schools 109
   closures 3, 52, 190
   establishment 76, 116, 135, 143, 159, 181
   and family learning 191
   implications of downward trend in provision and enrolments 123–124, 191
   and mātauranga Māori 119–121
   numbers of children attending 3, 91, 110, 117
   numbers of children going on to bilingual classes 121
   numbers of children going on to kura kaupapa 121
   and regional te reo and tikanga 191
   and te reo ability 11, 17, 22, 27–28, 77, 82, 109, 119, 120, 155, 213
   Te Tai Tokerau 117, 119–121, 123–124
   Tiriti o Waitangi claim 3
kōrero (talk, discussion) 133, 134, 139, 183, 205, 206, 207, 225
kōrero hītori (traditional stories) 74, 88–89, 90, 91, 130, 155, 205, 206, 213, 219–222, 223–224, 225, 230, 243
   intellectual property concerns 232, 235, 240
   non-verbal gestures 227–228
kotahitanga (unity) 54, 196, 197, 199
kuia (female elders) 16, 26, 44, 45, 74, 99, 106, 130, 131, 132, 135, 137, 155, 184, 222
   Te Wehi Nui a Mamao project 223–224
kura kaupapa Māori (Māori-language primary schools) 3, 4, 5, 75, 110, 112
   establishment 76, 116, 135, 143, 159, 181
   implications of downward trend in provisions and enrolments 123–124
   and mātauranga Māori 122, 123
   need for more kura, managed or overseen by Māori 176–177
   numbers of students attending 4, 91
   numbers of students who attended kōhanga reo 121
   and regional te reo and tikanga 191
   and te reo ability 17, 27–28, 77, 78, 82, 83–84, 121, 122, 123, 155, 176, 200–201
   Te Tai Tokerau 117–118, 119, 123–124, 171
kura-ā-iwi (Māori immersion schools adhering to identified iwi tikanga or dialect) 110, 111
Kurahaupō 12, 20, 22, 31

labour force, Māori 47, 49, 52
land
   alienation of Māori from land and resource base 49–50, 51, 52, 98, 226
   Ngata's schemes 49–50
   traditional knowledge 231
land wars 49–50, 58
languages, *see also* English language, New Zealand; indigenous languages; te reo Māori
   spoken by Māori 148
   used in Aotearoa 146–147
Lapita peoples 37–38
leadership (rangatiratanga)
   rangatira (kin leaders) 43, 44, 47, 59, 237
   and te reo 129–137, 191–193
leadership (rangatiratanga), and marae 21, 31, 42, 43, 44, 53, 58, 59, 187–190
   female leadership 20–21, 31, 132–133, 137
   younger generation 5–6, 133–134, 137, 187, 208

Mahaiatea marae, Tahiti 41
mana (prestige, respect) *16*, 27, 45, 48, 51, 52, 54, 58, 133, 205, 206, 207, 208
mana whenua 56
manaaki (hospitality) 51, 54
manaaki manuhiri (looking after guests) 98–99, 188
manaakitanga (duties of care and hospitality) 130, 187
manuhiri (guests) *16*, *20*, 26, 31, 130, 134, 135
mānuka honey business, Te Rarawa 100, 192
Maori Land Court minute books *19*, *29*, 47, 229
Māori language, *see* te reo Māori
Māori Language Act 1987 76
Māori Language Commission, *see* Te Taura Whiri i te Reo Māori (Māori Language Commission)
Māori-made mark 181
Māori-medium education 2, 76, 88, 91, 104–105, 106, 108, 109–113, 143, 181, *see also see also* kōhanga reo; kura kaupapa; puna reo; wānanga (Māori tertiary institutions)
 basic learning, fine-tuned within marae community 191
Matawaia Declaration 116–117
mission schools 114
 and te reo ability 3, 4, *11*, 22, 155
 Te Tai Tokerau 114, 115–116, 119, 123–124
 teaching of cultural knowledge 112, 119, 123, 191, 200, 203, 207
Māori Maps project (www.maorimaps.com) 2, 7, 9, 36, 43, 55–57, 205
Māori Television 2, *11*, *18*, 22, 29, 80, 181
marae, *see also* identity, Māori, and marae; leadership (rangatiratanga), and marae; papakāinga (home marae communities)
 balancing marae and day-to-day responsibilities 182, 188
 changing roles and protocols 132–137
 in crisis 1–2, 5, *21*, 31–32, 51–55, 182, 243
 and declining numbers of elders 132, 133–134, 135, 137, 182, 187–190, 192, 198
 declining use as forum for dispute resolution 177–178
 digital connection opportunities 57, 59, 100, 182, 192–193, 205–208
 and identity of Māori 2, 5, 36, 42, 55, 57, 58, 59, 98, 196, 197, 199, 215
 kin support necessary for survival 58–60, 98, 182, 197, 201
 'national marae', Waitangi Treaty Grounds 50
 Ōrākei 52–53
 rebuilding and rejuvenation 5, 50, 51, 181
 role in iwi and hapū learning 74, 88, 89, 90, 99, 121, 185–186, 191–192, 207–208, 243
 role in recovering wellbeing 54, 197
 role in te reo learning 79, 107, 186, 191–192
 rural marae 52, 98–101, 184, 185, 187–190
 school support of marae 185, 190, 207
 and taitamariki/rangatahi (young Māori) 5, 57, 58–59, 60, 85–86, 88, 89, 90, 121, 122, 182, 185, 195–203, 208
 and tamariki (children) 133, 193–194
 Te Rarawa marae 98–101
 Te Tai Tokerau 55–57
 tikanga *18*, *21*, 29, 31, 44–45, 129, 130–137, 188, 198, 199, 207–208
 and Treaty claims and settlements 5, 54–55, 59, 181, 184–185, 186–188, 192
 tū marae (protocol) *16*, 27
 urban marae 52, 185
 usage of term in New Zealand English 85
 whanaungatanga 187
marae, ancient origins 36–42, 58
 continuous transformation 41
 evidence of ritual space resembling marae 38–39
 matua (parent) marae 40
 navigationally associated marae complexes 40, 41–42
 traditional creation story 39

transformation into complex, highly
    ritualised spaces 40
values associated with land distinct
    from oceanic resources 41
marae ātea 40, 41, 42–43, 44, 58, *see also*
    ātea (basalt plaza of Pacific marae)
marae, evolution in Aotearoa 42–51, 58
    hapū development of marae 43–44
    unifying role during negative
        experience of colonisation 49–51
Marion du Fresne, Marc-Joseph 46
market gardens 47
Marsden, Maori 52
mātauranga Māori (Māori knowledge,
    world view), *see also* wānanga
    (tribal knowledge); and individual
    aspects of mātauranga Māori, e.g.
    whakapapa
  hapū guardianship and
    transmission 74, 103–104, 121,
    192, 228–229, 231, 233
  and identity 225, 227, 228, 234, 243
  internet transmission: risks, benefits
    and protection 206–208, 221,
    228–231, 233, 235–238, 239, 240,
    243
  iwi guardianship and transmission 66,
    68, 103–104, 112–113, 121, 175,
    228–229, 233
  language barrier to transfer of
    knowledge 90
  only te reo can capture the
    essence 20, 30
  'ownership' 230, 233
  taitamariki/rangatahi (young
    Māori) 71, 72, 74–75, 85–86,
    88–91, 104, 119–124, 182, 222, 224,
    236, 243
  as taonga 205, 227, 234, 235, 238
  whānau guardianship and
    transmission 74, 84, 89, 103–104,
    191
Matauri Bay 223
Matawaia Declaration 116–117
maunga (mountains) 74, 88, 89, 91, 120,
    122
Maungawhau pā 46
mauri (life force) 85, 86
mihi whakatau (formal welcome) 131,
    134, 135

mihimihi (formal greetings) 44, 77, 84,
    183
Ministry of Education, *see* Education
    Department/Ministry
missionary stations, and pā 47
moa, as analogy for loss of te reo and
    identity 72, 84
mokopuna (grandchildren, young
    children) 56, 57, 82, 136–137, 155,
    197
mōteatea (songs of lament) 75, 77, 131,
    137
Motutī Road, Hokianga 97–101
musket wars 48
muskets
  impact on pā and hapū 46, 47
  and literacy 113–114

National Certificate of Educational
    Achievement (NCEA) 108
Native Schools Act 1867 114–115
Native Schools Code 1880 115
navigation, Pacific ancestors of
    Māori 36, 37, 38, 39, 41
  ancestrally encoded 40, 41–42
New Zealand Council for Educational
    Research (NZCER)
  Māori Unit 116
  survey of te reo (Benton) 2, 75, 76, 78,
    80, 115
New Zealand Curriculum 124
Ngā Haeata Mātauranga – Annual
    Report on Maori Education 110
Ngāi Takoto 12, 22, 161, 162, 186
Ngāpuhi 13, 18, 24, 29, 35, 36, 65, 67,
    113–114, 130, 133, 134, 161, 162,
    163, 164, 187
Ngāpuhi ki Whaingaroa 161, 162, 163,
    164
Ngata, Sir Apirana 49–50, 51, 220
Ngāti Kahu 12, 22, 161, 162, 163, 164,
    165, 166
Ngāti Kahu ki Whaingaroa 161, 162,
    163, 164, 165, 166
Ngāti Kahungunu 3
  Cultural Standards Project 112
Ngāti Koata 3
Ngāti Kurī 15, 16, 20, 25, 26, 27, 31,
    161, 162, 163, 164, 165, 166, 169,
    187

Ngāti Murikahara 12, 22
Ngāti Poneke Young Māori Club 142
Ngāti Porou 3, 15, 25, 113
Ngāti Wai 161, 162, 163, 164, 165, 166
Ngāti Whātua 161, 162, 163, 164, 165, 166, 169, 186, 187
Ngāti Whātua ō Ōrākei 52–53
Ngunguru sandspit 231
noa (freedom from restriction) 45
Northland, *see* Tai Tokerau

ora (wellbeing) 54
Ōrākei claim 52–53
oral history 219, 220–221, 239, 242
   differences from oral tradition 224–228
   responsibilities when recording 224
   television and radio recordings 234–235
oral tradition 219–222, 223, *see also* kōrero hītori (traditional stories)
   differences from oral history 224–228
'ownership' 230

pā, *see also* papakāinga
   impact of firearms 46
Pacific basalt-terraced elevations 41, 42, 43
   part of marae evolution 42
   protection of marae ātea 42–43
   sighted and recorded by early Europeans 46
   tapu as a result of sickness and death 46
   transformation from hilltop to lowland pā 47, 58
   Tupaea's and Cook's descriptions 43
Pacific ancestors of Māori
   cessation of Māori contact with East Polynesian communities 43
   exploration and colonisation of Pacific 37, 38, 41–42
   Lapita peoples, Near Oceania 37–38
   navigation 36, 37, 38, 39, 40, 41–42
   new oceanic expansion, out of marae-centred culture 41–42
   trading 37
   wave of exploration into Remote Oceania 38
pā–kāinga, *see* papakāinga

pan-Māori organisations 52
papa, *see* pā
Papa tū ā Nuku (Earth Mother) 39
Papa tū ā Nuku (Pacific island groups) 40
papakāinga (home marae communities) 43, 47, 220
   economic isolation from lands 49, 50, 51, 58
   kin support necessary for survival 58–60
   migration away from 36, 51–52, 59
   Te Tai Tokerau 56
Pārengarenga 12, 19, 20, 23, 30
Patukoraha 12, 22
pepeha (tribal sayings) 19, 29, 74, 77, 84, 88, 89, 90, 91, 120, 121, 182, 206, 239
'pepper potting' policy 142
Pēwhairangi, *see* Bay of Islands (Pēwhairangi)
Pōhurihanga 12, 20, 22, 31
population, Māori 144–145, 146
   Te Tai Tokerau 151, 189–190
post-modern theory of language and identity 72
post-Treaty governance entities (PSGEs) 59
pōtiki 33
pōwhiri (welcome) 44, 107, 184
preschools, Māori-language-learning, *see* kōhanga reo; puna reo
Proclamation of Masterpieces of the Oral and Intangible Heritage of Humanity 239
Proto-Austronesian class of peoples 37
Puhitīare 12, 22
Pukana television programme 87
   ngā puna kōhungahunga (play groups) 109
puna reo 3, 109, 110

Queen Victoria School, Auckland 13, 23

radio, Māori 2, 181
   promotion of te reo and culture 2, 144, 234
rangatahi, *see* taitamariki/rangatahi (young Māori)

rangatiratanga, *see* leadership (rangatiratanga); tino rangatiratanga (sovereignty, self-determination)
Rangihoua 114
Ranginui (night sky heavens) 40
Ranginui (Sky Father) 39
Rātana Church *14–15, 21,* 25–26, 31, 58
recessions 52, 53, 58
Recognised Iwi Organisations (RIOs) 54–55
religious activity, te reo usage 80–81
renaissance, Māori 75, 143, 175, 176, 178, 220, 239, 243
reo Māori, *see* te reo Māori
reo rua (bilingual school units) 110, 111, 143, 191
Reversing Language Shift (RLS) 105–106
ringa wera 136
Rio Declaration on Environment and Development 232
Rūatoki 116
rumaki (Māori immersion units in schools) 110, 111, 118, 143
rural areas
  impact of recessions 52, 53
  marae 52
  and new media 220, 237
  Ngata's schemes 49–50
  Te Rarawa communities 98–101
  and te reo 75, 112
  Te Tai Tokerau, pre-World War II 141–142

schools, *see also* education; kōhanga reo; kura kaupapa; Māori-medium education; puna reo
  internet access 237–238
  mission schools 114
  native schools system 114–115
  potential to take over or regenerate socialising functions of families 107
  role in decline of te reo 2, *12, 17, 23,* 27, 104, 108–109, 114–115, 116, 132, 142, 170
  role in language and cultural regeneration 108–113, 124, 184, 200, 203, 207
  studying te reo as a separate subject 111, 118–119, 120
  te reo heard frequently in mainstream schools 79–80
Sinoto, Yoshiko 41
social networking and media 57, 59, 182, 208
social welfare, government policy 99
socio-economic status of Māori 49, 53–54, 226
Statistics New Zealand 4, 76, 141, 145
stories, traditional, *see* kōrero hītori (traditional stories)

Tai Tokerau 6, 46, 55–57, 59, 89, 104, 105, 112, 130, 133, 134, *see also* Te Wehi Nui a Mamao project; and names of individual iwi and places
  boundaries 104
  Māori population 151, 189–190
  numbers of te reo speakers 148–150
  return home of families who have spent some time away 185, 191
  schooling: historical context 113–117
  schooling: today 117–118
  strategies for revitalisation of te reo 144
  study of te reo use by tamariki 139–171
  Te Puni Kōkiri report on health of te reo 77–78
  te reo use by district, age, iwi and gender 150–169, 170–171
Tai-nui marae, Tahiti 41
taitamariki/rangatahi (young Māori)
  identity 73, 87–88, 169, 184, 195–196
  leadership potential 5–6, 133–134, 137, 187, 208
  and marae 5, 57, 58–59, 60, 85–86, 88, 89, 90, 121, 122, 182, 185, 195–203, 208
  mātauranga Māori 71, 72, 74–75, 85–86, 88–91, 104, 119–124, 222, 224, 236, 243
  te reo 71, 72, 73, 74, 75, 76–88, 90–91, 106, 156, 157, 158, 176–177, 182, 200–201
tamariki (children)
  allowed into wharenui during tangihanga 133

INDEX · 255

tamariki (children) *(cont.)*
  apprenticeships, marae and rituals 133
  frequency of visits to marae 193–194
  future 2
  influence of global culture 170
  living away from marae 99
  te reo ability *17–18*, 28, 155, 156, 157, 158, 162, 163, 164, 165, 168, 169, 170–171
  Te Tai Tokerau population 189
tāngata whenua (local people; people of the land) 39, 45, 52, 130, 155
Tangata Whenua television programme 234
tangihanga (funerals) *15*, 26, 44, 50, 98–99, 100, 107, 130–132, 136, 188, 199, 200, 201, 202, 214
  children allowed into wharenui 133
  and nursing mothers 136–137
taonga (ancestral treasures) *15–16*, *19*, 26, 29, 30, 45, 204–207, 221–222, 227, 234, 235
tapu (sacred, restricted) 40, 41, 43, 44, 45, 46, 134, 136–137, 205, 206, 225
  lifting speeches at tangihanga 134
Taputapuatea marae 40–41, 42
Taranaki 48
taumata (representative speakers) 133, 134, 135–136, *see also* kaikōrero (speaker)
  manuhiri kaumātua 135–136
  utilisation of young, inexperienced tāne 134–135
Tawhiwhirangi, Dame Iritana 181
Te Arawa *16*, 27, 44
Te ātaarangi language schools 143
Te Aupōuri 161, 162, 163, 164, 165, 166
Te Hāpua *12*, *13*, *14*, *15*, 22–23, 24, 25, 26
Te Hiku o Te Ika, *see* Far North (Te Hiku o Te Ika)
Te Hoe Nuku Roa study 193–194, 203, 207
Te Kawerau 161, 162, 163, 164, 165, 166
Te Kōhanga Reo National Trust 109
te mita o te reo, *see* te reo Māori – regional dialects (te mita o te reo)
Te Paepae Motuhake, 'Te Reo Mauriora' 66, 68

Te Potiki National Trust 56
Te Puni Kōkiri 76, 77–78, 141, 159, 171
Te Putahitanga Mātauranga 112
Te Rarawa *12*, 22, 97–101, 161, 162, 164, 165, 166, 186, 187, 192
Te Rauparaha 47
te reo Māori, *see also* kaikōrero; kōrero; Māori-medium education; mōteatea; pepeha; radio, Māori; television; waiata; whaikōrero; whakataukī
  and age group 3, 78, 155–158, 162–165, 167–168, 169
  code mixing 84, 85, 86
  colonisation impacts 103, 104
  competitions 5–6
  decline and crisis of 1–2, 5, *11*, *17–20*, 22, 27–30, 65–68, 90–91, 175, 178, 243
  decrease in numbers of fluent speakers 4, 65–66, 67–68, 72–73, 75, 77–78, 115, 163, 164, 167–168, 175, 182, 243
  diglossic approaches 107
  formulaic (ritual) 83, 84
  and gender 141, 162–164, 165–166, 167, 169
  and global culture 170
  and identity of Māori 2, 5, 66, 68, 71–94, 169, 177
  intergenerational transmission 80, 81–82, 116, 139
  and leaders 191–193
  and mātauranga Māori 20, 30
  places heard most frequently by taitamariki 78–81
  regional dialects (te mita o te reo) 3, 4–5, 6, *13*, 24, 74, 91, 99, 100–101, 112, 113, 182, 191, 204, 207, 239
  revitalisation 3, 75, 143–144, 159, 171, 181
  role of schooling in loss 2, *12*, 17, 23, 27, 104, 108–109, 114–115, 116, 132, 142, 170
  spoken in homes *12*, 17, *21* 22, 27–28, 32, 65, 66, 67, 68, 79, 80, 81–82, 116, 171, 177, 191, 192
  statistics of use by Māori, in total, by geographic region and by

iwi 148–150, 151, 159–165, 167, 168–169
statistics of use in Aotearoa 146, 147
studying as a separate subject at school 111, 118–119, 120
taitamariki/rangatahi (young Māori) 7, 71, 72, 76–88, 90–91, 106, 156, 157, 158, 176–177, 182, 200–201
tamariki (children) 17–18, 28, 155, 156, 157, 158, 162, 163, 164, 165, 168, 169, 170–171
Te Rarawa programme 100–01
Tiriti o Waitangi claim 2, 73, 75–76, 191, 204
and transfer of knowledge 90, 116
wairua 18, 19, 29
te reo Māori me ōna tikanga (Māori language and associated customs) 11, 12, 16, 19, 26, 29, 87, 112, 116–117, 124, 184, 191
Te Reo Mihi marae 14–15, 25, 26
Te Reo o Te Tai Tokerau 144
Te Ringamaui 12, 22
Te R.I.T.O. Māori project 112
Te Roroa 135, 161, 162, 163, 164, 165, 166
Te Tai Tokerau, see Tai Tokerau
Te Taura Whiri i te Reo Māori (Māori Language Commission) 2, 4, 76, 141, 143, 159, 171
Mā Te Reo fund 143
Te Uri-o-Hau 161, 162, 163, 164
Te Wehi Nui a Mamao project 71, 74–75, 76–88, 105, 117, 118–124, 183, 188, 195–203, 209, 222, 223–224, 227, 239
Te Wehi Nui website 72, 74, 91, 123, 203–208, 221, 224, 233, 236–237, 238, 239, 240, 242–243
Te Whānau Moana 12, 22
television
  influence on youth 87
  promotion of te reo and culture 2, 11, 18, 22, 29, 144, 155, 181, 234
  use of te reo 79, 80, 87, 107, 155
tikanga Māori (custom, correct procedure) 16, 26, 65, 66, 67, 68, 77, 79, 87, 99, 112, 116, 129, 130, 184

knowledge of taitamariki/rangatahi 72, 74
marae 18, 21, 29, 31, 44–45, 129, 130–137, 188, 198, 199, 207–208
te reo Māori me ōna tikanga (Māori language and associated customs) 11, 12, 19, 21, 22, 29, 31, 87, 112, 116–117, 124, 184, 191
tuakana/teina 130
Tinirau-Hui-Mataitepapa marae complex 41
tino rangatiratanga (sovereignty, self-determination) 48, 51, 55, 178
Tiriti o Waitangi 47–48, see also Waitangi Tribunal
centenary 50
Tiriti o Waitangi claims and settlements
  cultural initiatives 220
  and economic development 192, 220
  impact on marae and leadership 5, 54–55, 59, 181, 184–185, 186–188, 192
  and involvement of Māori in policy and decision-making 229
  kōhanga reo claim 3
  Ōrākei claim 52–53
  and taonga 204–205
  te reo Māori claim 2, 73, 75–76, 191, 204
  Wai 262: flora and fauna claim 232
tohunga (customary specialist) 39
tohunga āhurewa (revered navigator, spiritual specialist descended from navigators) 42, 43
trade, Māori 47–48
Treaty of Waitangi, see Tiriti o Waitangi
tūāhu, see āhu
tuakana/teina tikanga 130, 135
Tuhawaiki 47
Tūhoe 16, 27
tuku 205
Tupaea 40, 43
tūpāpaku (deceased) 85, 201
tūpuna (ancestors) 15, 19, 26, 30, 65, 67, 83, 84, 89, 120, 122, 129, 136, 137, 197, 198, 199, 205, 222, 224, 227
tūrangawaewae (place to stand) 84

ūkaipō (birth place) 130
unemployment 52, 53, 99

INDEX · 257

UNESCO Convention for the Safeguarding of Intangible Cultural Heritage 239
United Nations Declaration on the Rights of Indigenous Peoples 233
urban migration and life 36, 51–52, 57, 59, 65, 67, 75, 98, 99, 132, 142–143, 166–167, 182, 188–189, 190, 192, 202, 208, 220, 226, 236
urupā (cemeteries) 74, 120, 122
utu (payment, reciprocity) 45, 215

wāhi tapu 231
wāhine (women), *see also* kaikaranga (female leader who performs customary calls of welcome); kuia (female elders)
    female leadership on marae 20–21, 31, 132–133, 137
waiata (songs) 16, 21, 26, 31, 44–45, 75, 77, 87–88, 89, 90, 91, 107, 120, 122, 184, 205, 206, 224, 225, 239, 243
Waikato 48
Waiora marae 15, 26
wairua (spirit) 18, 19, 29, 134, 216
Waitangi Tribunal 75, 229, 236, *see also* Tiriti o Waitangi claims and settlements
    focus on Recognised Iwi Organisations (RIOs) 54–55
waka 45
Waka Huia television programme 234
wānanga (learning opportunities) 89, 136, 186
wānanga (Māori tertiary institutions) 2, 110, 116, 143, 181
wānanga (tribal knowledge) 42, 44, 58–59, 112, *see also* mātauranga Māori (Māori knowledge, world view)
wānanga reo (week-long immersion courses) 143
websites, *see* internet
Weriweri pā 46
wero (ceremonial challenge) 44
Whaia te Iti Kahurangi partnership 113
whaikōrero (formal speech exchanges) 6, 16, 18, 21, 26–27, 29, 31, 98–99, 107, 130, 185, 188, 208, 225
    decline of/challenges for 21, 31, 65–68, 188, 208
whakairo (carvings) 50
whakapapa (genealogy) 12, 20, 22, 30–31, 45, 53, 54, 89, 130, 159, 168, 183, 196, 197–198, 205, 212, 215, 220
whakataukī (proverbs) 16, 27, 74, 75, 77, 84, 88, 89, 90, 91, 205, 239
Whakatupuranga Rua Mano (Generation 2000) 143
whānau (family) 49, 50, 54, 56, 168
    diversity 211–216
    guardianship and transmission of cultural knowledge and values 74, 84, 89, 103–104, 191
    involvement in marae 98, 192, 196, 197, 199, 200, 201
    role in survival of te reo 11, 12, 17, 21 22, 27–28, 32, 65, 66, 67, 68, 79, 80, 81–82, 116, 143, 144, 155, 171, 177, 191–192
    usage of term in New Zealand English 85
whānau pani (bereaved family) 85, 199, 201
whanaungatanga (familial connectedness) 187, 214
Whangārei district 99, 117, 152–153, 167, 223
wharekai (dining hall) 50, 89, 133
    as whare wānanga 134
wharenui/whare hui (meeting house) 48, 56, 89, 120, 122, 130, 134
    children allowed into, during tangihanga 133
    and nursing mothers 136–137
Where Words Touch the Earth First Nations video documentary 240–241
women, *see* wāhine (women)
World Intellectual Property Organization 238, 239–240
World War II 50, 51, 131, 132

young Māori, *see* taitamariki/rangatahi (young Māori)